AF538948

ALFRED TENNYSON

SELECT POEMS

Alfred Tennyson

SELECT POEMS

[Edited with Complete Introduction to the Poet and His Poetry, Background Context , Text Summary and Analysis and Study Questions]

Anshu Mallika Sawhney
M.A. English, Delhi University
M. Phil., Himachal Pradesh University

ANMOL PUBLICATIONS PVT. LTD.
NEW DELHI - 110 002 (INDIA)

ANMOL PUBLICATIONS PVT. LTD.

H.O.: 4374/4B, Ansari Road, Darya Ganj,
New Delhi-110 002 (India)
Ph.: 23278000, 23261597

B.O.: No. 1015, Ist Main Road, BSK IIIrd Stage
IIIrd Phase, IIIrd Block
Bangalore - 560 085 (India)
Visit us at: www.anmolpublications.com

Select Poems

First Published, 2009

PRINTED IN INDIA

Printed at Mehra Offset Press, Delhi.

Contents

Preface

Alfred Tennyson (1809 - 1892) is regarded as one of the significant representative of Victorian Age. This English poet was the successor to William Wordsworth as a Poet Laureate. He was the son of George Clayton Tennyson, a clergyman and rector. He was suffering from depression and was absent minded. Tennyson was immensely influenced by the great Lord Byron and used to write poetry in his style. Major poetic achievements of Tennyson is the elegy mourning the death of his friend Arthur Hallam, "In Memoriam" (1850). The patriotic poem "Charge of the Light Brigade", published in Maud (1855), is one of Tennyson's best known works.

Tennyson is also referred as the "Poet of the People". Interestingly, his poetry was ironically private. One of the finest example of his great poetry is the "The Charge of the Light Brigade". In order to narrate the progression of events, Tennyson effectively uses repetition of last line of each stanza.

Author

Chapter 1

Introduction

In poetry, apart from the drama, the Victorian period is the greatest in English literature. Its most representative, though not it's greatest, poet is Alfred Tennyson. Tennyson, the fourth of a large family of children, was born in Somersby, Lincolnshire, in 1809. That year, as it happened, is distinguished by the birth of a large number of eminent men, among them Gladstone, Darwin, and Lincoln.

Tennyson's father was a clergyman, holding his appointments from a member of the landed gentry; his mother was peculiarly gentle and benevolent. From childhood, the poet though physically strong, was moody and given to solitary dreaming; from early childhood he composed poetry, and at the age of seventeen he and one of his elder brothers brought out a volume of verse, immature, but of distinct poetic feeling and promise. The next year they entered Trinity College, Cambridge, where Tennyson, too reserved for public prominence, nevertheless developed greatly through association with a gifted group of students. Called home by the fatal illness of his father shortly before his four year's completed, he decided, as Milton had done, and as Browning was even then doing, to devote himself to his art. But, like Milton, he equipped himself, now and throughout his life, by hard and systematic study of many of the chief branches of knowledge, including the sciences. His next twenty years were of difficulty and sorrow. The critics greeted two volumes of poems that published in 1830 and 1832 with their usual harshness, which deeply wounded his sensitive spirit and checked his further publication for ten years. However, the second of these volumes contains some pieces that, in their later, revised, form, are among his chief lyric triumphs. In 1833 his warm friend Arthur Hallam, a young man of extraordinary promise and engaged to one of Tennyson's sisters, died suddenly without warning. Tennyson's grief, at first overwhelming, was long a main factor in his life and during many years found slow artistic expression in 'In Memoriam' and other poems. A few years later came another deep sorrow. Tennyson formed an engagement of marriage with Miss Emily Sellwood, but his lack of worldly prospects led her relatives to cancel it.

Tennyson now spent much of his time in London, on terms of friendship with many literary men, including Carlyle, who almost made an exception in his favour from his general fanatical contempt for poetry. In 1842 Tennyson published two volumes of poems, including the earlier ones revised; he here won an undoubted popular success and was accepted by the best judges as the chief living productive English poet. Disaster followed in the shape of an unfortunate financial venture which for a time reduced his family to serious straits and drove him with shattered nerves to a sanitarium. Soon, however, he received from the government as recognition of his poetic achievement a permanent annual pension of two hundred pounds, and in 1847, he published the strange but delightful 'Princess.' The year 1850 marked the decisive turning point of his career. He was able to renew his engagement and be married. The publication of 'In Memoriam' established him permanently in a position of such popularity as only a few living poets have ever enjoyed and after the death of Wordsworth, he was appointed as Poet Laureate.

The prosperity of the remaining half of his life was a full recompense for his earlier struggles, though it is marked by few notable external events. Always a lover of the sea, he soon took up his residence in the Isle of Wight. His poetry was steady with great variety. The largest of all his single achievements was the famous series of 'Idylls of the King,' which formed a part of his occupation for many years. In much of his later work there is a marked change from his earlier elabourate decorativeness to a style of vigourous strength.

At the age of sixty-five, fearful that he had not yet done enough to insure his fame; he gave a remarkable demonstration of poetic vitality by striking out himself into the new field of poetic drama. His important works here are the three tragedies in which he aimed to complete the series of Shakespeare's chronicle-history plays; but he lacked the power of dramatic action, and the result is rather three fine poems than successful plays. In 1883, after having twice refused a baronetcy, he, to the regret of his more democratic friends, accepted a peerage (barony).

Tennyson disliked external show, but he was always intensely loyal to the institutions of England, he felt that literature was been honoured in his person, and he was willing to secure a position of honour for his son, who had long rendered him devoted service. He died quietly in 1892, at the age of eighty-three, and buried in Westminster Abbey besides Browning, who had found a resting-place there three years earlier. His personal character, despite some youthful morbidity, was unusually delightful, marked by courage, honesty, sympathy, and straightforward manliness. He had a fine voice and took undisguised pleasure in reading his poems aloud. The chief traits of his poetry in form and substance may be suggested in a brief summary.

Most characteristic, perhaps, is his exquisite artistry (in which he learned much from Keats). His appreciation for sensuous beauty, especially colour, is acute; his command of poetic phraseology is unsurpassed; he suggests shades of, feeling and elusive aspiration with, marvelously subtle power; his descriptions are magnificently beautiful, often with much detail; and his melody is often the perfection of sweetness. Add the truth and tenderness of his emotion, and it results that he is one of the finest and most moving of lyric poets. Nor is all this beauty vague and unsubstantial. Not only was he the most careful of English poets, revising his works with almost unprecedented pains, but his scientific habit of mind insists on the greatest accuracy; in his allusions to Nature he often introduces scientific facts in a way thitherto unparalleled, and sometimes even only doubtfully poetic. The influence of the classic literatures on his style and expression was great; no poet combines more harmoniously classic perfection and romantic feeling.

The variety of his poetic forms is probably greater than that of any other English poet. In summary catalogue may be named: lyrics, both delicate and stirring; ballads; romantic dreams and fancies; descriptive poems; sentimental reveries, and idylls; long narratives, in which he displays perfect narrative skill; delightfully realistic character-sketches, some of them in dialect; dramas; and meditative poems, long and short, on religious, ethical, and social questions. In almost all these forms, he has produced numerous masterpieces.

His chief deficiency is in the dramatic quality. No one can present more finely than he moods (often carefully set in a harmoniously appropriate background of external nature) or characters in stationary position; and there is splendid spirit in his narrative passages of vigourous action. Nevertheless his genius and the atmosphere of his poems are generally dreamy, romantic, and aloof from actual life. A brilliant critic has caustically observed that he 'withdraws from the turmoil of the real universe into the fortress of his own mind, and beats the enemy in toy battles with toy soldiers.' He never succeeded in presenting to the satisfaction of most good critics a vigourous man in vigourous action.

The ideas of his poetry are noble and on the whole clear. He was an independent thinker, though not an innovator, a conservative liberal, and was so widely popular because he expressed in frank but reverent fashion the moderately advanced convictions of his time. His social ideals, in which he is intensely interested, are those of Victorian humanitarianism. He hopes ardently for a steady amelioration of the condition of the masses, proceeding toward a time when all men shall have real opportunity for full development; and freedom is one of his chief watchwords. But with typical English conservatism he believes that progress must be gradual, and that it should be controlled by order, loyalty, and reverence. Like a true Englishman, also, he is sure that the institutions of England are the best in the world, so that he is a strong supporter of the monarchy and the hereditary aristocracy. In religion, his inherited belief, rooted in his deepest fibres, early found itself confronted by the discoveries of modern science, which at first seemed to him to proclaim that the universe is much what it seemed to the young Carlyle, a remorseless monster, 'red in tooth and claw,' scarcely thinkable as the work of a Christian God who cares for man. Tennyson was too sincere to evade the issue, and after years of inner struggle, he arrived at a positive faith in the central principles of Christianity, broadly interpreted, though it was avowedly a faith based on instinct and emotional need rather than on unassailable reasoning.

His somewhat timid disposition, moreover, never allowed him to enunciate his conclusions with anything like the buoyant aggressiveness of his contemporary, Robert Browning. How greatly science had influenced his point of view appears in the conception which is central in his later poetry, namely that the forces of the universe are governed by unchanging Law, through which God works. The best final expression of his spirit is the lyric 'Crossing the Bar,' which every one knows and which at his own request is printed last in all editions of his works.

Chapter 2

Alfred Tennyson: Biography

Born: 5-Aug-1809
Birthplace: Somersby, Lincolnshire, England
Died: 6-Oct-1892
Location of death: Aldworth House, Hazlemere, Surrey, England
Cause of death: Influenza
Remains: Buried, Poets' Corner, Westminster Abbey
Gender: Male
Race or Ethnicity: White
Sexual orientation: Matter of Dispute
Occupation: Poet
Nationality: England
Executive summary: The Charge of the Light Brigade

English poet, born at Somersby, Lincolnshire, on the 6th of August 1809. He was the fourth of the twelve children of the Rev. George Clayton Tennyson and his wife Elizabeth Fytche. The Tennyson's were an old Lincolnshire family settled at Bayon's Manor. The poet's grandfather, George Tennyson, M.P., had disinherited the poet's father, who was settled hard by in the rectory of Somersby, in favour of the younger son, Charles Tennyson D'Eyncourt.

The rich pastoral scenery of this part of Lincolnshire influenced the imagination of the boy, and is plainly reflected in all his early poetry, although it has now been stated with authority that the localities of his subject-poems, which had been ingeniously identified with real brooks and granges, were wholly imaginary. At a very early age he began to write in prose and verse. At Christmas 1815 he was sent to the grammar school at Louth, his mother having kept up a connection with this typical Lincolnshire borough, of which her father, the Rev. Stephen Fytche, had been vicar. Tennyson was at this school for five years, and then returned to Somersby to be trained by his father. In the rectory, the boys had the run of an excellent library, and here the young poet based his wide knowledge of the English classics.

The news of Lord Byron's death (19th April 1824) made a deep impression on him: it was a day, he said, when the whole world seemed to be darkened for me; he went out into the woods and carved "Byron is dead" upon a rock. Tennyson was already writing copiously — "an epic of 6000 lines" at twelve, a drama in blank verse at fourteen, and so on: these exercises have not been properly printed, but the poet said of them at the close of his life, "It seems to me, I wrote them all in perfect meter."

The family was in the habit of spending the summer holidays at the coast of the county, commonly at Mablethorpe, and here Tennyson gained his impressions of the vastness of the sea. Fitzgerald very justly attributed the landscape character of Tennyson's genius to the impress left on his imagination by "old Lincolnshire, where there were not only such good seas, but also such fine hill and dale among the worlds."

In 1827 Frederick Tennyson, the eldest surviving brother, uniting with his younger brothers Charles and Alfred, published at Louth an anonymous collection of Poems by Two Brothers. The two were Charles and Alfred (whose contributions predominated), and who shared the surprising profits, £20. On the 20th February 1828 Charles and Alfred matriculated at Trinity College, Cambridge, where Frederick was already a student.

The poet subsequently told Edmund Gosse that his father would not let him leave Somersby until, on successive days; he had recited from memory the whole of the odes of Horace.

The brothers took rooms at 12 Rose Crescent, and afterwards moved into Trumpington Street (now 157 Corpus Buildings). They were shy, and made at first few friends; but they gradually gathered selected associates around them, and Alfred grew to be looked up to in Cambridge "as to a great poet and an elder brother" by a group which included Richard Chenevix Trench, Monckton Milnes (Lord Houghton), James Spedding, W. H. Thompson, Edward Fitzgerald, W. H. Brookfield, and, above all, A. H. Hallam (1811-1833).

Charles Tennyson afterwards took the additional name of Turner. He published four volumes of sonnets which have been highly praised. In June 1829 Alfred Tennyson won the Chancellors prize medal for his poem called "Timbuctoo." With great imperfections, this study in Miltonic blank verse displays the genius of a poet, in spite of a curious obscurity both of thought and style. Here are already both richness and power, although their expression is not yet clarified by taste. But by this time Tennyson was writing lyrics of still higher promise, and, as Arthur Hallam early perceived, with an extraordinary earnestness in the worship of beauty.

The results of this enthusiasm and this labour of the artist appeared in the volume of Poems, chiefly Lyrical, published in 1830. This book would have been astonishing as the production of a youth of twenty-one, even if, since the death of Byron six years before, there had not been a singular dearth of good poetry in England. Here at least, in the slender volume of 1830, was a new writer revealed, and in "Mariana", "The Poet", "Love and Death", and "Oriana", a singer of wonderful though still unchastened melody. Through these, and through less perfect examples, was exhibited an amazing magnificence of fancy, at present insufficiently under control, and a voluptuous pomp of imagery, tending to an over-sweetness. The veteran Samuel Taylor Coleridge, praising the genius in the book, blamed the metrical imperfection of it.

For this criticism he has himself constantly been reproved, and Tennyson (whose impatience of anything like censure was phenomenal) continued to resent it to the end of his life. Yet

Coleridge was perfectly just in his remark; and the metrical anarchy of the "Madelines" and "Adelines" of the 1830 volume showed that Tennyson, with all his delicacy of modulation, had not yet mastered the arts of verse.

In the summer of 1830 Tennyson and Hallam volunteered in the army of the Spanish insurgent Torrijos, and marched about a little in the Pyrenees, without meeting with an enemy. He came back to find his father ailing, and in February 1831 he left Cambridge for Somersby, where a few days later Dr. George Tennyson died. The new incumbent was willing that the Tennysons should continue to live in the rectory, which they did not leave until six years later. Arthur Hallam was now betrothed to Emily Tennyson (afterwards Mrs. Jesse, 1811-1889), and stayed frequently at Somersby.

This was a very happy time, and one of great physical development on Alfred's part. He took his share in all kinds of athletic exercises, and it was now that Brookfield said, "It is not fair that you should be Hercules as well as Apollo." This high physical zest in life seems to have declined after 1831, when his eyes began to trouble him, and he became liable to depression. The poetical work of these three years, mainly spent at Somersby, was given to the world in the volume of Poems which (dated 1833) appeared at the end of 1832. This was certainly one of the most astonishing revelations of finished genius ever produced by a young man of less than twenty-four. Here were to be read "The Lady of Shallot", "The Dream of Fair Women", "Oenone", "The Lotos-Eaters", "The Palace of Art", and "The Miller's Daughter", with a score of other lyrics, delicious and divine.

The advance in craftsmanship and command over the materiel of verse shown since the volume of 1830 is absolutely astounding. If Tennyson had died of the savage article which presently appeared in the Quarterly Review, literature would have sustained terrible losses, but his name would have lived forever among those of the great English poets. Indeed, it may be doubted whether, in several directions, he ever surpassed the glorious things to be found in this most exquisite and most precious book. It was well that its publication was completed before the blow fell upon Tennyson that took for a while all the light out of him. In August 1833, Arthur Hallam started with his father, the great historian, for Tirol.

They went no farther than Vienna, where Hallam, returning to the hotel on 15 September 1833, found his son lying dead on a sofa: a blood-vessel had broken in his brain. His body was brought back to England, and buried at Clevedon on the 3rd of January 1834. These events affected Tennyson extremely. He grew less than ever willing to come forward and face the world; his health became "variable and his spirits indifferent." The earliest effect of Hallam's death upon his friend's art was the composition, in the summer of 1834, of The Two Voices; and to the same period belong the beginnings of the Idylls of the King and of In Memoriam, over both of which he meditated long.

In 1835 he visited the Lakes, and saw much of Hartley Coleridge, but would not "obtrude on the great man at Rydal", although "Wordsworth was hospitably disposed." Careless alike of fame and of influence, Tennyson spent these years mainly at Somersby, in a uniform devotion of his whole soul to the art of poetry.

In 1837, to their great distress, the Tennysons were turned out of the Lincolnshire rectory where they had lived so long. They moved to High Beech, in Epping Forest, which was their home until 1840. The poet was already engaged, or "quasi-betrothed", to Emily Sellwood, but ten years more had to pass before they could afford to marry. At Torquay, in 1838, he wrote Audley Court on one of his rare excursions, for he had no money for touring, nor did he wish for change: he wrote at this time, "I require quiet and myself to myself, more than any man when I write." In 1840 the Tennysons moved to Tunbridge Wells, and a year later to Boxley, near Maidstone, to be close to Edmund Lushington, who had now married Cecilia Tennyson. Alfred was from this time more and more frequently a visitor in London.

In 1842 the two-volume edition of his Poems broke the

ten years' silence which he had enforced himself to keep. Here, with many pieces already known to all lovers of modern verse, were found rich and copious additions to his work. These he had originally intended to publish alone, and an earlier privately printed Morte d'Arthur, Dora, and other Idylls, of 1842, is the despair of book-collectors. Most of those studies of home-life in England, which formed so highly popular a section of Tennyson's work — such as "The Gardener's Daughter", "Walking to the Mail", and "The Lord of Burleigh" — were now first issued, and, in what we have grown to consider a much higher order, "Locksley Hall", "Ulysses", and "Sir Galahad."

To the older and more luxurious lyrics, as reprinted in 1842, Tennyson did not spare the curbing and pruning hand, and in some cases went too far in restraining the wanton spirit of beauty in its youthful impulse. It is from 1842 that the universal fame of Tennyson must be dated; from the time of the publication of the two volumes he ceased to be a curiosity, or the darling of an advanced clique, and took his place as the leading poet of his age in England. Among the friends whom he now made, or for the first time cultivated, were Thomas Carlyle, Rogers, Charles Dickens, and Elizabeth Barrett Browning.Material difficulties now, however, for the first time intruded on his path.

He became the victim of a certain "earnest-frothy" speculator, who induced him to sell his little Lincolnshire estate at Grasby, and to invest the proceeds, with all his other money, and part of that of his brothers and sisters, in a "Patent Decorative Carving Company": in a few months the whole scheme collapsed, and Tennyson was left penniless. He was attacked by so overwhelming hypochondria that his life was despaired of, and he was placed for some time under the charge of a hydropathic physician at Cheltenham, where absolute rest and isolation gradually brought him around to health again.

The state of utter indigence to which Tennyson was reduced, greatly exercised his friends, and in September 1845, at the suggestion of Henry Hallam, Sir Robert Peel was induced to bestow on the poet a pension of £200 a year. Never was public money expended in a more patriotic fashion. Tennyson's health slowly became restored, and in 1846, he was hard at work on The Princess; in the autumn of this year, he took a tour in Switzerland, and saw great mountains and such "stateliest bits of landskip" for the first time. In 1847 nervous prostration again obliged him to undergo treatment at Prestbury: "They tell me not to read, not to think; but they might as well tell me not to live."

Dr. Gully's water-cure was tried, with success. The Princess was now published, in a form afterwards considerably modified and added to. Carlyle and Fitzgerald "gave up all hopes of him after The Princess", or pretended that they did. It was true that the bent of his genius was slightly altered, in a direction which seemed less purely and austerely that of the highest art; but his concessions to public taste vastly added to the width of the circle he now addressed. The home of the Tennysons was now at Cheltenham: on his occasional visits to London he was in the habit of seeing William Makepeace Thackeray, Coventry Patmore, Robert Browning and William Charles Macready, as well as older friends, but he avoided "society."

In 1848, while making a tour in Cornwall, Tennyson met Robert Stephen Hawker of Morwenstow, with whom he seems — but the evidence is uncertain — to have talked about King Arthur, and to have resumed his intention of writing an epic on that theme. In his absent-minded way Tennyson was very apt to mislay objects; in earlier life he had lost the manuscript of Poems, chiefly Lyrical, and had been obliged to restore the whole from scraps and memory.

Now a worse thing befell him, for in February 1850, having collected into one "long ledger-like book" all the elegies on Arthur Hallam which he had been composing at intervals since 1833, he left this only manuscript in the cupboard of some lodgings in Mornington Place, Hampstead Road. By extraordinary good chance it had been overlooked by the landlady, and Coventry Patmore was able to recover it. In this way In Memoriam was dragged back from the very verge of destruction, and could be published, in its original anonymous form, in May 1850. The public was at first greatly mystified by the nature and object of this poem, which was not merely a chronicle of Tennyson's emotions under bereavement, nor even a statement of his philosophical and religious beliefs, but, as he long afterwards explained, a sort of Divina Commedia, ending with happiness in the marriage of his youngest sister, Cecilia Lushington.

In fact, the great blemishes of In Memoriam, its redundancy and the dislocation of its parts, were largely due to the desultory manner of its composition. The poet wrote the sections as they occurred to him, and did not think of weaving them together into a single poem until it was too late to give them real coherency. The meter, which for a curious naive Tennyson was his own invention, served to bind the sections together, and even to give an illusion of connected movement to the thought.

The sale of Tennyson's poems now made it safe for him to settle, and on the 13th of June 1850 he was married at Shiplake to Emily Sarah Sellwood. Of this union no more need be said than was recorded long afterwards by the poet himself, "The peace of God came into my life before the altar when I wedded her." Every species of good fortune was now to descend on the path of the man who had struggled against bad luck so long. William Wordsworth died, and on 19th of November 1850 Queen Victoria appointed Tennyson poet laureate. The salary connected with the post was very small, but it had a secondary value in greatly stimulating the sale of his books, which was his main source of income.

The young couple took a house at Warninglid, in Sussex, which did not suit them, and then one in Montpelier Row, Twickenham, which did better. In April 1851 their first child was born dead. At this time Tennyson was brooding much upon the ancient world, and reading little but Milton, Homer and Virgil. This condition was elegantly defined by Carlyle as "sitting on a dung heap among innumerable dead dogs."

In the summer of 1851 was made the tour in Italy, of which The Daisy is the immortal record. Of 1852 the principal events were the birth of his eldest son Hallam, the second Lord Tennyson, in August, and in November the publication of the Ode on the Death of the Duke of Wellington. In the winter of 1853 Tennyson entered into possession of a little house and farm called Farringford, near Freshwater, in the Isle of Wight, which he leased at first, and afterwards bought: this beautiful place, ringed around with ilexes and cedars, entered into his life and coloured it with its delicate enchantment.

In 1854 he published The Charge of the Light Brigade, and was busy composing Maud and its accompanying lyrics; and this volume was published in July 1855, just after he was made D.C.L. at Oxford: he was received on this occasion, which may be considered his first public appearance, with a "tremendous ovation." The reception of Maud from the critics, however, was not the worst trial to his equanimity, which Tennyson had ever had to endure, nor had the future anything like it in store for him. He had risen in Maud far above his ordinary serenity of style, to ecstasies of passion and audacities of expression which were scarcely intelligible to his readers, and certainly not welcome.

It is odd that this irregular poem, with its copious and varied music, its splendid sweep of emotion, its unfailing richness of texture — this poem in which Tennyson rises to heights of human sympathy and intuition which he reached nowhere else, should have been received with bitter hostility, have been styled "the dead level of prose run mad", and have been reproved more absurdly still for its "rampant and rabid bloodthirstiness of soul." There came a reaction of taste and sense, but the delicate spirit of Tennyson had been wounded. For some years the world heard nothing from him; he was at Farringford, busying himself with the Arthurian traditions. He had now become an object of boundless personal curiosity, being already difficult to find, and the centre of amusing legends.

It was in 1857 that Bayard Taylor saw him, and carried

away the impression of a man "tall and broad-shouldered as a son of Anak, with hair, beard and eyes of southern darkness." This period of somewhat mysterious withdrawal from the world embraced a tour in Wales in 1857, a visit to Norway in 1858, and a journey through Portugal in 1859. In 1857 two Arthurian poems had been tentatively and privately printed, as Enid and Nimue, or the True and the False, to see how the idylllic form would be liked by the inner circle of Tennyson's friends. In the summer of 1859 the first series of Idylls of the King was at length given to the world, and achieved a popular success far beyond anything experienced before by any English poets, save perhaps Byron and Scott. Within a month of publication, 10,000 copies had been sold. The idylls were four in number, "Enid", "Vivien" (no longer called "Nimue"), "Elaine" and "Guinevere."

These were fragments of the epic of the fall of King Arthur and the Table Round which Tennyson was so long preparing, and which he can hardly be said to have ever completed, although nearly thirty years later he closed it. The public and the critics alike were entranced with the "sweetness" and the "purity" of the treatment. A few, like John Ruskin, were doubtful about "that increased quietness of style"; one or two already suspected that the "sweetness" was obtained at some sacrifice of force, and that the "purity" involved a concession to Victorian conventionality. It was not perceived at the time that the four idylls were parts of a great historical or mystical poem, and they were welcomed as four polished studies of typical women: it must be confessed that in this light their even perfection of workmanship appeared to greater advantage than it eventually did in the general texture of the so-called "epic."

In 1859 "Boadicea" was written, and "Riflemen, Form!" published in The Times. Urged by the Duke of Argyll, Tennyson now turned his attention to the theme of the Holy Grail, though he progressed with it but fitfully and slowly. In 1861, he traveled in Auvergne and the Pyrenees, with Clough, who was to die a few months later; to this year belong "Helen's Tower" and the "Dedication" of the Idylls to the prince consort,

"These to his Memory." The latter led to Tennyson's presentation in April 1862 to the queen, who "stood pale and statue-like before him, in a kind of stately innocence", which greatly moved his admiring homage. From this time forth the poet enjoyed the constant favour of the sovereign, though he could never be moulded into a conventional courtier. He now put the Arthurian legends aside for a time, and devoted himself to the composition, in 1862, of "Enoch Arden", which, however, did not appear until 1864, and then in a volume which also contained "Sea Dreams", "Aylmer's Field" and, above all, "The Northern Farmer", the first and finest of Tennyson's remarkable studies in dialect.

In April of this year Giuseppe Garibaldi visited Farringford; in February 1865 Tennyson's mother died at Hampstead in her eighty-fifth year; in the ensuing summer he traveled in Germany. The time slipped by with incidents but few and slight, Tennyson's popularity in Great Britain growing all the time to an extent unparalleled in the whole annals of English poetry. This universality of fame led to considerable practical discomfort; he was besieged by sightseers, and his nervous trepidation led him perhaps to exaggerate the intensity of the infliction.

In 1867 he determined to make for himself a haven of refuge against the invading Philistine, and bought some land on Blackdown, above Haslemere, then a secluded corner of England; here James Knowles began to build him a house, ultimately named Aldworth. This is the time of two of his rare, privately printed pamphlets, The Window; or, the Loves of the Wrens (1867), and The Victim (1868).

The noble poem Lucretius, one of the greatest of Tennyson's versified monographs, appeared in May 1868, and in this year The Holy Grail was at last finished; it was published in 1869, together with three other idylls belonging to the Arthurian epic, and various miscellaneous lyrics, besides Lucretius. The reception of this volume was cordial, but not as universally respectful as that which Tennyson had grown to expect from his adoring public. The fact was that the heightened reputation of Browning and still more the sudden vogue of Algernon Charles Swinburne, Morris and Rossetti (period 1866-70), considerably disturbed the minds of Tennyson's most ardent readers, and exposed him to a severer criticism than he had lately been accustomed to endure.

He went on quite calmly, however, sure of his mission and of his music. His next volume (1872), Gareth and Lynette and The Last Tournament, continued, and, as he then supposed, concluded The Idylls of the King, to the great satisfaction of the poet, who had found much difficulty in rounding off the last sections of the poem. Nor, as he was to find, was the poem yet completed, but for the time being he dismissed it from his mind. In 1873 he was offered a baronetcy by Gladstone, and again by Disraeli in 1874; in each case the honour was gracefully declined. Believing that his work with the romantic Arthurian epics was concluded, Tennyson now turned his attention to a department of poetry which had long attracted him, but which he had never seriously attempted — the drama. He put before him a scheme, which he cannot be said to have carried far, that of illustrating "the making of England" by a series of great historical tragedies.

His Queen Mary, the first of these chronicle plays was published in 1875, and played by Sir Henry Irving at the Lyceum in 1876. Although it was full of admirably dramatic writing, it was not theatrically well composed, and it failed on the stage. Extremely pertinacious in this respect, the poet went on attempting to storm the theater, with assault upon assault, all practically failures until the seventh and last, which was unfortunately posthumous.

To have really succeeded on the stage would have given Tennyson more gratification than anything else, but he was not permitted to live long enough to see this blossom also added to the heavy garland of his glory. Meanwhile Harold, a tragedy of doom, was published in 1876; but, though perhaps the finest of its author's dramas, it has never been acted. During these years Tennyson's thoughts were largely occupied with the building of Aldworth. His few lyrics were spirited ballads of adventure, inspired by an exalted patriotism — "The Revenge" (1878), "The Defence of Lucknow" (1879) — but he reprinted and finally published his old suppressed poem, The Lover's Tale, and a little play of his, The Falcon, versified out of Boccaccio, was produced by the Kendals at their theater in the last days of 1879.

Tennyson had reached the limits of the age 70, and it was tacitly taken for granted that he would now retire into dignified repose. In point of fact, he now started on a new lease of poetical activity. In 1880, he published the earliest of six important collections of lyrics, this being entitled Ballads and other Poems, and containing the somber and magnificent "Rizpah". In 1881 "The Cup" and in 1882 "The Promise of May", two little plays, were produced without substantial success in London theaters, the latter is perhaps the least successful of all the poet's longer writings, but its failure annoyed him unreasonably. This determination to be a working playwright, pushed on in the face of critical hostility and popular indifference, is a very curious trait in the character of Tennyson. In September 1883 Tennyson and Gladstone set out on a voyage around the north of Scotland, to Orkney, and across the ocean to Norway and Denmark.

At Copenhagen they were entertained by the king and queen, and after much fêting, returned to Gravesend: this adventure served to cheer the poet, who had been in low spirits since the death of his favourite brother Charles, and who now entered upon a phase of admirable vigour. During the voyage Gladstone had determined to offer Tennyson a peerage. After some demur, the poet consented to accept it, but added, "For my own part, I shall regret my simple name all my life." On the 11th of March 1884 he took his seat in the House of Lords as Baron Tennyson of Aldworth and Farringford.

He voted twice, but never spoke in the House. In the autumn of this year his tragedy of Becket was published, but the poet at last despaired of the stage, and disclaimed any hope of "meeting the exigencies of our modern theater." Curiously enough, after his death Becket was the one of all his plays which enjoyed a great success on the boards.

In 1885 was published another interesting miscellany, Tiresias and other Poems, with a posthumous dedication to Edward Fitzgerald. In this volume, it should be noted, The Idylls of the King was completed at last by the publication of "Balin and Balan"; it contained also the superb address "To Virgil." In April 1886 Tennyson suffered the loss of his second son, Lionel, who died in the Red Sea on his return from India.

The untiring old poet was steadily writing on, and by 1886 he had another. collection of lyrics ready, Locksley Hall Sixty Years After, etc.; his eyes troubled him, but his memory and his intellectual curiosity were as vivid as ever. Late in 1888 he had a dangerous attack of rheumatic gout, from which it seemed in December that he could scarcely hope to rally, but his magnificent constitution pulled him through. He was past eighty when he published the collection of new verses entitled Demeter and other Poems (1889), which appeared almost simultaneously wilh the death of Browning, an event which left Tennyson a solitary figure indeed in poetic literature.

In 1891 it was observed that he had wonderfully recovered the high spirits of youth, and even a remarkable portion of physical strength. His latest drama, The Foresters, now received his attention, and in March 1892 it was produced at New York, with Miss Ada Rehan as Maid Marian. During this year Tennyson was steadily engaged on poetical composition, finishing "Akbar's Dream", "Kapiolani" and other contents of the posthumous volume called The Death of Oenone (1892). In the summer, he took a voyage to the Channel Islands and Devonshire; and even this was not his latest excursion from home, for in July 1892 he went up for a visit to London.

Soon after entering his eighty-fourth year, however, symptoms of weakness set in, and early in September his condition began to give alarm. He retained his intellectual lucidity and an absolute command of his faculties to the last, reading Shakespeare with obvious appreciation until within a few hours of his death. With the splendor of the full moon falling upon him, his hand clasping his Shakespeare, and looking, as we are told, almost unearthly in the majestic beauty of his old age, Tennyson passed away at Aldworth on the night of the 6th of October 1892. Cymbeline, the play he had been reading on the last afternoon, was laid in his coffin, and on the 12th he was publicly buried with great solemnity in Westminster Abbey. Lady Tennyson survived until August 1896.

The physical appearance of Tennyson was very remarkable. Of his figure at the age of thirty-three Carlyle has left a superb portrait: "One of the finest-looking men in the world. A great shock of rough, dusky, dark hair; bright, laughing, hazel eyes; massive aquiline face, most massive yet most delicate; of sallow brown complexion, almost Indian-looking, clothes cynically loose, free-and-easy, smokes infinite tobacco. His voice is musical, metallic, fit for loud laughter and piercing wail, and all that may lie between; speech and speculation free and plenteous; I do not meet in these late decades such company over a pipe."

He was unusually tall, and possessed in advanced years a strange and rather terrifying air of somber majesty. But he was, in fact, of a great simplicity in temperament, affectionate, shy, still exquisitely sensitive in extreme old age to the influences of beauty, melancholy and sweetness. Although exceedingly near-sighted, Tennyson was a very close observer of nature, and at the age of eighty his dark and glowing eyes, which were still strong, continued to permit him to enjoy the delicate features of country life around him, both at Aldworth and in the Isle of Wight. His Life, written with admirable piety and taste by his son, Hallam, second Lord Tennyson, was published in two volumes in 1897.

Father: Rev. George Clayton Tennyson (b. 1778, d. 1831)
Mother: Elizabeth Fytche (b. 1781, d. 1865)
Brother: Frederick Tennyson (b. 1807, d. 1898)
Brother: Charles Tennyson (b. 1808, d. 1879)
Wife: Emily Sarah Sellwood (b. 1813, m. 13-Jun-1850, d. 1896)

Chapter 3

Tennyson: Chronology

1809	Born at Somersby, Lincolnshire, England; fourth of twelve children
1820-1827	Educated at home by his father
1821	Tennyson composes a 6,000 line epic poem
1823-1824	Composes "The Devil and the Lady"
1827	Enters Cambridge University
	Publishes, with brother Charles, Poems by Two Brothers
1829	Meets his best-friend-to-be, Arthur Henry Hallam
	Wins Chancellor's Prize Medal with his poem "Timbuctoo"
1830	Publishes Poems, Chiefly Lyrical
	With Hallam, joins insurgent army in Spain for a time
1831	Father dies
	Tennyson leaves Cambridge
1833	Publishes Poems
1836	Begins courtship of Emily Sellwood
1842	Republishes Poems, with additions; Tennyson's fame established
1850	Publishes In Memoriam (to the memory of Arthur Hallam)
	Marries Emily Sellwood
	Queen Victoria appoints poet laureate of England
1851	The Tennyson's first child is born dead
1852	Birth of his eldest son, Hallam Tennyson (to become the second Lord Tennyson)

1855	Publishes Maud, and Other Poems
1859	Publishes first poems of Idylls of the King; 10,000 copies sell in one month
1864	Publishes Enoch Arden
1865	Tennyson's mother dies
1869	Publishes the Holy Grail and Other Poems
1871	Publishes "The Last Tournament"
1872-1874	Tennyson completes Idylls of the King (except for "Balin and Balan")
1880	Publishes Ballads and Other Poems
1883	Tennyson made a Baron
1885	Publishes Tiresias and Other Poems
1889	Publishes Demeter and Other Poems
1892	Tennyson dies after a long illness

Chapter 4

Introduction to Victorian Literature

The important writing of the Victorian period is largely the product of a double awareness. This was a literature addressed with great immediacy to the needs of the age, to the particular temper of mind which had grown up within a society seeking adjustment to the conditions of modern life. And to the degree that the problems which beset the world of a century ago retain their urgency and still await solution, the ideas of the Victorian writers remain relevant and interesting to the twentieth century.

Any enduring literature, however, must transcend topicality; and the critical disesteem into which so much Victorian writing has fallen may be traced to the persistent notion that the literary men of that time oversubscribed to values with which our own time is no longer in sympathy. Yet this view ignores the fact that nearly all the eminent Victorian writers were as often as not at odds with their age and that in their best work they habitually appealed not to, but against the prevailing mores of that age.

The reader who comes to the Victorians without bias must be struck again and again by the underlying tone of unrest which pervades so much that is generally taken as typical of the period.

Sooner or later he begins to wonder whether there is any such thing as a representative Victorian writer, or at any rate, whether what makes him representative is not that very quality of intransigence as a result of which he repudiated his society and sought refuge from the spirit of the times in the better ordered realm of interior consciousness. Since, however, any tendency to exalt individual awareness at the expense of conventionally established attitudes ran counter to the concept of the role of the artist which the Victorian age tried to impose on its writers, there resulted a conflict which has been too often ignored, but which must be taken into account in reaching any satisfactory evaluation of Victorian literature. This was a conflict, demonstrable within the work of the writers themselves, between the public conscience of the man of letters who comes forward as the accredited literary spokesman of his world, and the private conscience of the artist who conceives that his highest allegiance must be to his own aesthetic sensibilities.

Most Victorian writers still thought of themselves as men of letters in the full meaning of the term. Victorian literature was predominantly a literature of ideas, and of ideas, furthermore, brought into direct relation with the daily concerns of the reading public. To a degree now inconceivable the influential literary types of the nineteenth century were expository in character-the essay, tract, and treatise. The student who wishes to understand the Victorian world begins with such works as Past and Present, The Stones of Venice, On Liberty, Culture and Anarchy.

The assumption that a writer's first responsibility is to get into close correspondence with his audience induced a great many of the original thinkers in the period to turn aside from their fields of special knowledge, to the end of making their theories more generally accessible. So Mill, Carlyle, Ruskin, Arnold, Morris, Huxley, after achieving distinction along specialized lines, gave up exclusive concentration on these in order to apply the disciplines they had mastered to subjects of the broadest human import. Or, to consider the novel, Dickens, George Eliot, Disraeli, Kingsley, Mrs. Gaskell, and Charles Reade all quite evidently chose themes with an eye to their social significance.

Yet, paradoxically, it becomes increasingly difficult to

think of the great Victorians as other than solitary and unassimilated figures within their century. Deeply as they allowed themselves to be involved in the life of the times, familiarity seemed only to breed contempt.

Their writings, inspired by a whole-hearted hostility to the progress of industrial culture, locate the centres of authority not in the existing social order but within the resources of individual being. Nor was this procedure merely a reaction to the isolation which is traditionally visited on prophets without honour, although for many the years brought disillusionment and bitterness over the debacle of cherished programmes of reform.

The prestige of a Carlyle or Ruskin or Newman may almost be said to have risen in inverse proportion to the failure of their preachments. At the core of the malaise that pervades so much that is best in Victorian literature lays a sense, often inarticulate, that modern society has originated tendencies inimical to the life of the creative imagination. By mid-century the circumstances of successful literary production had begun to make demands on writers which strained to the breaking point their often very considerable capacities for compromise. Among novelists, the careers of Dickens and Thackeray epitomize the all but intolerable difficulties of reconciling popular appeal with artistic integrity.

A new generation, led by Rossetti and Swinburne, was to resolve the dilemma by an outspoken assertion of the artist's apartness; but for the writers who came of age in the 1830's and 1840's no such categorical disavowal of social commitment was admissible. As a result, there is recognizable in their work a kind of tension originating in the serious writer's traditional desire to communicate, but to do so without betraying the purity of his creative motive even in the face of a public little disposed to undergo the rigors of aesthetic experience.

Even when, as was too often the case, their love of fame overcame their artistic restraint, traces of the initiating conflict remain imbedded in what they wrote; and it is these constantly recurring evidences of a twofold awareness which, perhaps more than any other trait, give its distinctive quality to the writing of the Victorian age.

In criticizing Victorian poetry it is necessary to keep this ambivalence in mind; and this is especially true for Tennyson, Browning, and Arnold, the poets who touched their period at the greatest number of points. The history of nineteenth century English poetry records a gradual, but radical shift in the relationship of the artist to his public with the three poets just mentioned occupying a position at dead centre of the forces which were in opposition.

A divorce between the artist and society first became conspicuous as an element of the Romantic Movement; but even though they had to endure abuse or neglect, the Romantics did not in any sense thought of themselves as abdicating the poet's traditional right to speak for his age. Blake, Coleridge, Wordsworth, Byron, Shelley, Keats were all, it is true, keenly sensitive to their generation's reluctance to pay attention to what they were saying, but they accepted isolation as a necessary consequence of their revolutionary programme. That they should confess defeat, with the alternatives either of self-withdrawal or compromise, never seriously occurred to them.

On the contrary, they declared open warfare on the prejudices which would dispossess them and continued to assert that the poet's vision is transcendently of intellectual and spiritual truth. Before the end of the century, however, the conflict thus resolutely engaged had been lost, and the artist had come to accept as a foregone conclusion his inefficacy as of his contemporaries. In compensation, he now espoused the aesthetic creed which goes by the name of art for art's sake, and with Pater and then Wilde as his apologists and Rossetti and Swinburne as his models, embraced his alienation from all but a coterie of initiates persuaded like himself to value the forms of art above its message.

Between the Romantics and the Pre-Raphaelites lie Tennyson, Browning, and Arnold, leading the poetic chorus of the great Victorian noonday. In addition, by virtue of this midway position between the two extremes represented by the schools of poetry which came before and after, their work brings into sharp focus the choice which has been forced on the modern artist. In the common view, these mid-Victorian poets, either unable or unwilling to maintain the spirit of bellicose self-sufficiency, which sustained their Romantic forbears, achieved rapprochement with their audience by compromising with the middle-class morality of the time, and in so doing, deliberately sacrificed artistic validity.

So flagrant a betrayal of the creative impulse, the argument then continues, provoked a reaction in the following generation, whereby the pendulum swung back towards the belief that art is and must be its own justification irrespective of ulterior motive. But this version of the poetic situation in the nineteenth century gravely misrepresents the real meaning of an endeavor on which Tennyson, Browning, and Arnold were alike engaged. For each of them was ultimately seeking to define the sphere within which the modern poet may exercise his faculty, while holding in legitimate balance the rival claims of his private, aristocratic insights and of the tendencies existing in a society progressively vulgarized by the materialism of the nineteenth and twentieth centuries. Thus it came about that the double awareness, which so generally characterized the Victorian literary mind, grew almost into a perpetual state of consciousness in these poets through their efforts to work out a new aesthetic position for the artist.

The literary careers of Tennyson, Browning, and Arnold present a number of striking parallels that, since their poetic endowments were so divergent; that could be explained in terms of influences impinging on them from the outside. In the early manner of each there is an introspective, even a cloistral element which was later subdued in an obvious attempt to connect with contemporary currents of thought.

Of the three, Tennyson succeeded most quickly in conforming to the Victorian ideal of the poet as popular bard; his reward was the laureateship as Wordsworth's successor. Browning's progress in public favour was more gradual, but the formation of the Browning Society in 1881 signalized his eventual arrival within the select company of Victorian idols of the hearth. Less versatile in poetic range, Arnold became a full-fledged man of letters and won the prestige of the Oxford Professorship of Poetry only after turning to prose. It is perhaps worth pondering whether his inability to bring his poetry into closer accord with the demands of the age does not account for the fact that he has attracted a greater amount of serious critical attention in recent years than either Tennyson or Browning.

The Victorian writer, of course, had to acclimate himself to a reading public vastly bigger in size and more diverse and unpredictable in its literary requirements than any that had existed hitherto. There is something astonishing, even slightly appalling, in the unselective voracity with which the Victorians wolfed down In Memoriam and Bailey's Festus, The Origin of Species, and Samuel Smiles' Self-help, the novels of Dickens and the tales of Harriet Martineau. The ill success of their first volumes early awakened Tennyson, Browning, and Arnold to a realization that under existing conditions originality was no passport to artistic acclaim. The critics were for the most part hostile; but it was the disapprobation of intimate friends which carried the greatest weight.

For while the poets might turn a deaf ear to the voice of the age as it spoke through the weekly and monthly journals which had feebly replaced the Edinburgh and Quarterly Reviews as arbiters in literary matters, the well-intended strictures of a Hallam or Elizabeth Barrett or Clough were another matter. In addition, friends and foes were at one in their insistence that the poets take a broader view of their responsibilities as men of letters.

In general, their work drew reproof on three counts, one major and two incidental thereto. It was unduly introspective and self-obsessed and as a result, it was too often obscure content and precious in manner. All three faults are chargeable to immaturity; but as attributed indiscriminately to Tennyson, Browning, and Arnold, they carry additional implications suggestive of the tyranny, which the age was to exercise over its artists. For the invariable inference in the attacks on these poets is that their faults could easily be remedied by more attention to normal human thoughts and activities, and correspondingly by less infatuation with their own private states of being.

The experiments in the narrative and dramatic modes to which Tennyson, Browning, and Arnold turned so early in their careers were certainly undertaken out of a desire to counteract objections of this kind. Yet it is apparent from the vagaries of their critical reputations that they were never sure enough of their audience to be able to estimate its response with any degree of reliability. The appearance of a Maud or Sordello or Empedocles on Etna, interspersed among more admired efforts, is continuing evidence that the best will in the world could not compensate for temperamental variances with prevailing tastes which went much deeper than the authors themselves always recognized.

That they should have professed impatience with the often obtuse and ill-considered estimates of their poetry is not in itself surprising; but it is to be noted that as time went on they tended increasingly to transfer this resentment to the reading public at large. In their later days, Tennyson and Arnold would have agreed with Browning's statement in Red Cotton Night-Cap Country about "artistry being battle with the age it lives in!" There is, of course, an element of the disingenuous in such professions of disdain for popular favour; and their assumed indifference cannot disguise the fact that all three poets were keenly sensitive to the fluctuations of their literary stock. In this respect, they were no more than exhibiting awareness natural to men of letters possessed of an inherent belief in the instrumentality of literature as a social force.

Yet again, the conventional explanation does not cover the facts; and we are brought back to the dichotomy which emerges from any close analysis of the relations between the artist and society in the Victorian period. The hallmark of the literary personalities of Tennyson, Browning, and Arnold alike is a certain aristocratic aloofness, a stubborn intractability which is likely to manifest itself at just those points where the contemporary social order assumed automatic conformity with its dictates. Thus, their refusal to be restricted by current suppositions is less often a subterfuge to cover a fear of failure than a forthright avowal of the artist's independence from societal pressures whenever these threaten to inhibit the free play of his imaginative powers.

Tennyson, Browning, and Arnold never went to the lengths of the poets who came after in disassociating themselves from their audience. On the other hand, there is a fundamental error in the prevalent notion that they uncritically shared most of the foibles that, rightly or wrongly, are attributed to the Victorians. Such an opinion overlooks that quality of double awareness which we are now to investigate as the crux of the Victorian literary consciousness.

With these remarks as a starting point, it is proposed in the ensuing chapters to survey the artistic careers of the three poets, testing for each in turn the truth of the following statements.

1. In their youthful poems Tennyson, Browning, and Arnold revealed the habits of mind, the emotional and intellectual leanings, the kinds of imaginative vision other words, the native resources at the disposal of each.
2. Subsequently, from a desire to gain a wide audience for their work and hence to play an influential part in the life of the times, all three poets showed a willingness to make concessions to literary fashions with which they were temperamentally out of sympathy.
3. Resolved, nevertheless, that conformity should involve as little artistic loss as possible, Tennyson, Browning, and Arnold perfected remarkable techniques for sublimating their private insights without materially falsifying the original perceptions at the heart of their creative impulse.

4. The identification of these insights, along with the recognition of their concealed but vivifying action within poems ostensibly concerned with subjects of different and sometimes contradictory import, draws attention to the true centres of poetic intent in Tennyson, Browning, and Arnold, and thus provides a basis for reassessing their total achievement.

Chapter 5

Victorian Poetry

Conventionally, the Victorian age overlaps with the reign of Queen Victoria, from her coronation, in 1837, to her death, in 1901. Geopolitically, it is the age of the British Empire which occupied one third of the world and declared it to be British. From its insular headquarters, the British Empire extended in Asia to Afghanistan and Tibet, covering the whole of India, which was thirty-four times the size of England; by 1877 actually Queen Victoria was proclaimed Empress of India. The British Empire extended to Hong-Kong, New Zealand and Australia (where Magwitch in "Great Expectations" or Hetty Sorrell in "Adam Bede" by George Eliot and many a real Victorian villain got transported in a kind of surrogate of a criminal's execution).

The British Empire also extended to Canada, 40 times the size of England. In Africa, the British Empire occupied Nigeria and Egypt to the North, after the Purchase in 1875 of the Suez Canal, and went as far down as the tip of the continent where it conquered South Africa after the Boer War, in the 1890s. A clear outline of the British conquest of the world in the Victorian age is offered by G. M. Trevelyan, in his "Illustrated History of England", 1962, translated into Romanian in 1975.

Britain's geopolitical power in the 19th century was due to its being the first industrialized country in the world, because of the scientific and technological progress it had been involved in since the end of the 18th century. In the span of a single century, the history of science unites in Britain the names of James Watt, Michael Faraday, William Thomson, Lord Kelvin, George Boole, James Clerk Maxwell. The technological advances include the invention of the telegraph, the intercontinental cable, the generalisation of steam power (with the large-scale implementation of the steam hammer, the steam turbine, the steam loom and the steam plough) or the universal milling machine. The communication industry saw revolution by the invention and the worldwide spreading of the telegraph, the intercontinental cable or photography and the rotary printing press.

Land transportation developed tremendously in Britain with the building of the first successful railroad system in the world – followed by the construction of the first underground railway system, the Metropolitan, in 1860. The electric lamp increased the urbanization standards, too; the commodity industry was changed by the introduction of the vacuum cleaners, and the war industry "thrived" after the invention of the automatic guns, the shell gun and the Winchester gun.

All this spelled progress, Progress with a capital letter, and proposed England as" the greatest and most civilized people".

At a closer look at the age, progress meant a great deal of environmental change: the change of the countryside and the city alike. Quite often, a plain would be spectacularly transformed into a canyon by the sprouting railways that cut through meadows in depth or cut tunnels through the mountains. All these site changes amounted to a special kind of environmental events, thought worthy of being celebrated in work songs about the naives (or railway workers) and their prowess in taming nature. (as the theme park folklore demonstrates today, in the most recent and fashionable kind of muse graphical exhibition in Britain, aimed at recreating the commoners' everyday life in the regional British near past).

Urbanization became overriding, with the displacement of the rural population in the mass. In literature, this was reflected by the nostalgic remembrance of the rural past in quite a number of success, or simply representative, Victorian novels, such as the majority of George Eliot's novels or the rural gentry and family chronicles that spawned into a picturesque Victorian genre.

Sociologically, the Victorian age was the first mass age in history, the precursor, therefore, of the 20th century mass society. The main difference from the 20th century mass society, however, resided in the respect paid to the middle-class owners of property and their sense of prosperity, with the leaders regarded by Victorian standards as heroic protagonists of progress. Consequently, the dominant middle-class ethics of progress involved materialistic optimism (the cult of which could be seen and achieved with skill, passion and pride), mercantilism and the hypocritical praise of excessive pragmatism.

The "virtues" of a new made class, which were brilliantly satirized by Dickens in the description of the Veneering at the beginning of his last finished novel, "Our Mutual Friend". The upper mobility of the middle classes also and especially involved a considerable amount of cultural ambition too, an urge for intensive instruction of the "bran new" leaders; culture will therefore be "translated" to make it accessible to the understanding of the middle-class average men and the major effect of this was the popularity of culture. Culture will be used and administered in the Victorian age of utilitarianism as a kind of community good or public service; it will be wrapped in a didactic, widely communicative finish.

Politically, the Victorian or liberal state was essentially non-interventionist as it was dominated by the mercantile regulations of the free market. It was based on the political doctrine of "laissez-faire" that gave free reign to the private capitalistic enterprise without regard to the public welfare. Thus, the liberal legislation was double-edged: protectionist, for the capitalistic, entrepreneurial class and impoverishing when not simply indifferent or even oppressive towards the working class. From a populist or social-democratic viewpoint, this could be seen as a" cruel" state.

Two sets of examples will be offered for defining two

Victorian socio-political trends: on the one hand, the liberal laws that defined the age as an age of reformism meant to empower the new Whig class as typified by William Ewart Gladstone's Liberal Party; on the other hand, the social unrest caused by the same political wiggery which this otherwise triumphant age managed or failed to appease.

Firstly, the liberal laws which enfranchised the man of property were called "Reform Bills", since they completely changed the voting qualifications at the beginning from nominal to real property qualifications by eliminating the old "rotten" boroughs and the appointment of constituencies by royal charter. The Reform Bill of 1832 enfranchised all the male owners of property worth at least 10 pounds in annual rent; the Reform Bill of 1867 doubled the number of voters; and the 1884 Bill brought about the universal male enfranchisement.

The parliamentary battle was fought throughout the 19th century between the representatives of the two political parties, the Liberals and the Conservatives. William Ewart Gladstone, nicknamed "The Old Man" at the head of the Liberal Party and four times as the head of the executive as the British Prime Minister, between 1868-74, 1880-85, 1885-6 and 1892-3; the other mandates were held for the Conservatives by Sir Robert Peel, first, then by Benjamin Disraeli, Queen Victoria's friend and British Prime Minister between 1874-1880. The two parties are also distinguished by their foreign policy, in so far as the Tories advocated a "big England", imperial policy, while the Liberals were the "little England" party.

Between the two of them, the Tories and the Liberals carried through the property-strengthening and free trade measures required by a successful political machine meant to sustain the kind of progress associated with the British power in control of a newly industrial economy and a modern empire. Thus, in 1846, the old Corn Laws were repealed, which had offered protectionist tariffs for British agriculture. This was the pre-requisite for effectively securing free trade, by 1860.

The year 1846 also saw the achievement of Catholic Emancipation, which meant the modernization of the British polity now capable of making allowance for other than its own Reformed, Anglican political formations. A similar modernization embraced the British polity services and institutions, thanks to the measures passed by Gladstone's administration during the 1868-1874 mandates. In education, reformism meant that essential education was generalised, so that the 1870 Education Act opened the way to generalised literacy in Britain. By 1871, the abolition of the university tests virtually transformed the leading universities of Oxford and Cambridge into lay, metropolitan, "universalist" universities. The quality of urban life improved by reforms in the fields of public administration and municipal management.

As a result, what we know today, as roughly modern city life became a reality translated into higher living standards and the increased number of commodities. The Victorian periodical, serialised pamphlets, the formal discourses, not to mention the fiction and satirical documents of the age retain numerous traces of the eventful addition to cities of public baths and laundries, museums, libraries (public reading rooms), parks, public gardens and later trams, gas and electricity facilities or water networks.

Secondly, the poverty problem that represented the reverse of the great imperial and colonial coin included in the Victorian age the passing of a number of poor laws, such as the 1834 Poor Law Amendment that created the workhouses or prisons in disguise for containing what was considered to be, at the time, the social scum of the street villains. The poor street population literally haunted the Dickensian imaginary in so many of his youthful novels. The Chartist Movement of 1836–1854 proved that beyond the middle-class modern paradise there reined supreme social chaos. For almost the entire first half of the age, the Victorian masses demonstrated in the streets and sent petitions of rights (charts) signed by ever-increasing numbers of people to the leaders of the nation but they were never listened to the 1840 Chart, for example, was signed by over three million three hundred people.

This prolonged street demonstration reminds one of the

long demonstrations for democracy in Bucharest, in the Piata Universitatii Square at the beginning of the 1990's. under Chartist inspiration, there were organised strikes, such as the first general strike of 1842 but all these got practically nowhere and had to continue their "fight" by the better organised trade-unionist movement of the 1860s and 1870s. This proved that there existed virtually "two nations" in Britain, as Benjamin Disraeli put it, the rich and the poor. The rich passed and enacted quite a big number of consistent laws for the poor, but it appears that the former were too busily engrossed in their business to devote enough attention or resources to rescuing the poor.

The Factory Acts of the period 1833–1878, however, eliminated child labour and gross overworking in factories. Some support was granted also by the government's Public Health Acts of 1871 – 1875 which granted some measure of medical assistance to the poor as well. Still, for all the echoes of the social unrest and unhealthy living conditions of the poor in the printed Victorian media, including the literature of the age, the 1880s saw the rise of more radical social movements. Such as the widespread socialism of the Fabian brand or the utopian socialism of the intellectuals and of Marxian communism, some time after the publication of the Communist Party Manifesto by Karl Marx, in 1859. By 1903, the Socialist Labour Party had also been formed as a potential opposition force on the political stage.

Culturally and critically, the main question remains to what extent Great Britain was great in the Victorian age, when regarding it from outside the magic circle of its own, self-sufficient statement about its greatness in being "the greatest and most civilized people". The cultural arguments pro-greatness would include its generalised mass literacy and its modernization of education, its quality journalism reflected in the wide circulation of prestigious magazines (such as the Blackwood's Magazine, the Cornhill Magazine, the Edinburgh Review, the Westminster Review or the Athenaeum), out of a total of 115 periodicals started in London only.

One monthly issue of a literary periodical would contain scientific or general critical essays, poetry and serialised fiction. Statistically speaking, for a wide circulation magazine totalizing 20,000 copies, there existed about five people who would read each copy. The readership amounted to one hundred thousand per issue, people who kept themselves up –to-•date with fiction, poetry and the essay, which form the subject of these lectures in Victorian literature. We can assume, therefore, for the profile of the age, that it was endowed with very strongly informed - and ample - currents of opinion and shared learning or entertainment.

This recommends the Victorian age as one of the most paradoxically learned modern ages. It was modern in so far as it was a mass communication age and learned in as much as it entertained itself with encyclopedic conversationalist and serious debate in the widely-read essays. With encyclopedic fiction in Northrop Frye's terms, encyclopedic literature being any successfully comprehensive, all-encompassing fictional forms functioning as ambitious tantalizations of the basic historical knowledge and experience on a given topic at a given moment - and the novel or the great poetic epic tends to be precisely that. In poetry, the Victorian age entertained itself with a rather ample poetry of ideas that the age had inherited from its immediate precursors, the Romantics; in fact one label attached to the Victorian poets was that of " the post-romantics".

In the novel, the Victorian popular spirit proved equally ambitious and "eminent", i.e., serious and didactic in its outreach, tone and subject matter. When we read the fully realistic existential dossiers of the novelistic prose we are invited to make major sense of the fictive life presented by Dickens, Thackeray, the Bronte sisters or George Eliot; the same is true for Thomas Hardy's naturalistic and universal plus almost, avant-la-lettre, ample existentialist case studies. A similarly didactic tone pervades the "interminable briefs" (as Dickens put it in his introductory chapter to "Bleak House") of the social cases and ideological debates presented in the essays by Thomas Carlyle, John Henry Newman, John Ruskin, John Stuart Mill, Matthew

Arnold or Walter Pater. In fact it is one function of the essay to popularize a multitude of traditions, some of which are advocated, like in a royal court room or like in the Greek Areopagus or Roman forum, while others are more or less ceremoniously rejected.

The Victorian essay student is suddenly caste in the reading role of a judge or a scholar of medievalism, the Renaissance, classicism - which Matthew Arnold terms Hellenism. Hebraism as another name given by Matthew Arnold to the Puritanical Victorianism of his day, of romanticism, or hedonism as revived by the painters and poets of the Pre-Raphaelite brotherhood or at Oxford by Walter Pater, of aestheticism and socialism as invented in and for the Victorian Brits by John Ruskin, Walter Pater, Oscar Wilde and William Morris. A direct, dramatic discussion of the same "-isms" as cultural fashions or phenomena occurs in George Bernard Shaw's plays, in the novel "Middlemarch" by George Eliot, or in Lord Alfred Tennyson's and Robert Browning's poetry, in the species called "the dramatic monologue", one of the favourite Victorian literary species in addition to the idyll or the long allegorical poem.

Understanding Victorianism in Broader Cultural Terms

An explanatory and critical discussion of 'Victorian-ism' itself from the distant vantage point of the end of the 20th century involves adding our reasonable, later experience to both the Bloomsbury detractors' fury in the first decades of our century and to the Victorians' own opinionated views. The circle of leading anti-Victorian intellectuals and creators in London's Bloomsbury circle included people like Lytton Strachey and Virginia Woolf who left reference documents of their hatred of Victorianism.

Lytton Strachey's book of 1918 was ironically titled "Eminent Victorians" and Virginia Woolf's essays on Victorian writers in "The Common Reader" series of the 1920s and 30s, respectively, are written in a dismissive tone. Their main polemical aim was to demolish the aura of respectability surrounding the edifice of Victorian culture. Reading their refutation of Victorianism we can ask why the Victorians invested so much ambition and time and money in the written entertainment, in culture or humanism, as the generic term for the above mentioned "-isms" (medievalism, Pre-Raphaelitism, classicism/ Hellenism, Puritanism/Hebraism, romanticism, aestheticism, liberalism) would be humanism. On a materialistic and cynical assumption, we may rhetorically ask if the fact that the Victorians got so closely involved with reading on a popular basis was not simply a fad – in Romanian,"un moft".

Next, we may need to wonder about the dangers of associating culture to materialism in yet another sense. How damaging is it to commit literature to a polity's shared utilitarian values, as many a Victorian writer of essays but also of fiction or poetry did? What are the effects of casting culture in the role of a public service ministering to the spiritual needs of the historical British community? as had ministered the improvement in material commodities in urban life in general during the industrialised 19th century. Among the observable effects of the Victorian sense of a useful culture is the ideological prolixity and didactic tone of Victorianism, even in the literature of pure invention, in the novel and in poetry. This is due to the fact that Victorianism ostensibly addresses a newly made gentlemanly class which it wants to educate and make commensurably important from a cultural point of view, directly proportional to its greatness in point of material wealth and progress.

The Victorian public, the cultural protagonists and cultural agents could be accused of impairing the quality of art by subordinating it to seriousness in the virtuously moral sense, and to propagandistic utilitarianism. For, instead of being in accordance with 20th century standards professionally serious or genuine in its own terms, Victorian literature spent itself in creating, defending and publically enforcing its cultural dogmas which can be quite irritating for any representatives of the 20th century, especially as was the case of the artists for art's sake in our century's opening decades. The missionary culturalism of the Victorians promotes a conventional and didactic rather than original version of culture, adapted and subordinated as it is to the needs of the laymen or the masses, to the utilitarian view of culture as a gain from the "the greatest happiness of the greatest numbers" standpoint.

In the guise of a devil's advocate, however, we may defend the late outburst of replica humanism in the Victorian age by stating that the means employed by these humanists in their literary periodicals raised the standard of mass education to such an extent, that while losing perhaps in originality as one component of spiritual progress, Victorian culture managed, nevertheless to statistically increase the participation of the masses to the phenomenon of culture so that the Victorian age functions as an age of generalised quality press.

The issues, eloquence and format of the Victorian quality press are almost inconceivable today, in the context of the trash informational explosion of the late 20th century media hype and consumerism. Also, in referring to the Victorian cultural makers or teachers as a whole, the means they employed for their business of cultural legitimation and transmission are exemplary too: they employed several humanistic traditions critically and liberally, i.e. progressively, as they were prompted by faith.

The recipe of their faith is eclectic and maybe no longer compatible with 20th century wisdom, but it nevertheless is faith, secular faith, which in the context of these lectures will be referred to by different names, such as medievalism, liberalism, hedonism. The same otherwise utilitarian intellectuals were careful to limit the materialistic effects of their age of progress; they were in two minds about their own excellence, which proves that their Bloomsbury detractors were narrow-minded, they ignored the overall picture of Victorianism, when they allowed themselves to get carried away by their high-modernist targeted fury.

These modernist writers disparaged the British bourgeois class, judging it by French avant-garde standards, because by the time of the First World War, the term "middle-class" had already become charged with the full range of negative connotations put in circulation by fashionable dandies. Maybe it is no longer necessary to join in the high intellectualist revolt against the massification implicit in Victorian culture and begin to regard the high-modernist savagely disrespectful anti-Victorianism as a case of typical revolt of the sons against their fathers. Demonstrably, the high-modernist poets in Britain, W. B. Yeats and T.S. Eliot obviously built their own prophetic dark edifice of historical lucidity and decadence with the same genealogically recognisable "bricks"; it was only that their cultural edifice opened onto a different post- war (and post-colonial) vista. With its back turned on the parental hearth and home, the modernist edifice had its tired/tiresome eyes riveted on a historical turned cultural desert or "Waste Land" as T.S.Eliot's thematic title "The Waste Land" implied.

One should focus on man's position in the universe during the Victorian age for understanding Victorianism more radically, though neither polemically, nor apologetically. The first important observation is that there existed a discrepancy between man's powers and his position within the natural world. On the one hand, his powers over external nature or the natural environment had been spectacularly increased owing to the scientific and technological progress of the first industrialization age. It was first to match this sense of greater power over nature that man developed a commensurate ambition in the management of his own material, social and historical affairs, i.e., in the man-created environment or social milieu.

As the optimistic component of man's ambition, the orthodox Puritanism of the average man as manager and, theoretically speaking, producer of materialistic success was an uncritical ethically religious doctrine or ideology that pragmatically invoked and used the Biblical spirituality to support the exemplary ascent of the Victorian imperial, industrial "first and greatest and most civilised" nation. The success of this exemplary people (styling itself a nation in the 19th century) was modeled on the success of the chosen Hebrew people as chronicled in the historical books of the Old Testament who demonstrably thrived due to God's graceful benevolence "unto them".

The Puritans, be they the historical Hebrews, the 17th century American founding fathers and pilgrims or the 19th century Victorians during the reign of Queen Victoria, took the written word of the Old or New Testament indiscriminately (read "analogically") as a kind of testimony, authority or precedent for their invented ideology of social success. Victorianism added the specific stamp of its own optimism to this social archetype: utilitarianism. Invented shortly before the beginning of the 19th century, utilitarianism was based on the work of Adam Smith, the Scottish economist, who, in his 1776 treaty "The Wealth of Nations", had been the first to assume that progress of civilisation should be naturally associated to increasing national wealth".

Utilitarianism also rested on the pragmatic philosophy principles regulating social happiness by a set of well-chosen checks and balances, as they had been stipulated in Jeremy Bentham's "Introduction to the Principles of Morals and Legislation" of 1789. (An extensive critical assessment of Bentham's role in the history of culture and utilitarianism is to be found in John Stuart Mill's essay "Bentham", anthologized in the first volume of "Proza eseistica victoriana", edited for the Romanian students' use by professors Ana Cartianu and Stefan Stoenescu at the Bucharest English Department in 1969. This three-volume book will be referred to by the acronym PEV- I, II or III - in what follows. In fiction, Dickens's "Hard Times" works as a savage caricature of the principles of utilitarian education as outrageously applied by Mr. Gradgrind in his own family.

The other component of man's ambition in his immediate plans in the 19th century was less optimistic and, psychoanalytically speaking, more compensatory. All the more ambitious was man in his immediate plans in the 19th century as he had become rationally aware and scientifically convinced of the cruelty of time and nature in the long run, especially as measured against the geological scale. By the study of rocks and fossils, the remote past of the planet was scientifically revealed to be a scene of cyclical creation and destruction irrespective and in despite of man. Man, therefore, saw himself as a puny creature whose survival was a matter of intense, ambitious presentness. To compensate for this recently proved human because biological frailty at the planetary scale and in the long-term perspective, or to compensate for man's newly discovered decentred position in the universe at large, a kind of present living frenzy and awareness took possession of energetic humanity, delivering it whole-sale into the hands of scientific, social or historical rationalism permeated by a high responsibility towards the whole human species which needed to be turned at all costs into a surviving species.

The name given to all this is materialism, and if regarded from the opposite, puritanical fold, secularism or agnosticism. The fear, however, of failure in such a grandiose project was what animated the great intellectual Victorian skeptics like the poet Matthew Arnold or the novelist Thomas Hardy or Samuel Butler, the author of the Victorian dystopia "Erewhon" and the novel "The Way of All Flesh". In typically post-romantic tones, Matthew Arnold's classicist sonnet "In Harmony with Nature" savagely deplores nature's cruelty and warns man against its deceitful example. Similarly, Thomas Hardy's powerful fiction seems to be written with the express purpose of exposing the implacable and, for man, merciless mechanisms of nature and society, as they will clash in history.

It is customary to refer to Victorianism as, on the one hand the earlier puritanical orthodoxy, while, on the other hand, to distinguish it from the adverse reactions of late Victorianism. By applying a formalist, rhetorical criterion rather than a purely ideological one, here we tend to look at the various manifestations of Victorianism as understandable human reactions to the environment, materialised in kinds of discourse as follows. First, an emotion dominated/ceremonial discourse kind, in reaction to the environment and its changes; secondly, a rationally constructive/deliberative discourse in response to the same; thirdly, as a combination of the two previous cases, a morally responsible ethical discourse that tends to be either ceremonially high-flown or, on the contrary, deprecatory. The discourse of pure ideology. This affords a classification together of both the mentalities or attitudes and the discursive stances that underlay Victorianism as a whole.

Thus, in the prose of ideas, when, taking himself very seriously, Victorian man reacted emotionally first, he asserted his own spiritual, supernatural worth very powerfully in the face of cynical materialism. This was the plea and pledge of Thomas Carlyle's vitalism or transcendentalism, which regarded man as the repository of a higher-quality, because more energetic, order than the order of the observable one.

When, in the first lecture on the essay, Carlyle's work will be studied in detail, we shall refer to his complementary dismissively emotional reactions to the man-created industrialized, urbanized environment as his medievalist anarchism paired with his ethical praise of industrious work as a means of salvation, which is termed activism. After noting that medievalism is the generic cultural term embracing all the forms of early Victorian criticism of the materialistic present, just as individualistic hedonism with its variants Pre-Raphaelitism, Renaissance revivalism, pan-aestheticism or Utopian socialism correspond to the later Victorian criticism of the pervading materialism ingrained in the first industrialised age. It is necessary to stress the overall emotional tone of the medievalist discourse that is called by Northrop Frye, in the last part of his fourth essay of the "Anatomy of Criticism", "tantrum prose".

The pervading emotional overtone of the ceremonial discourse may be either celebratory or vituperative, as the case may be, but it is nevertheless firstly impassioned and only secondly or secondarily rational/deliberative or moral/ethical. Yet another necessary remark has to do with the underlying puritanical idealism of medievalism which can be more precisely defined as a kind of alternative faith militating against the materialistic, secular limitations of the present. Another rectification of the materialistic faith came from a chronologically different quarter in Matthew Arnold's long essay of 1869 "Culture and Anarchy" which advocates a neo-classicist cult of Hellenism as an obviously ethical cure through culture of utilitarian materialism; Arnold labels the puritanical materialism of the middle-classes "Hebraism" and considers it synonymous with "narrow-mindedness". Thus, in the middle of the Victorian age, Arnold's culturalism aims at saving utilitarianism from its ignominious present by endowing it with the ethical virtues of an enlightened, utopian future that he considers to be made effective by poetry as a criticism (i.e., an enhanced understanding) of life.

Arnold will repeatedly declare that" the future of poetry is immense, because in poetry, where it is worthy of its high destinies, our race, as time goes on will find an ever surer and surer stay." ("Essays in Criticism - Second Series: The Study of Poetry", 1888). Arnold has in view the decay of every other form of creed or tradition when he declares that poetry will never be shaken but increase, since "it attaches its emotion to the idea", "which is the fact", ditto, quoted. As a typically ideological discourse that marries the ceremonially emotional strategy with the rationally deliberative one, Matthew Arnold's tone strikes a happy, didactic balance between emotion, reason and ethics.

With Arnold's criticism of life we arrive at the dominant component of Victorianism as mirrored at the cultural level of the discourse, namely liberalism. Liberalism will be proved in the second lecture on the essay to pervade the debates on (public, general or higher) education, civic existence and public communication, reaching into the more spiritually self-sufficient departments or institutions of religion or the discussion of artistic and literary creation.

The liberal discourse in either science, politics, (cultural) sociology or religion, as wielded by John Stuart Mill, Cardinal

John Henry Newman or John Henry Huxley, the popularizer of Darwin's thinking, or as typified by the aesthetic critic Walter Pater or even by the not-too-well beloved in (post-)communist Romania materialistic thinker Karl Marx, who wrote his "Manifesto" and capital "Das Kapital" in London, in the British Museum library - the liberal discourse, therefore, in each and every one of these cases is a typically deliberative, logical and rational discourse, the discourse of enlightened pragmatism or practical philosophy in its highest theoretical sense, devoid of any ideological ulterior uses or even mystifications.

Liberalism starts from the demonstration and construction of knowledge. Knowledge is the basic notion of all deliberative activities as the only logical source of theoretical or practical justice. Starting from justice and knowledge any liberally constructed social intention or project or enterprise, any important decision is arrived at in anybody's sight and never dogmatically "given". Liberalism is, like democracy, a transparent public deed (a res publica) that can be understood and verified by any reasonable human being. Cultural liberalism is probably the greatest contribution of an age of individualistic initiative and progress, as the Victorian age was, to the edifice of human history, debatable though it may be in many material or spiritual respects.

It is as a result of the accumulation and correct management of knowledge as information in an age of active mass communication that the 19th century liberal thinking can be credited with having set up new disciplines, each functioning owing to its own legitimate corpus, laws and discourse: social analysis and criticism amounting to either the theoretical discipline of sociology or the applicative one of political economy; modern hermeneutics as comparist humanism or culturalism, as aesthetics, as literary criticism; historical comparatism branching into specialised domains such as historiography, and with Sir James Frazer, at the end of the Victorian age, anthropology.

And no mention has been made as yet of the less directly humanistic disciplines of geology or biology as branches of natural science with whose spectacular development it is again the 19th century that must be credited. One major source of 19th century materialism or positivism is precisely the application of the natural science models to every department of knowledge and to any social project. It was against this levelling of human understanding that the majority of the humanists such as Carlyle, Ruskin and Arnold, then the socialists and the other brands of modern (ist) thinkers protested in the latter half of the 19th century and afterwards

Analysis of Common Themes in Victorian Poetry

Many of the themes and meanings of Victorian poetry reflect a conflicted sense of self. At once, many poems by Robert Browning and Elizabeth Barrett Browning portray a longing for the ideals of the Romantic period in literature but they are stunted as the unique period and its use of new language. The changing and ever-growing economy in the bustling city of London, and of course, the changing views of religion and its place in such a complex world. Through the poems from the Victorian era of both Robert and Elizabeth Barrett Browning and Matthew Arnold, the recurrent themes of shifting religious ideas, language usage, and the economy are clear.

During the long reign of Elizabeth religious dissent was growing and the Church broke off into three distinct branches. This schism was also coupled with the fact that new discoveries were being made, most notably by the controversial theories of Darwin, but by other thinkers as well that argued for a more rational existence. Influenced by the works of Percy and Mary Shelley, Robert Browning already had atheistic ideas and although his feelings dissipated to some degree later in his life, his numerous criticisms of religion are obvious in his poem "Fra Lippo Lippi" is a tale, in the form of a narrative poem complete with slang and comedy, of a man that was not destined to be in the Church and chooses to heed his more physical impulses instead of conforming to the will of the Church. " Browning seems to be engaging in a dialogue with the Church regarding celibacy—both in the artistic and sexual sense.

The feelings of the poem's narrator in "Fra Lippo Lippi" by Browning can easily be seen as Browning's own critique and while the main theme concerns art, the strict sense in which the church views artistic pursuits and products is similar to the way it requires priests to live celibate lives. While the church's main argument is that art should be presented as something "higher" than the base representation of the human form, this denies the essential humanity of the subject, God's people. Along these same lines, the way the church frowns upon sexual, lustful activity on the part of its clergy by demanding celibacy is exactly the same request as for the artist. Both demands of the church, artistic and sexual are idealized conceptions of how humans should be represented and both, according to the narrator of the poem, are entirely unrealistic and misguided. Through this poem, Browning is arguing against mandatory celibacy for priests and is suggesting, through the story and artistic struggle of Fra Lippo Lippi, that the demands of the church go against human nature.

We are all, to use Browning's word, "beasts" thus prone to the same desires that the church wishes to "rub out". The narrator of this poem from the Victorian period argues that his life in cloister has been unnatural and restraining and bemoans the lack of life he is allowed to experience (although he obviously breaks the rules). The mandatory celibacy is made even more absurd when the Fra point out, "You should not take a fellow eight years old/ and make him swear to never kiss the girls". Earlier in the poem, he speaks of this in terms of other boys that had been brought into cloister by openly saying, "Trash, such as these poor devils of Medicine have given their hearts to—all at eight years old".

He seems to see this celibacy as a terrible waste of youth and life—both of which he values above all else. He seeks to represent truth through art, despite the fact that everything in his life is geared towards a completely celibate existence—both in art, sexuality, and life. The story of his life can be summed up in the simple phrase on line, "Rub all out!' Well, well, there's my life in short." He has been told to extinguish the art and the humanity, thus the keen sexual desire that longs to be free. This goes against human nature—an idea that was taking firm root after the more scientific observations about the self and the natural world and thus religion is represented as the antithesis of all that is natural.

What is most interesting about this religious criticism in the Victorian era as seen in some of its poetry is that there is also a certain yearning for the old days of religious order. For example, in "Sonnets from the Portuguese" Elizabeth Barrett Browning bemoans her loss of faith when she equates her lover as something she cannot quite grasp, something that is far away but familiar, the "lost Saints" that once presided over her world. It is almost a romantic-era poem but in the last stanza, I love thee freely, as men strive for right; / I love thee purely, as they turn from Praise" then goes on... "I love thee with a love I seemed to lose with my lost Saints" and the general tone of the poem indicates that there is something missing and remote about the speaker's existence. She is not quite connected with the world of God and Saints yet she is also not connected with the Romantic ideas from earlier poetry.

In true Victorian style, she seems unable to extricate religion from the picture; it is something she seems to yearn for, much like a lost or dead lover from glorious days gone by. The Introduction to Victorian puts it rather succinctly as "All of the Victorian poets show the strong influence of the Romantics, but they cannot sustain the confidence that the Romantics felt in the power of the imagination. Victorians often rewrite poems from the Romantic Movement with a sense of belatedness and distance (1060). One cannot help but wonder if it is the "religion question" that is perturbing their brilliance or just a melancholy from the fast-paced, industrialized, modern world that had sprung up in this era.

Although Elizabeth Barrett Browning was more conservative in her expression of religious criticism, even her husband expresses some sense of loss over the grand days when faith and religion were apparent. In his poem, "Love Among the Ruins" he details a city that has fallen, but nonetheless it is romanticized and described as a place where "they built their gods a brazen pillar high / As the sky". It is interesting to note how Robert Browning's language changes when he speaks of these more traditional and lofty ideas about religion and spirituality and it is worth noting that Robert Browning is a master of using different voices and language to convey different meaning.

The language of the Victorian period is most traditionally associated with that of Tennyson whose poetry used grand language that was not of the Victorian age, but rather conjured up a romantic image of days gone by and glorious places and events from history. In many ways then, instead of having Tennyson stand out as the quintessential Victorian (or even English) poet, it seems more fitting that Robert Browning should have the honour because he was capable of using the grandiose language of older more traditional poets, yet was also able to invoke slang and rhymes that are almost childish in their simplicity—both in terms of language and structure. For instance, his poem "Two in the Campagna" delicately conjures the Romantic era with a tinge of Tennyson thrown in—almost for effect. The second stanza is flowery and stands in stark contrast to the bold language of "Fra Lippo Lippi".

"Help me to hold it! First it left / The yellow fennel, run to seed / There, branching from the brickwork's cleft, / Some old tomb's ruin: yonder weed / Took up the floating weft". It seems he is unable to resist the traditional pastoral impulse and delights in using the tone and form of such poems but to look at such a poem provides a vastly incomplete picture of Browning as a poet.

The fact that he was able to harness everyday language and combine it with his knowledge of classical and traditional language is symbolic of the sense of encroaching modernity of the Victorian period. The economy was growing, the nobility was becoming less important, and all of the class structures that once propagated such "flowery" Romantic poetry were disappearing. There is a visible (and even audible) search occurring with Victorian poets to find a voice that is uniquely of their time and place and although Tennyson was perhaps the most prosaic, he did not capture the essence, the almost post-modern (by our definition) self-conscious co-mingling of so many decades, forms, structures, and movements. Although Elizabeth Barrett Browning has notable skill, there is not such an edge that separates her from other poets of the time. While it is true that she represents one of the few distinctive women's voices in Victorian poetry, her words do not slice; they soothe. Unlike other, later Victorian poets, Elizabeth Barrett Browning's assertions of love and "lost Saints" sounds a bit hollow when one understands that on the level of language alone, English poetry was undergoing a massive (and often, or so it seems) fruitless search for a distinct identity.

In Robert Browning's "Love Among the Ruins" one cannot help but think of the new economy that was growing exponentially during the middle part of the Victorian period—the period in which he was doing much of his writing. He is wistful and as mentioned above he imagines this different society building "brazen pillars" to their gods. This is a bustling city he represents in the poem "Love Among the Ruins" and money and the economy is at the forefront—mentioned even before the allusions to a grander view of religion. Instead of making this ruined city fall only because of war, he sees the ills of money and remarks, "And that glory and that shame alike, the gold/ Bought and sold".

The ever-growing capitalist economy was not only changing culture as a whole, but the very language and images used in Victorian poetry. In fact, this slant on economic history can form an important point of analysis of "Love Among the Ruins" by Robert Browning.

While there was a great deal of wealth and gold, there was a darker side to this as well which Matthew Arnold explores in his poem, "To a Republican Friend" he reminds the reader of the sad side of the new economy and the potential for greed in such a rapidly progressing system of commerce and industrialization. Matthew Arnold closes the poem with the resonating yet simply worded lines, "The armies of the homeless and unfed: — / If these are yours, if this is what you are, / Then am I yours, and what you feel, I share". Instead of setting, his language on high, as Tennyson and the poet John Keats were wont to do; he brings it down to a lower level and exposes the dirty side of the new economy and subsequent politics. During the Victorian age there was an increased sense of treating workers well and although one might to consider this to be a reminder to be a humanitarian, it is a reminder of what they flowery language of the earlier never spoke.

Between these three poets of the Victorian period, it is possible to see the themes of religious questioning and turmoil, the changes and revisions of language in order to find a distinctively Victorian form of poetry and syntax, and an ever-present but implicit awareness of the economic issues of the world outside the of the speakers' lines. While it has been stated above that Robert Browning captures these ideas perfectly because he is able to combine all of the themes without backing himself in a corner as far as language is concerned, perhaps it is unfair to try to pinpoint any particular poet as representative of an age that was progressing too rapidly to be pinned down.

Chapter 6

Tennyson as a Victorian Poet

Introduction: The Victorian Zeitgeist. Mannerism and the Post-Romantic Heritage

Just as the title suggests, in analyzing the poetry of Lord Alfred Tennyson, a 20th century reader gains almost direct access to the Victorian Zeitgeist that he can be said to typify. This is mainly due to Tennyson's sharing in the quality that most Victorian poetry has that of being a form of fictionalized public letter writing. This is striking for someone reading poetry after nearly one century of experimentally obscure lyricism in the symbolist key, or the surrealistic (Dadaist) key, or, again, the factual classicism of the American imagism/vorticism - in short, after the modernist revolution in letters in general and in poetry in particular.

Thus, Victorian poetry is complicated and difficult in a very different way from the complications/difficulties we have grown accustomed with in the 20th century. (This does not mean that, as it will be seen immediately, Victorian fashions in poetry have been entirely shed or forgotten nowadays; on the contrary, they have added up to the conglomerate of conventions behind which the common mind of the 20th century has been hiding. And it is the purpose of today's lecture on Victorian poetry – and the others to follow - to make the readers aware of the Victorian heritage to the poetry and poets still cherished today in the space of the English language poetic craft).

The first thing worth noting is that the same didactic vein pervading Victorian literature in an age of realism in fiction paradoxically makes Victorian poetry be anything but realistic. This comes from its quality as public poetry in an age when the dominant ideology dictated a dogmatic turning to the past for discovering spectacular models of public action and public feeling materialised as "commendable, great literature". In plainer terms, therefore, Victorian poetry, just like the Victorian essay, is obsessed by the great ideas of a fictionalised past, it functions as a popular encyclopedia or commentary to myth or folklore and it is, consequently, a fashionable manneristic commentary to a variety of ideas. Consequently, the primary task of the 20th century student is to identify the idea(s) that a particular Victorian poem illustrates and to discover the precise manner in which it achieves this. This is, of course, in direct opposition with the warning launched by the 20th century American formalist critics, W. Wimsatt or Cleanth Brooks against "the heresy of paraphrase",

This leads to the second general observation about Victorian poetry: if it is lyrical, a Victorian poem is so in an oblique, indirect way. In his 1932 text "New Bearings in English Poetry", F. R. Leavis refers to "the mischeviousness of the 19th century conventions of 'the poetical' " (apud Donald Thomas's excellent file of illuminating contemporary and later criticism in Victorian poetry represented by the lost book of the British Council Library in Bucharest, "The Post-Romantics" – which it unfortunately represents today in absentia. Among these mischievousness, Leavis enumerates:

- The dramatized poetic voice, which prompts to us here a jocose statement: poetry becomes ventriloquy (sic!), being voiced through a mask;
- Poetry amounts to allegory, voiced as fairytale or as medieval legend. More often than not, the reader of Victorian poetry has to grapple with streams of historically obscure consciousness projected outwardly or packed for the use of the Victorian

public, with the Victorian public's own psychological or moral dominants.

A pattern of double obliqueness or difficulty or, from the point of view of direct lyricism, double difficulty, underwrites any Victorian poem, whose sentiment hides behind two "veils": the historically remote one, classicist or medievalist, in Tennyson's allegorical poetry and the, nowadays, remote veil of the intended Victorian lesson in spirituality. With Tennyson, the intended lesson in spirituality embraces the realm of art versus conventional life (in"The Lady of Shallot"), or the opposition between the man of aspiration, in general, as compared to the man of convention (in"Ulysses").

Grotesquely between the sentimental craving of man and his limited life doomed to defeat, old age dwindling and ultimately, decrepitude (as typified in"Tithonus"). Victorian lyricism in general is steeped in sadness and melancholy and seeks the weak consolations of oblivion, more often than not lethal oblivion. Orthodox Victorian poetry is, therefore, a kind of morbidly elegiac lyrical poetry, feeble, decadent and even – stuffy.

The resulting lack in lyrical vigour was translated by literary history into a label for Victorian poetry as a whole: "Post-romantic poetry". When analysing this label from the point of view of Northrop Frye's "Anatomy of Criticism", the first essay, it is possible to detach a number of retained features that the Romantics had added to poetry, features that were not lost in Victorian verse.

– Regarding the poet, the Victorian poet, just like the Romantic, moves back in time and space, higher too and beyond the conventional experience, into a more imaginative order of experience. But whereas the Romantic remains lyrically elevated in/by that imaginative transport, the Victorian poet returns wiser and embittered, to his present-day audience for whose sole benefit. It appears he has soared into the provisional infinite; hence, the shared elegiac tone associated to Victorian lyricism. On a formal level, this points to the difference between the romantic love of (organic) metaphor and the Victorian alternative love of allegory, simile and dramatic representation in general. It is not by accident that the Victorian poets selected the form of the dramatic monologue as their favourite form of self-expression. But the dramatic monologue will be analysed later, in connection with its greatest Victorian protagonist, Robert Browning.

- Regarding the formal features shared by the Victorian with the Romantic poets, Frye mentions the tendency of the Romantics to develop encyclopedic, grand, long poems in the form of epics, which is retained in Victorian poetry. The structures and motivations of these long epics can only be elucidated when relating the poetry to the poet's own design. The range of encyclopedic epics includes:
- Victorian replicas of mythological and religious or folk epics (respectively in Tennyson's Arthurian" Idylls of the King", 1859, Gerard Manley Hopkins's" The Wreck of the Deutschland", 1875 or Matthew Arnold's longer verse narratives" Empedocles on Etna", 1852 and"The Scholar Gipsy", 1853);
- Allegorical epics (such as Tennyson's"The Palace of Art" or the feminist fable of"The Princess");
- Psychological epics of all hues: extensive and comprehensive spiritual autobiographies in a major elegiac key (e.g. Tennyson's peerless "In Memoriam" or Matthew Arnold's "Thyrsis"); dramatised alienist confessions (Tennyson's monodrama "Maud" or Robert Browning's long psychological and philosophical thriller "The Ring and the Book" 1868-9
- High-mimetic novels in plain verse (Elizabeth Barrett Browning's" Aurora Leigh", 1857)

But there are obviously missing features in the Victorian

poems as compared to the Romantic ones: in addition to the above-mentioned failure of the Victorian poets to radically turn away from the contemporary social or public thinking, as the high Romantics had done, the nature poetry of the Victorians lacks the nature – inspired sense of power, and it is bland and outspoken or simply elegiac, where Romantic poetry had been mystical. As F. R. Lewis put it in the same text already quoted in Donald Thomas's book: "It was possible for the poets of the Romantic period to believe that the interests animating their poetry were the forces moving the world, or that might move it. But Victorian poetry admits implicitly that the actual world is alien, recalcitrant and unpoetical and that no protest is worth making except the protest of withdrawal". Lastly, the direct belief in the creative genius of the poet underpinning the fabric of any Romantic poem be it great or small in size, is missing from each and every Victorian poem.

This belief is translatable as a kind of repressed manifestation of a stunted when not downwardly ironic Victorian poet who is necessarily wearing a didactic, moralising mask. Even the least sophisticated Victorian poet puts on an allegorical mask - pastoral, professorial, clinical – in the verse narratives. These can no longer be called "ballads" because they are too learned to qualify for mere ballads; also they are by no means intended as lyrical, because they are learned allegories addressing well-informed gentlemen and ladies, as in Tennyson's "The Lady of Shallot" gathering for the purposes of poetic communion the typically elegant audience of "Knight and burgher, lord and dame". The more talented Victorian poet, however, has a correspondingly more difficult alternative: that of assuming the voice of a local persona who is heard speak in the dramatic monologue on a very partially visible scene.

The last consequence of all this is that, as in Matthew Arnold's poetry, the lyricism of the Victorian poet is, as the French would put it, "dirb", or as Northrop Frye would qualify it, a (self-) ironic lyricism dismayed by the specter of the Greek sparagmos, the tearing to pieces of man to whom "heroism and effective action" are denied. Now, Frye decidedly considers that sparagmos is"the archetypal theme of irony and satire". This obviously leads one to the conclusion that as a whole and through its post-Romantic qualities, Victorian poetry exists within the horizon of the ironic mode. Thus, a major de-synchronization operates in the Victorian age. Victorian poetry, when lyrical, more decidedly manifests lay, modern man's universal and personal despair as (tragic) irony, whereas fiction still toys with romance and the self-important high mimetic forms of realism. (And this ultimately, and ironically speaking, "recommends" the Victorian age as a cultural age lacking in true, inherent stylistic and aesthetic greatness. The Victorian age is great as a modern commentator only, as an impersonator or teacher of traditions and counter-traditions fabricated by other ages and other people. Even more so is the Victorian age essential for a Romanian modern student of letters, whom it can equip with the cultural background and critical spirit compulsory for a metropolitan intellectual. In a way, the average Romanian student as a potential representative of a provincial, mass culture is in the position of Matthew Arnold's Philistine who is in need of major cultural instruction or, as John Henry Newman would put it, of Liberal Education in a University.

Applying the General Features of Victorian Poetry to Tennyson's Poems

The first consequence of Tennyson's transposition of Victorian orthodox ideas in the neo-classicist key superimposed upon the key of late medievalism is the idyllic tone of a pastoral poetry which is elevating before being lyrical. Secondly, Tennyson's poems oscillate between a resulting epical grandeur (you can read here "grandiloquence") and a picturesque artificiality meant to move even the less refined middle-class average readers in the otherwise busy entrepreneurial circles, in their spare time.

Tennyson had a magus-like power of instilling dignity and picturesque in the domestic, everyday Victorian life as well as in many a public occasion, when people were eager to rejoice or mourn in public. For such occasions, Tennyson had ready many a pastoral allegory or elegy, elevating the factual above itself, rendering it closer to the ideal.

All this means that Tennyson's participative readiness fitted him, as a writer of occasional poetry for complying with the consumerist taste that was shared by this first age of mass communication which the Victorian age was.

(It is quite clear that the Victorian consumerism was of an intellectual brand, not the raw, material consumerism advertised in today's media). As the contemporary Victorian literary critic Walter Bagehot put it in his review of Tennyson's "Idylls of the King"as excerpted by Donald Thomas in his book: there were "two audiences for Tennyson's poetry: those with more youthful enthousiasm, the poet's admirers, and the wider public alienated from poetry".

Actually, from the common status he was the fourth child of eight sons born – in 1809 - to the Lincolnshire rector (in Romanian "vicar") of Somersby, Tennyson rose to the dignity of a national bard and the friend of the Royal Pair, being nominated "Poet Laureate", after Wordsworth, in 1850 and was chosen by Thomas Alva Edison to record his voice, among only three other famous 19th century voices (as Donald Thomas shows in his introduction to the Tennyson casebook in his "Post –Romantics").

From the point of view of the 20th century reader, there are two poets Tennyson, one readable, the other unreadable today, respectively, the lyrical poet and the occasional, public poet. This is mainly due to the fact that we are a different audience for poetry today than the public Tennyson enjoyed in the 19th century.

We are neither enthusiastic in the youthful, naïve sense, nor alienated from poetry in the same way as the Victorian wider public. Rather, we form a middle (but not" middle-class"!) category of public who like to think of themselves as neither wide nor too enthusiastic readers of literature this is the point of view of the average reader.

Tennyson the Lyrical Poet

Tennyson the lyrical poet fits almost perfectly the identikit portrait offered for the generic Victorian poet in this lecture's introduction, under this portrait might well remain an abstraction, were it not actually obtained by ad hoc extrapolation from Tennyson's particular case).

Anyone can follow extensively in Tennyson's lyrical poetry what T. S. Eliot described in his essay on the Metaphysical poets as "the dissociation of sensibility", more and more refined language with feeling remaining more crude; or as Matthew Arnold complained, in the Preface to his First Edition of "Poems", morbid sufferance, sufferance, in excess to accompany just rudimentary human action. Tennyson's poetry, which Walter Bagehot terms"ornate", exaggerates in all these ways the basic assumptions of lyricism.

It is, just like Matthew Arnold's poetry, poetry suffused in "a universal note of sadness". This vein pervades Tennyson's poetry from his first volume, "Juvenilia", through the great elegiac sequence of "In Memoriam" which poetically attempted to come to terms with the death of a beloved friend and it echoed forth in the "Idylls of the King".

It has the power, praised by E. A. Poe in "The Poetic Principle", to offer "the elevating excitement of the soul", but it has two shortcomings: it is the only tonality of Tennyson's lyrical poems, always written in the elegiac, sick key and it is derived from a predictable plot describing human and universal decline. This makes one read the same basic poem with few variations, irrespective of the title and the superficial accidents.

It is worth comparing the feelings induced by the setting of the nature poem "Song", with the background of a poem about a dying swan in the same first volume, "Juvenilia", or with ... "other poems" in the later collections "The Lady of Shallot and Other Poems" and "English Idylls and Other Poems":

Heavily hangs the broad sunflower
Over its grave i'the earth so chilly:

Heavily hangs the hollyhock,
Heavily hangs the tiger-lily.

II

The air is damp, and hush'd and close,
As a sick man's room when he taketh repose
An hour before death;
My very heart faints and my whole soul grieves
At the moist rich smell of the rotting leaves,
And the breath
Of the fading edges of box beneath,
And the year's last rose.
Heavily hangs the broad sunflower
Over its grave i'the earth so chilly:
Heavily hangs the hollyhock,
Heavily hangs the tiger-lily.
("Song")
The wild swan's death-hymn took the soul
Of that waste place with joy
Hidden in sorrow: at first to the ear
The warble was low, and full and clear;
And the creeping mosses and clambering weeds,
And the willow-branches hoar and dank,
And the wavy swell of the soughing reeds,
And the wave-worn horns of the echoing bank,
And the silvery marsh – flowers that throng
The desolate creeks and pools among,
Were flooded over with eddying song.
("The Dying Swan")
or, at the beginning of "The Lotos-Eaters"
In the afternoon they came unto a land
In which it seemed always afternoon.
All round the coast the languid air did swoon,
Breathing like one that hath a weary dream.
Full-faced above the valley stood the moon;
And like a downward smoke, the slender stream
Along the cliff to fall and pause and fall did seem.

A land of streams! some, like a downward smoke,
Slow-dropping veils of thinnest lawn, did go;
And some thro' wavering lights and shadows broke,
Rolling a slumberous sheet of foam below

From this atmosphere, Tennyson awakens into existence equally melancholy shadows of characters, incarnations of sad,.slothful dreams themselves:

The charmed sunset linger'd low adown
In the red West: thro' mountain clefts the dale
Was seen far inland, and the yellow down
Border'd with palm, and many a winding vale
And meadow, set with slender gallingale;
A land where all things always seem'd the same!
And round about the keel with faces pale,
Dark faces pale against that rosy flame,
The mild-eyed melancholy Lotos-eaters came.
Branches they bore of that enchanted stem,
Laden with flower and fruit, wherof they gave
To each, but whoso did receive of them,
And taste, to him the gushing of the wave
Far far away did seem to mourn and rave
On alien shores; and if his fellow spake,
His voice was thin, as voices from the grave;
And deep-asleep he seem'd, yet all awake,
And music in his ears his beating heart did make.

With these lines extending into a whole fable of languidness, forgetfulness and doom enacted through the story of the public orgy represented by the opiate Lotos eating. It is as if, from this suffused, oppressing memory, the great Romantic dreams and visions are projected as pale phantoms onto the Victorian canvass destined for public shows and not for visions.

Then at the opening of the other Greek fable of "Tithonus", the climactic outpour of similar imagery:

The woods decay, the woods decay and fall,
The vapours weep their burthen to the ground,
Man comes and tills the field and lies beneath.

And after many a summer dies the swan.

This overwhelming, nightmarish sentiment in the decadent romantic key will be further and systematically explored by Tennyson, and also to its ultimate transcendental implications, in the cumulative sequence of 131 philosophical lyrics forming "In Memoriam". These poems transmute the underlying phantom of death that haunted the Victorian universe of experience by directly confronting it. "In Memoriam" thus functions as a great exorcising poem on death and the human limitation regarded against the wider canvass of the world and time, for this age that feared its own shadow, in Jungian terms. In poems such as III, XI and L, Victorian sentiments got expressed in the purest vein of lyricism, with a directness and clarity that amount the great action of coming to terms with experience rather than self-complacently toying with it. This last observation can be proved by comparing Tennyson's earlier sleep/languish poems, with the straightforward meditative discursiveness of poem IV in the sequence:—

Victorian artists manneristically find refuge in various alternatively favourite histories. The Pre-Raphaelite brotherhood painters and poets get transported to that period which marks the threshold between the Middle Ages and the Renaissance, which they identify from beyond its actual span as the period of the old Pre-Raphaelite school painters, Giotto, Angelico, Orcagna, John Bellini.

The poet Browning - who was also a man of subtle artistic tastes - and Walter Pater, the Oxford don and art theorist - who influenced all the later generations of Victorian artists and aesthetic theorists - opened the windows of their contemporary Victoriansm into the Renaissance itself. Matthew Arnold proclaimed a more general standard or ideal in any "epoch of expansion", be it past or foreign, the period of Pericles' century in Athens, the Elizabethan period in England, the period of French academism which he saw to be successfully extended into the 19th century culture of France. Last but not least, the poet Gerard Manley Hopkins selected as his private model age that of the Oxford eccentric Duns Scotus's anti-Thomist scholasticism, which he revived through his militant devotional verse. In this way, Victorian escapism ends where it had started with Thomas Carlyle, namely in the Middle Ages of heroic ethics and enhanced vision.

To Sleep I give my powers away;
My will is bondsman to the dark;
I sit within a helmless bark,
And with my heart I muse and say:
O heart, how fares it with thee now,
That thou should'st fail from thy desire,
Who scarcely darest to inquire,
'What is it makes me beat so low'
Something it is which thou hast lost,
Some pleasure from thine early years.
Break thou deep vase of chilling tears,
That grief hath shaken into frost!
Such clouds of nameless trouble cross
All night below the darken'd eyes:
With morning wakes the will, and cries,,
'Thou shalt not be the fool of loss.'

III

O Sorrow, cruel fellowship,
O Priestess in the vaults of Death,
O sweet and bitter in a breath,
What whispers from thy lying lip
The stars,' she whispers, 'blindly run;
A web is wov'n across the sky;
From out waste places comes a cry,
nd murmurs from the dying sun:
'And all the phantom, Nature, stands-
With all the music in her tone,
A hollow echo of my own,-
A hollow form with empty hands."
And shall I take a thing so blind,
Embrace her as my natural good;

Or crush her, like a vice of blod,
Upon the threshold of the mind

XI

Calm is the morn without a sound,
Calm as to suit a calmer grief,
And only thro' the faded leaf
The chestnut pattering to the ground:
Calm and deep peace on this high wold,
And on these dews that drench the furze,
And all the silvery gossamers
That twinkle into green and gold:
Calm and still light on yon great plain
That sweeps with all its autumn bowers,
And crowded farms and lessening towers,
To mingle with the bounding main:
Calm and deep peace in this wide air,
These leaves that redden to the fall;
And in my heart, if calm at all,
If any calm, a calm despair:
Calm on the seas, and silver sleep,
And waves that sway themselves in rest,
And dead calm in that noble breast
Which heaves but with the heaving deep.

L

Be near me when my light is low
When the blood creeps, and the nerves prick
And tingle; and the heart is sick
And all the wheels of Being slow.
Be near me when the sensuous frame
Is rack'd with pangs that conquer trust;
And Time, a maniac scattering dust,
And Life, a Fury slinging flame.
Be near me when my faith is dry,
And men the flies of latter spring,
That lay their eggs, and sting and sing,

And weave their petty cells and die.
Be near me when I fade away,
To point the term of human strife,
And on the low dark verge of life
The twilight of eternal day.

The Public Poet Tennyson

Just like Dickens, Tennyson died rich and lionized by ordinary readers and officials alike, in 1892, and buried in the Poet's Corner in Westminster Abbey. While still living he was also knighted as first Baron Tennyson of Aldworth and Farringford. All this was in recognition to his great merits as a public poet. Today we may venture to read his official poetry for its documentary value if we want to study the ideas, environment, general mentality and lifestyle of the Victorian men.

The superior, gentlemanly ethics and refinement often voiced as a brand of chivalrous feminism as it happens in "The Princess", which being a long poem bears the subtitle of "A Medley". It allegorically sweeps through Victorian domestic and industrial life regarded in the light of Victorian culture as refinement and learning, Victorian colonial leisure, Victorian urbanity, Victorian fashion and sporting during a leisure day in the outing.

As "The Prologue" explains, the setting is a Victorian big house or mansion in the countryside which idyllically recreates urban values, ambitions and intellectual debates from the elegant vista of Sir Walter Vivian's little palace which seems to concentrate in little the whole Victorian material and intellectual universe. Facetiously and graciously then, this world will be counteracted by the poet's"fearful", actually farcical fairy-tale or fable of the all-feminine University-Convent of the Princess Ida, a man-eater who threatened the male I of the storyteller Prince with her whole army of chaste women or cultural amazons.

From The Prologue
Sir Walter Vivian all a summer's day
Gave his broad lawns until the set of sun

Up to the people: thither flocked at noon
His tenants, wife and child, and thither half
The neighbouring borough with their Institute
Of which he was the patron. I was there
From college, visiting the son, - the son
A Walter too,- with others of our set,
Five others: we were seven at Vivian-place.
And me that morning Walter show'd the house,
Greek, set with busts: from vases in the hall
Flowers of all heavens, and lovelier than their names,
Grew side by side; and on the pavement lay
Carved stones of the Abbey-ruin in the park,
Huge Ammonites, and the first bones of Time;
And on the tables every clime and age
Jumbled together; celts and calumets,
Claymore and snowshoe, toys in lava, fans
Of sandal, amber, ancient rosaries,
Labourious orient ivory sphere in sphere,
The cursed Malayan crease, and battle-clubs
From the isles of palm: and higher on the walls,
Betwixt the monstrous horns of elk and deer,
His own forefathers' arms and armour hung.
And 'this' he said 'was Hugh's at Agincourt;
And that was old Sir Ralph's at Ascalon:
A good knight he! We keep a chronicle
With all about him' – which he brought, and I
Dived in a hoard of tales that dealt with knights,
Half-legend, half-historic, counts and kings
Who laid about them at their wills and died.

While the visitors are given a tour of the park, in which the reader may visually participate like in a documentary movie on today's cable television, or like in a Zefirelli super-production set in the Victorian age. One seems to overcome by the uninterrupted chain of gracious miracles and technological toys meant precisely for such a day of sporting, which playful miracles transform this park into a land of the 19th century fairies, or into an imagined International

Exhibition of 1851 – only here imagined a few years in advance (as "The Princess" was first published in 1847):

....round the lake
A little clock-work steamer paddling plied
And shook the lilies: perch'd about the knolls
A dozen angry models jetted steam:
A petty railway ran; a fire balloon
Rose gem-like up before the dusky groves
And dropt a fairy parachute and past:
And there thro' twenty posts of telegraph
They flash'd a saucy message to and fro
Between the mimic stations; so that sport
Went hand in hand with Science;

The same pairing of science with prowess, this time seriously rather than in jest, occurs in the strange poem "Locksley Hall", a concessive and didactic narrative and a thwarted love story yoking together feminism with progress:

"Here about the beach, I wander'd, nourishing a youth sublime With the fairy tales of science, and the long results of Time This poem contains some incredible injunctions, such as the following:

.... forward, forward let us range

Let the great world spin forever down the ringing grooves of change the heroic Homeric echo of"the ringing plains of Troy" makes one vacillate between despair, disdain and mere laughter. But, the poem continues with its heroic couplets in exactly the same incredibly encomiastic tone:

There methinks would be enjoyment more than in this march of mind. In the steamship, in the railway, in the thoughts that shake mankind. After all this praise of science and progress, we cannot wonder at the tone of Tennyson's topical" Ode Sung at the Opening of the International Exhibition"

I

Uplift a thousand voices full and sweet,
In this wide hall with earth's invention stored,
And praise the invisible universal Lord,

Who lets once more in peace the nations meet,
Where Science, Art, and Labour have outpour'd
Their myriad horns of plenty at our feet

Analytically speaking now, Tennyson as a public poet is obviously full of contradictions, because his occasional verse should be capable of flexibly moving from required lyricism to grandiloquence, as the case may be; sometimes, his public service as a Laureate required him to be sentimental; at other times, didactic. When sentimentally grandiloquent, Tennyson writes idylls. As a kind of fixed allegorical poem, conventionally presenting a scene of rural, pastoral life, giving a sense of tranquil happiness ranging from serenity to euphoria (as J. A. Cuddon defines it in his "Dictionary of Literary Terms and Theory", Penguin, 1992) and again, conventionally transporting the reader to an idealized, remotely attainable past. When didactically grandiloquent, Tennyson writes odes (i.e., ceremonial, celebratory verse) dedicated to science and progress, to this or that member of the Royal Family.

To this or that historical victory on the battle fields of the Continent or at home, as at the opening of the International Exhibition in London in 1851. The poems of "Locksley Hall" are precisely that, and Tennyson's explicit odes "To the Queen" "A Welcome to Alexandra", "A Welcome to Her Royal Highness Marie Alexandrovna, Duchess of Edinburgh", "The Charge of the Light Brigade", "Ode on the Death of the Duke of Wellington" or "The Third of February, 1852").All these occasional poems may be read as documents illustrating the age just like paintings in "The National Portrait Gallery" in London, and then their high-flown language is atoned for, and they will immediately assume a humbler and more acceptable position among the Victorian Age exhibits.

This lassification of Tennyson's of ficial, "collabourationist" or occasional poetry into idylls and odes, brings us to one of Tennyson's most successful legitimating narratives in verse: his Arthurian "Idylls of the King" (1859- occasioned by the death of Prince Albert, the Royal Consort). Written in order to dignify in retrospect the life of the Royal Pair and to console the Queen for the loss of the Prince, they identified the dead Prince with King Arthur. ("The Passing of Arthur" being especially topical, while it was also followed by the already quoted ode "To the Queen") and inaugurated a parallel soon to become the fashion, between the Victorian society as a whole and the legendary knightly court of King Arthur et comp.

In this way, the social and moral mythology of the inflated Victorian excellence and virtuous aspiration became a publicly shared ideology. The epic thread of the twelve poems that make up the sequence has to do with the recognition of Arthur's excellence in war and in marriage, his fight for the moral restoration of the knights who have lost their power and purity by a life of sin.

There is an entire catalogue of allegorical virtues, vices and beneficial transformations high-mimetically connecting the Victorians with the Knights of the Round Table. Thus, Sir Lancelot is the (sensual) good man who stands in need of being tamed; Queen Guinevere concentrates all the emotional hues of the human personality and points towards the need of controlling one's self through reason; the Sword Excalibur is the exemplary straightened and repository of the guiding Spirit in general. A pattern of mutual explicit obtains therefore between the literal and the figurative levels of the allegory, which enriches both levels in their signifying power.

To Sleep I give my powers away;
My will is bondsman to the dark;
I sit within a helmless bark,
And with my heart I muse and say:
O heart, how fares it with thee now,
That thou should'st fail from thy desire,
Who scarcely darest to inquire,
'What is it makes me beat so low'
Something it is which thou hast lost,
Some pleasure from thine early years.
Break thou deep vase of chilling tears,
That grief hath shaken into frost!
Such clouds of nameless trouble cross

All night below the darken'd eyes:
With morning wakes the will, and cries,,
'Thou shalt not be the fool of loss.'

III

O Sorrow, cruel fellowship,
O Priestess in the vaults of Death,
O sweet and bitter in a breath,
What whispers from thy lying lip
'The stars,' she whispers, 'blindly run;
A web is wov'n across the sky;
From out waste places comes a cry,
And murmurs from the dying sun:
'And all the phantom, Nature, stands-
With all the music in her tone,
A hollow echo of my own,-
A hollow form with empty hands."
And shall I take a thing so blind,
Embrace her as my natural good;
Or crush her, like a vice of blod,
Upon the threshold of the mind

XI

Calm is the morn without a sound,
Calm as to suit a calmer grief,
And only thro' the faded leaf
The chestnut pattering to the ground:
Calm and deep peace on this high wold,
And on these dews that drench the furze,
And all the silvery gossamers
That twinkle into green and gold:
Calm and still light on yon great plain
That sweeps with all its autumn bowers,
And crowded farms and lessening towers,
To mingle with the bounding main:
Calm and deep peace in this wide air,
These leaves that redden to the fall;

And in my heart, if calm at all,
If any calm, a calm despair:
Calm on the seas, and silver sleep,
And waves that sway themselves in rest,
And dead calm in that noble breast
Which heaves but with the heaving deep.

L

Be near me when my light is low
When the blood creeps, and the nerves prick
And tingle; and the heart is sick
And all the wheels of Being slow.
Be near me when the sensuous frame
Is rack'd with pangs that conquer trust;
And Time, a maniac scattering dust,
And Life, a Fury slinging flame.
Be near me when my faith is dry,
And men the flies of latter spring,
That lay their eggs, and sting and sing,
And weave their petty cells and die.
Be near me when I fade away,
To point the term of human strife,
And on the low dark verge of life
The twilight of eternal day.

Chapter 7

Text and Summary

[SH]"The Lady of Shallot"

Complete Text

PART I

On either side the river lie
Long fields of barley and of rye,
That clothe the wold and meet the sky;
And thro' the field the road runs by
To many-tower'd Camelot;
And up and down the people go,
Gazing where the lilies blow
Round an island there below,
The island of Shallot.
Willows whiten, aspens quiver,
Little breezes dusk and shiver
Thro' the wave that runs for ever
By the island in the river
Flowing down to Camelot.
Four gray walls, and four gray towers,
Overlook a space of flowers,
And the silent isle imbowers
The Lady of Shallot.
By the margin, willow veil'd,
Slide the heavy barges trail'd
By slow horses; and unhail'd

The shallop flitteth silken-sail'd
Skimming down to Camelot:
But who hath seen her wave her hand
Or at the casement seen her stand
Or is she known in all the land,
The Lady of Shallot
Only reapers, reaping early
In among the bearded barley,
Hear a song that echoes cheerly
From the river winding clearly,
Down to tower'd Camelot:
And by the moon the reaper weary,
Piling sheaves in uplands airy,
Listening, whispers " 'Tis the fairy
Lady of Shallot."

PART II

There she weaves by night and day
A magic web with colours gay.
She has heard a whisper say,
A curse is on her if she stay
To look down to Camelot.
She knows not what the curse may be,
And so she weaveth steadily,
And little other care hath she,
The Lady of Shallot.
And moving thro' a mirror clear
That hangs before her all the year,
Shadows of the world appear. .
There she sees the highway near
Winding down to Camelot:
There the river eddy whirls,
And there the surly village-churls,
And the red cloaks of market girls,
Pass onward from Shallot.
Sometimes a troop of damsels glad,
An abbot on an ambling pad,

Sometimes a curly shepherd-lad,
Or long-hair'd page in crimson clad,
Goes by to tower'd Camelot;
And sometimes thro' the mirror blue
The knights come riding two and two:
She hath no loyal knight and true,
The Lady of Shallot.
But in her web she still delights
To weave the mirror's magic sights,
For often thro' the silent nights
A funeral, with plumes and lights
And music, went to Camelot:
Or when the moon was overhead,
Came two young lovers lately wed:
"I am half sick of shadows," said
The Lady of Shallot.

PART III

A bow-shot from her bower-eaves,
He rode between the barley-sheaves,
The sun came dazzling thro' the leaves,
And flamed upon the brazen greaves
Of bold Sir Lancelot.
A red-cross knight for ever kneel'd
To a lady in his shield,
That sparkled on the yellow field,
Beside remote Shallot.
The gemmy bridle glitter'd free,
Like to some branch of stars we see
Hung in the golden Galaxy.
The bridle bells rang merrily
As he rode down to Camelot:
And from his blazon'd baldric slung
A mighty silver bugle hung,
And as he rode his armour rung,
Beside remote Shallot.
All in the blue unclouded weather

Thick-jewell'd shone the saddle-leather,
The helmet and the helmet-feather
Burn'd like one burning flame together,
As he rode down to Camelot.
As often thro' the purple night,
Below the starry clusters bright,
Some bearded meteor, trailing light,
Moves over still Shallot.
His broad clear brow in sunlight glow'd;
On burnish'd hooves his war-horse trode;
From underneath his helmet flow'd
His coal-black curls as on he rode,
As he rode down to Camelot.
From the bank and from the river
He flash'd into the crystal mirror,
"Tirra lirra," by the river
Sang Sir Lancelot.
She left the web, she left the loom,
She made three paces thro' the room,
She saw the water-lily bloom,
She saw the helmet and the plume,
She look'd down to Camelot.
Out flew the web and floated wide;
The mirror crack'd from side to side;
"The curse is come upon me," cried
The Lady of Shallot.

PART IV

In the stormy east-wind straining,
The pale yellow woods were waning,
The broad stream in his banks complaining,
Heavily the low sky raining
Over tower'd Camelot;
Down she came and found a boat
Beneath a willow left afloat,
And round about the prow she wrote
The Lady of Shallot.

And down the river's dim expanse
Like some bold seër in a trance,
Seeing all his own mischance—
With a glassy countenance
Did she look to Camelot.
And at the closing of the day
She loosed the chain, and down she lay;
The broad stream bore her far away,
The Lady of Shallot.
Lying, robed in snowy white
That loosely flew to left and right—
The leaves upon her falling light—
Thro' the noises of the night
She floated down to Camelot:
And as the boat-head wound along
The willowy hills and fields among,
They heard her singing her last song,
The Lady of Shallot.
Heard a carol, mournful, holy,
Chanted loudly, chanted lowly,
Till her blood was frozen slowly,
And her eyes were darken'd wholly,
Turn'd to tower'd Camelot.
For ere she reach'd upon the tide
The first house by the water-side,
Singing in her song she died,
The Lady of Shallot.
Under tower and balcony,
By garden-wall and gallery,
A gleaming shape she floated by,
Dead-pale between the houses high,
Silent into Camelot.
Out upon the wharfs they came,
Knight and burgher, lord and dame,
And round the prow they read her name,
The Lady of Shallot.
Who is this and what is here

And in the lighted palace near
Died the sound of royal cheer;
And they cross'd themselves for fear,

All the knights at Camelot:
But Lancelot mused a little space;
He said, "She has a lovely face;
God in his mercy lend her grace,
The Lady of Shallot."

Summary

Part I: The poem begins with a description of a river and a road that pass through long fields of barley and rye before reaching the town of Camelot. The people of the town travel along the road and look toward an island called Shallot, which lies further down the river. The island of Shallot contains several plants and flowers, including lilies, aspens, and willows. On the island, a woman known as the Lady of Shallot imprisoned within a building made of "four gray walls and four gray towers."

Both "heavy barges" and light open boats sail along the edge of the river to Camelot. But has anyone seen or heard of the lady who lives on the island in the river Only the reapers who harvest the barley hear the echo of her singing. At night, the tired reaper listens to her singing and whispers that he hears her: "'Tis the fairy Lady of Shallot."

Part II: The Lady of Shallot weaves a magic, colourful web. She has heard a voice whisper that a curse will befall her if she looks down to Camelot, and she does not know what this curse would be. Thus, she concentrates solely on her weaving, never lifting her eyes.

However, as she weaves, a mirror hangs before her. In the mirror, she sees "shadows of the world," including the highway road, which also passes through the fields, the eddies in the river, and the peasants of the town. Occasionally, she also sees a group of damsels, an abbot (church official), a young shepherd, or a page dressed in crimson. She sometimes sights a pair of knights riding by, though she has no loyal knight of her own to court her. Nonetheless, she enjoys her solitary weaving, though she expresses frustration with the world of shadows when she glimpses a funeral procession or a pair of newlyweds in the mirror.

Part III: A knight in brass armor ("brazen greaves") comes riding through the fields of barley beside Shallot; the sun shines on his armor and makes it sparkle. As he rides, the gems on his horses bridle glitter like a constellation of stars, and the bells on the bridle ring. The knight hangs a bugle from his sash, and his armor makes ringing noises as he gallops alongside the remote island of Shallot.

In the "blue, unclouded weather," the jewels on the knight's saddle shine, making him look like a meteor in the purple sky. His forehead glows in the sunlight, and his black curly hair flows out from under his helmet. As he passes by the river, his image flashes into the Lady of Shallot's mirror and he sings out "tirra lirra." Upon seeing and hearing this knight, the Lady stops weaving her web and abandons her loom. The web flies out from the loom, and the mirror cracks, and the Lady announces the arrival of her doom: "The curse is come upon me."

Part IV: As the sky breaks out in rain and storm, the Lady of Shallot descends from her tower and finds a boat. She writes the words "The Lady of Shallot" around the boat's bow and looks downstream to Camelot like a prophet foreseeing his own misfortunes. In the evening, she lies down in the boat, and the stream carries her to Camelot.

The Lady of Shallot wears a snowy white robe and sings her last song as she sails down to Camelot. She sings until her blood freezes, her eyes darken, and she dies. When her boat sails silently into Camelot, all the knights, lords, and ladies of Camelot emerge from their halls to behold the sight. They read her name on the bow and "cross...themselves for fear." Only the great knight Lancelot is bold enough to push aside the crowd, look closely at the dead maiden, and remark "She has a lovely face; God in his mercy lend her grace."

Form

The poem is divided into four numbered parts with discrete, isometric (equally-long) stanzas. The first two parts contain four stanzas each, while the last two parts contain five. Each of the four parts ends at the moment when description yields to directly quoted speech: this speech first takes the form of the reaper's whispering identification, then of the Lady's half-sick lament, then of the Lady's pronouncement of her doom, and finally, of Lancelot's blessing. Each stanza contains nine lines with the rhyme scheme *AAAABCCCB*. The "B" always stands for "Camelot" in the fifth line and for "Shallot" in the ninth. The "A" and "C" lines are always in tetrameter, while the "B" lines are in trimeter. In addition, the syntax is line-bound: most phrases do not extend past the length of a single line.

Commentary

Originally written in 1832, this poem was later revised, and published in its final form in 1842. Tennyson claimed that he had based it on an old Italian romance, though the poem also bears much similarity to the story of the Maid of Astolat in Malory's *Morte d'Arthur.* As in Malory's account, Tennyson's lyric includes references to the Arthurian legend; moreover, "Shallot" seems quite close to Malory's "Astolat."

Much of the poem's charm stems from its sense of mystery and elusiveness; of course, these aspects also complicate the task of analysis. That said, most scholars understand "The Lady of Shallot" to be about the conflict between art and life. The Lady, who weaves her magic web and sings her song in a remote tower, can be seen to represent the contemplative artist isolated from the bustle and activity of daily life. The moment she sets her art aside to gaze down on the real world, a curse befalls her and she meets her tragic death. The poem thus captures the conflict between an artist's desire for social involvement and his/her doubts about whether such a commitment is viable for someone dedicated to art. The poem may also express a more personal dilemma for Tennyson as a specific artist: while he felt an obligation to seek subject matter outside the world of his own mind and his own immediate experiences—to comment on politics, history, or a more general humanity—he also feared that this expansion into broader territories might destroy his poetry's magic.

Part I and Part IV of this poem deal with the Lady of Shallot as she appears to the outside world, whereas Part II and Part III describe the world from the Lady's perspective. In Part I, Tennyson portrays the Lady as secluded from the rest of the world by both water and the height of her tower. We do not know how she spends her time or what she thinks about; thus we, too, like everyone in the poem, are denied access to the interiority of her world. Interestingly, the only people who know that she exists are those whose occupations are most diametrically opposite her own: the reapers who toil in physical labour rather than by sitting and crafting works of beauty.

Part II describes the Lady's experience of imprisonment from her own perspective. We learn that her alienation results from a mysterious curse: she is not allowed to look out on Camelot, so all her knowledge of the world must come from the reflections and shadows in her mirror. (It was common for weavers to use mirrors to see the progress of their tapestries from the side that would eventually be displayed to the viewer.) Tennyson notes that often she sees a funeral *or* a wedding, a disjunction that suggests the interchangeability, and hence the conflation, of love and death for the Lady: indeed, when she later falls in love with Lancelot, she will simultaneously bring upon her own death.

Whereas Part II makes reference to all the different types of people that the Lady sees through her mirror, including the knights who "come riding two and two" (line 61), Part III focuses on one particular knight who captures the Lady's attention: Sir Lancelot. This dazzling knight is the hero of the King Arthur stories, famous for his illicit affair with the beautiful Queen Guinevere. He is described in an array of colours: he is a "red-cross knight"; his shield "sparkled on the yellow field"; he wears a "silver bugle"; he passes through "blue unclouded weather" and the "purple night," and he has "coal-black curls." He is also adorned in a "gemmy bridle" and other bejeweled garments, which sparkle in the light. Yet in spite of the rich visual details that Tennyson provides, it is the sound and not the sight of Lancelot that causes the Lady of Shallot to transgress her set boundaries: only when she hears him sing "Tirra lirra" does she leave her web and seal her doom. The intensification of the Lady's experiences in this part of the poem is marked by the shift from the static, descriptive present tense of Parts I and II to the dynamic, active past of Parts III and IV.

In Part IV, all the lush colour of the previous section gives way to "pale yellow" and "darkened" eyes, and the brilliance of the sunlight is replaced by a "low sky raining." The moment the Lady sets her art aside to look upon Lancelot, she is seized with death. The end of her artistic isolation thus leads to the end of creativity: "Out flew her web and floated wide" (line 114). She also loses her mirror, which had been her only access to the outside world: "The mirror cracked from side to side" (line 115). Her turn to the outside world thus leaves her bereft both of her art object and of the instrument of her craft—and of her very life.

Yet perhaps the greatest curse of all is that although she surrenders herself to the sight of Lancelot, she dies completely unappreciated by him. The poem ends with the tragic triviality of Lancelot's response to her tremendous passion: all he has to say about her is that "she has a lovely face" (line 169). Having abandoned her artistry, the Lady of Shallot becomes herself an art object; no longer can she offer her creativity, but merely a "dead-pale" beauty (line 157).

"The Lotos-Eaters"

"Courage!" he said, and pointed toward the land,
"This mounting wave will roll us shoreward soon."
In the afternoon they came unto a land
In which it seemed always afternoon.
All round the coast the languid air did swoon,
Breathing like one that hath a weary dream.

Full-faced above the valley stood the moon;
And like a downward smoke, the slender stream
Along the cliff to fall and pause and fall did seem.
A land of streams! some, like a downward smoke,
Slow-dropping veils of thinnest lawn, did go;
And some thro' wavering lights and shadows broke,
Rolling a slumbrous sheet of foam below.
They saw the gleaming river seaward flow
From the inner land: far off, three mountain-tops,
Three silent pinnacles of aged snow,
Stood sunset-flush'd: and, dew'd with showery drops,
Up-clomb the shadowy pine above the woven copse.
The charmed sunset linger'd low adown
In the red West: thro' mountain clefts the dale
Was seen far inland, and the yellow down
Border'd with palm, and many a winding vale
And meadow, set with slender galingale;
A land where all things always seem'd the same!
And round about the keel with faces pale,
Dark faces pale against that rosy flame,
The mild-eyed melancholy Lotos-eaters came.
Branches they bore of that enchanted stem,
Laden with flower and fruit, whereof they gave
To each, but whoso did receive of them,
And taste, to him the gushing of the wave
Far far away did seem to mourn and rave
On alien shores; and if his fellow spake,
His voice was thin, as voices from the grave;
And deep-asleep he seem'd, yet all awake,
And music in his ears his beating heart did make.
They sat them down upon the yellow sand,
Between the sun and moon upon the shore;
And sweet it was to dream of Fatherland,
Of child, and wife, and slave; but evermore
Most weary seem'd the sea, weary the oar,
Weary the wandering fields of barren foam.
Then some one said, "We will return no more";

And all at once they sang, "Our island home
Is far beyond the wave; we will no longer roam."

Summary

Odysseys tell his mariners to have courage, assuring them that they will soon reach the shore of their home. In the afternoon, they reach a land "in which it seemed always afternoon" because of the languid and peaceful atmosphere. The mariners sight this "land of streams" with its gleaming river flowing to the sea, its three snow-capped mountaintops, and its shadowy pine growing in the vale.

The mariners are greeted by the "mild-eyed melancholy Lotos-eaters," whose dark faces appear pale against the rosy sunset. These Lotos-eaters come bearing the flower and fruit of the Lotos, which they offer to Odysseus's mariners. Those who eat the Lotos feel as if they have fallen into a deep sleep; they sit down upon the yellow sand of the island and can hardly perceive their fellow mariners speaking to them, hearing only the music of their heartbeat in their ears. Although it has been sweet to dream of their homes in Ithaca, the Lotos makes them weary of wandering, preferring to linger here. One who has eaten of the Lotos fruit proclaims that he will "return no more," and all of the mariners begin to sing about this resolution to remain in the land of the Lotos-eaters.

The rest of the poem consists of the eight numbered stanzas of the mariners' choric song, expressing their resolution to stay forever. First, they praise the sweet and soporific music of the land of the Lotos-eaters, comparing this music to petals, dew, granite, and tired eyelids. In the second stanza, they question why man is the only creature in nature who must toil. They argue that everything else in nature is able to rest and stay still, but man is tossed from one sorrow to another. Man's inner spirit tells him that tranquility and calmness offer the only joy, and yet he is fated to toil and wander his whole life.

In the third stanza, the mariners declare that everything in nature is allotted a lifespan in which to bloom and fade. As examples of other living things that die, they cite the "folded leaf, which eventually turns yellow and drifts to the earth, as well as the "full-juiced apple," which ultimately falls to the ground, and the flower, which ripens and fades. Next, in the fourth stanza, the mariners question the purpose of a life of labour, since nothing is cumulative and thus all our accomplishments lead nowhere. They question "what...will last," proclaiming that everything in life is fleeting and therefore futile. The mariners also express their desire for "long rest or death," either of which will free them from a life of endless labour.

The fifth stanza echoes the first stanza's positive appeal to luxurious self-indulgence; the mariners declare how sweet it is to live a life of continuous dreaming. They paint a picture of what it might be like to do nothing all day except sleep, dream, eat Lotos, and watch the waves on the beach. Such an existence would enable them peacefully to remember all those individuals they once knew who are now either buried ("heaped over with a mound of grass") or cremated ("two handfuls of white dust, shut in an urn of brass!").

In the sixth stanza, the mariners reason that their families have probably forgotten them anyway, and their homes fallen apart, so they might as well stay in the land of the Lotos-eaters and "let what is broken so remain." Although they have fond memories of their wives and sons, surely by now, after ten years of fighting in Troy, their sons have inherited their property; it will merely cause unnecessary confusion and disturbances for them to return now. Their hearts are worn out from fighting wars and navigating the seas by means of the constellations, and thus they prefer the relaxing death-like existence of the Land of the Lotos to the confusion that a return home would create.

In the seventh stanza, as in the first and fifth, the mariners bask in the pleasant sights and sounds of the island. They imagine how sweet it would be to lie on beds of flowers while watching the river flow and listening to the echoes in the caves. Finally, the poem closes with the mariners' vow to spend the rest of their lives relaxing and reclining in the "hollow Lotos land."

They compare the life of abandon, which they will enjoy in Lotos land, to the carefree existence of the Gods, who could not care less about the famines, plagues, earthquakes, and other natural disasters that plague human beings on earth. These Gods simply smile upon men, who till the earth and harvest crops until they either suffer in hell or dwell in the "Elysian valleys" of heaven. Since they have concluded, "slumber is more sweet than toil," the mariners resolve to stop wandering the seas and to settle instead in the land of the Lotos-eaters.

Form

This poem is divided into two parts: the first is a descriptive narrative (lines 1-45), and the second is a song of eight numbered stanzas of varying length (lines 46-173). The first part of the poem is written in nine-line Spenserian stanzas, so called because they were employed by Spencer in *The Faerie Queene*. The rhyme scheme of the Spenserian stanza is a closely interlinked *ABABBCBCC*, with the first eight lines in iambic pentameter and the final line an Alexandrine (or line of six iambic feet). The choric song follows a far looser structure: both the line-length and the rhyme scheme vary widely among the eight stanzas.

Commentary

This poem is based on the story of Odysseus's mariners described in scroll IX of Homer's *Odyssey*. Homer writes about a storm that blows the great hero's mariners off course as they attempt to journey back from Troy to their homes in Ithaca. They come to a land where people do nothing but eat Lotos (the Greek for our English "Lotos"), a flower so delicious that some of his men, upon tasting it, lose all desire to return to Ithaca and long only to remain in the Land of the Lotos. Odysseus must drag his men away so that they can resume their journey home. In this poem, Tennyson powerfully evokes the mariners' yearning to settle into a life of peacefulness, rest, and even death.

The poem draws not only on Homer's *Odyssey*, but also on the biblical Garden of Eden in the Book of Genesis. In the Bible, a "life of toil" is Adam's punishment for partaking of the fruit of the Tree of Knowledge: after succumbing to the temptation of the fruit, Adam is condemned to labour by the sweat of his brow. Yet in this poem, *fruit* (the Lotos) provides a *release* from the life of labour, suggesting an inversion of the biblical story.

Tennyson provides a tempting and seductive vision of a life free from toil. His description of the Lotos Land rivals the images of pleasure in Milton's "L'Allegro" and Marvell's "The Garden." Yet his lush descriptive passages are accompanied by persuasive rhetoric; nearly every stanza of the choric song presents a different argument to justify the mariners' resolution to remain in the Lotos Land. For example, in the second stanza of the song the mariners express the irony of the fact that man, who is the pinnacle and apex of creation, is the only creature made to toil and labour all the days of his life. This stanza may also be read as a pointed inversion and overturning of Coleridge's "Work without Hope," in which the speaker laments that "all nature seems at work" while he alone remains unoccupied.

Although the taste of the Lotos and the vision of life it offers is seductive, the poem suggests that the mariners may be deceiving themselves in succumbing to the hypnotic power of the flower. Partaking of the Lotos involves abandoning external reality and living instead in a world of appearances, where everything "seems" to be but nothing actually is: the Lotos Land emerges as "a land where all things always seemed the same" (line 24). Indeed, the word "seems" recurs throughout the poem, and can be found in all but one of the opening five stanzas, suggesting that the Lotos Land is not so much a "land of streams" as a "land of seems." In addition, in the final stanza of the choric song, the poem describes the Lotos Land as a "hollow" land with "hollow" caves, indicating that the vision of the sailors is somehow empty and insubstantial.

The reader, too, is left with ambivalent feelings about the mariners' argument for lassitude. Although the thought of life without toil is certainly tempting, it is also deeply unsettling. The reader's discomfort with this notion arises in part from the knowledge of the broader context of the poem: Odysseus will ultimately drag his men away from the Lotos Land disapprovingly; moreover, his injunction to have "courage" opens—and then overshadows—the whole poem with a sense of moral opprobrium. The sailors' case for lassitude is further undermined morally by their complaint that it is unpleasant "to war with evil" (line 94); are they too lazy to do what is right By choosing the Lotos Land, the mariners are abandoning the sources of substantive meaning in life and the potential for heroic accomplishment. Thus in this poem Tennyson forces us to consider the ambiguous appeal of a life without toil: although all of us share the longing for a carefree and relaxed existence, few people could truly be happy without any challenges to overcome, without the fire of aspiration and the struggle to make the world a better place.

"Ulysses"

It little profits that an idle king,
By this still hearth, among these barren crags,
Match'd with an aged wife, I mete and dole
Unequal laws unto a savage race,
That hoard, and sleep, and feed, and know not me.
I cannot rest from travel: I will drink
Life to the lees: All times I have enjoy'd
Greatly, have suffer'd greatly, both with those
That loved me, and alone, on shore, and when
Thro' scudding drifts the rainy Hyades
Vext the dim sea: I am become a name;
For always roaming with a hungry heart
Much have I seen and known; cities of men
And manners, climates, councils, governments,
Myself not least, but honour'd of them all;
And drunk delight of battle with my peers,
Far on the ringing plains of windy Troy.
I am a part of all that I have met;
Yet all experience is an arch wherethro'
Gleams that untravell'd world whose margin fades
For ever and forever when I move.
How dull it is to pause, to make an end,
To rust unburnish'd, not to shine in use!

As tho' to breathe were life! Life piled on life
Were all too little, and of one to me
Little remains: but every hour is saved
From that eternal silence, something more,
A bringer of new things; and vile it were
For some three suns to store and hoard myself,
And this gray spirit yearning in desire
To follow knowledge like a sinking star,
Beyond the utmost bound of human thought.
This is my son, mine own Telemachus,
To whom I leave the sceptre and the isle,—
Well-loved of me, discerning to fulfil
This labour, by slow prudence to make mild
A rugged people, and thro' soft degrees
Subdue them to the useful and the good.
Most blameless is he, centred in the sphere
Of common duties, decent not to fail
In offices of tenderness, and pay
Meet adoration to my household gods,
When I am gone. He works his work, I mine.
There lies the port; the vessel puffs her sail:
There gloom the dark, broad seas. My mariners,
Souls that have toil'd, and wrought, and thought with me—
That ever with a frolic welcome took
The thunder and the sunshine, and opposed
Free hearts, free foreheads—you and I are old;
Old age hath yet his honour and his toil;
Death closes all: but something ere the end,
Some work of noble note, may yet be done,
Not unbecoming men that strove with Gods.
The lights begin to twinkle from the rocks:
The long day wanes: the slow moon climbs: the deep
Moans round with many voices. Come, my friends,
'T is not too late to seek a newer world.
Push off, and sitting well in order smite
The sounding furrows; for my purpose holds
To sail beyond the sunset, and the baths

Of all the western stars, until I die.
It may be that the gulfs will wash us down:
It may be we shall touch the Happy Isles,
And see the great Achilles, whom we knew.
Tho' much is taken, much abides; and tho'
We are not now that strength which in old days
Moved earth and heaven, that which we are, we are;
One equal temper of heroic hearts,
Made weak by time and fate, but strong in will
To strive, to seek, to find, and not to yield.

Summary

Ulysses (Odysseus) declares that there is little point in his staying home "by this still hearth" with his old wife, doling out rewards and punishments for the unnamed masses who live in his kingdom.

Still speaking to himself he proclaims that he "cannot rest from travel" but feels compelled to live to the fullest and swallow every last drop of life. He has enjoyed all his experiences as a sailor who travels the seas, and he considers himself a symbol for everyone who wanders and roams the earth. His travels have exposed him to many different types of people and ways of living. They have also exposed him to the "delight of battle" while fighting the Trojan War with his men. Ulysses declares that his travels and encounters have shaped who he is: "I am a part of all that I have met," he asserts. And it is only when he is traveling that the "margin" of the globe that he has not yet traversed shrink and fade, and cease to goad him.

Ulysses declares that it is boring to stay in one place, and that to remain stationary is to rust rather than to shine; to stay in one place is to pretend that all there is to life is the simple act of breathing, whereas he knows that in fact life contains much novelty, and he longs to encounter this. His spirit yearns constantly for new experiences that will broaden his horizons; he wishes "to follow knowledge like a sinking star" and forever grow in wisdom and in learning.

Ulysses now speaks to an unidentified audience

concerning his son Telemachus, who will act as his successor while the great hero resumes his travels: he says, "This is my son, mine own Telemachus, to whom I leave the scepter and the isle." He speaks highly but also patronizingly of his son's capabilities as a ruler, praising his prudence, dedication, and devotion to the gods. Telemachus will do his work of governing the island while Ulysses will do his work of traveling the seas: "He works his work, I mine."

In the final stanza, Ulysses addresses the mariners with whom he has worked, traveled, and weathered life's storms over many years. He declares that although he and they are old, they still have the potential to do something noble and honourable before "the long day wanes." He encourages them to make use of their old age because "'tis not too late to seek a newer world."

He declares that his goal is to sail onward "beyond the sunset" until his death. Perhaps, he suggests, they may even reach the "Happy Isles," or the paradise of perpetual summer described in Greek mythology where great heroes like the warrior Achilles were believed to have been taken after their deaths. Although Ulysses and his mariners are not as strong as they were in youth, they are "strong in will" and are sustained by their resolve to push onward relentlessly: "To strive, to seek, to find, and not to yield."

Form

This poem is written as a dramatic monologue: the entire poem is spoken by a single character, whose identity is revealed by his own words. The lines are in blank verse, or unrhymed iambic pentameter, which serves to impart a fluid and natural quality to Ulysses's speech. Many of the lines are enjambed, which means that a thought does not end with the line-break; the sentences often end in the middle, rather than the end, of the lines. The use of enjambment is appropriate in a poem about pushing forward "beyond the utmost bound of human thought." Finally, the poem is divided into four paragraph-like sections, each of which comprises a distinct thematic unit of the poem.

Commentary

In this poem, written in 1833 and revised for publication in 1842, Tennyson reworks the figure of Ulysses by drawing on the ancient hero of Homer's *Odyssey* ("Ulysses" is the Roman form of the Greek "Odysseus") and the medieval hero of Dante's *Inferno*. Homer's Ulysses, as described in Scroll XI of the Odyssey, learns from a prophecy that he will take a final sea voyage after killing the suitors of his wife Penelope. The details of this sea voyage are described by Dante in Canto XXVI of the *Inferno*: Ulysses finds himself restless in Ithaca and driven by "the longing I had to gain experience of the world." Dante's Ulysses is a tragic figure who dies while sailing too far in an insatiable thirst for knowledge. Tennyson combines these two accounts by having Ulysses make his speech shortly after returning to Ithaca and resuming his administrative responsibilities, and shortly before embarking on his final voyage.

However, this poem also concerns the poet's own personal journey, for it was composed in the first few weeks after Tennyson learned of the death of his dear college friend Arthur Henry Hallam in 1833. Like *In Memoriam*, then, this poem is also an elegy for a deeply cherished friend. Ulysses, who symbolizes the grieving poet, proclaims his resolution to push onward in spite of the awareness that "death closes all" (line 51). As Tennyson himself stated, the poem expresses his own "need of going forward and braving the struggle of life" after the loss of his beloved Hallam.

The poem's final line, "to strive, to seek, to find, and not to yield," came to serve as a motto for the poet's Victorian contemporaries. The poem's hero longs to flee the tedium of daily life "among these barren crags" (line 2) and to enter a mythical dimension "beyond the sunset, and the baths of all the western stars" (lines 60-61); as such, he was a model of individual self-assertion and the Romantic rebellion against bourgeois conformity. Thus for Tennyson's immediate audience, the figure of Ulysses held not only mythological meaning, but stood as an important contemporary cultural icon as well.

"Ulysses," like many of Tennyson's other poems, deals with the desire to reach beyond the limits of one's field of vision and the mundane details of everyday life. Ulysses is the antithesis of the mariners in "The Lotos-Eaters," who proclaim, "We will no longer roam" and desire only to relax amidst the Lotos fields. In contrast, Ulysses "cannot rest from travel" and longs to roam the globe (line 6). Like the Lady of Shallot, who longs for the worldly experiences she has been denied, Ulysses hungers to explore the unraveled world.

As in all dramatic monologues, here the character of the speaker emerges almost unintentionally from his own words. Ulysses' incompetence as a ruler is evidenced by his preference for potential quests rather than his present responsibilities. He devotes a full 26 lines to his own egotistical proclamation of his zeal for the wandering life, and another 26 lines to the exhortation of his mariners to roam the seas with him. However, he offers only 11 lines of lukewarm praise to his son concerning the governance of the kingdom in his absence, and a mere two words about his "aged wife" Penelope. Thus, the speaker's own words betray his abdication of responsibility and his specificity of purpose.

"Tithonus"

Complete Text
The woods decay, the woods decay and fall,
The vapours weep their burthen to the ground,
Man comes and tills the field and lies beneath,
And after many a summer dies the swan.
Me only cruel immortality
Consumes; I wither slowly in thine arms,
Here at the quiet limit of the world,
A white-hair'd shadow roaming like a dream
The ever-silent spaces of the East,
Far-folded mists, and gleaming halls of morn.
Alas! for this gray shadow, once a man—
So glorious in his beauty and thy choice,
Who madest him thy chosen, that he seem'd

To his great heart none other than a God!
I ask'd thee, "Give me immortality."
Then didst thou grant mine asking with a smile,
Like wealthy men who care not how they give.
But thy strong Hours indignant work'd their wills,
And beat me down and marr'd and wasted me,
And tho' they could not end me, left me maim'd
To dwell in presence of immortal youth,
Immortal age beside immortal youth,
And all I was in ashes. Can thy love
Thy beauty, make amends, tho' even now,
Close over us, the silver star, thy guide,
Shines in those tremulous eyes that fill with tears
To hear me Let me go: take back thy gift:
Why should a man desire in any way
To vary from the kindly race of men,
Or pass beyond the goal of ordinance
Where all should pause, as is most meet for all
A soft air fans the cloud apart; there comes
A glimpse of that dark world where I was born.
Once more the old mysterious glimmer steals
From any pure brows, and from thy shoulders pure,
And bosom beating with a heart renew'd.
Thy cheek begins to redden thro' the gloom,
Thy sweet eyes brighten slowly close to mine,
Ere yet they blind the stars, and the wild team
Which love thee, yearning for thy yoke, arise,
And shake the darkness from their loosen'd manes,
And beat the twilight into flakes of fire.
Lo! ever thus thou growest beautiful
In silence, then before thine answer given
Departest, and thy tears are on my cheek.
Why wilt thou ever scare me with thy tears,
And make me tremble lest a saying learnt,
In days far-off, on that dark earth, be true
"The Gods themselves cannot recall their gifts."
Ay me! ay me! with what another heart

In days far-off, and with what other eyes
I used to watch (if I be he that watch'd)
The lucid outline forming round thee; saw
The dim curls kindle into sunny rings;
Changed with thy mystic change, and felt my blood
Glow with the glow that slowly crimson'd all
Thy presence and thy portals, while I lay,
Mouth, forehead, eyelids, growing dewy-warm
With kisses balmier than half-opening buds
Of April, and could hear the lips that kiss'd
Whispering I knew not what of wild and sweet,
Like that strange song I heard Apollo sing,
While Ilion like a mist rose into towers.
Yet hold me not for ever in thine East;
How can my nature longer mix with thine
Coldly thy rosy shadows bathe me, cold
Are all thy lights, and cold my wrinkled feet
Upon thy glimmering thresholds, when the steam
Floats up from those dim fields about the homes
Of happy men that have the power to die,
And grassy barrows of the happier dead.
Release me, and restore me to the ground;
Thou seest all things, thou wilt see my grave:
Thou wilt renew thy beauty morn by morn;
I earth in earth forget these empty courts,
And thee returning on thy silver wheels.

Summary

The woods in the forests grow old and their leaves fall to the ground. Man is born, works the earth, and then dies and is buried underground. Yet the speaker, Tithonus, is cursed to live forever. Tithonus tells Aurora, goddess of the dawn, that he grows old slowly in her arms like a "white-hair'd shadow" roaming in the east.

Tithonus laments that while he is now a "gray shadow" he was once a beautiful man chosen as Aurora's lover. He remembers that he long ago asked Aurora to grant him eternal life: "Give me immortality!" Aurora granted his wish generously, like a rich philanthropist who has so much money that he gives charity without thinking twice. However, the Hours, the goddesses who accompany Aurora, were angry that Tithonus was able to resist death, so they took their revenge by battering him until he grew old and withered. Now, though he cannot die, he remains forever old; and he must dwell in the presence of Aurora, who renews herself each morning and is thus forever young. Tithonus appeals to Aurora to take back the gift of immortality while the "silver star" of Venus rises in the morning. He now realises the ruin in desiring to be different from all the rest of mankind and in living beyond the "goal of ordinance," the normal human lifespan.

Just before the sun rises, Tithonus catches sight of the "dark world" where he was born a mortal. He witnesses the coming of Aurora, the dawn: her cheek begins to turn red and her eyes grow so bright that they overpower the light of the stars. Aurora's team of horses awakes and converts the twilight into fire. The poet now addresses Aurora, telling her that she always grows beautiful and then leaves before she can answer his request. He questions why she must "scare" him with her tearful look of silent regret; her look makes him fear that an old saying might be true—that "The Gods themselves cannot recall their gifts."

Tithonus sighs and remembers his youth long ago, when he would watch the arrival of the dawn and feel his whole body come alive as he lay down and enjoyed the kisses of another. This lover from his youth used to whisper to him "wild and sweet" melodies, like the music of Apollo's lyre, which accompanied the construction of Ilion (Troy).

Tithonus asks Aurora not to keep him imprisoned in the east where she rises anew each morning, because his eternal old age contrasts so painfully with her eternal renewal. He cringes cold and wrinkled, whereas she rises each morning to warm "happy men that have the power to die" and men who are already dead in their burial mounds ("grassy barrows"). Tithonus asks Aurora to release him and let him die. This way, she can see his grave when she rises and he, buried in the earth, will be able to forget the emptiness of his present state, and her return "on silver wheels" that stings him each morning.

Form

This poem is a dramatic monologue: the entire text is spoken by a single character whose words reveal his identity. The lines take the form of blank verse (unrhymed iambic pentameter). The poem as a whole falls into seven paragraph-like sections of varying length, each of which forms a thematic unit unto itself.

Commentary

Like Ulysses, Tithonus is a figure from Greek mythology whom Tennyson takes as a speaker in one of his dramatic monologues (see the section on "Ulysses"). According to myth, Tithonus is the brother of Priam, King of Troy, and was loved by Aurora, the immortal goddess of the dawn, who had a habit of carrying off the beautiful young men whom she fancied. Aurora abducted Tithonus and asked Zeus to grant him immortality, which Zeus did. However, she forgot to ask that he also grant eternal youth, so Tithonus soon became a decrepit old man who could not die. Aurora finally transformed him into a grasshopper to relieve him of his sad existence. In this poem, Tennyson slightly alters the mythological story: here, it is Tithonus, not Aurora, who asks for immortality, and it is Aurora, not Zeus, who confers this gift upon him. The source of suffering in the poem is not Aurora's forgetfulness in formulating her request to Zeus, but rather the goddesses referred to as "strong Hours" who resent Tithonus's immortality and subject him to the ravages of time.

Tennyson wrote the first version of this poem as "Tithon" in 1833, and then completed the final version for publication in 1859 in the *Cornhill Magazine* edited by William Makepeace Thackeray. The 1833 version contained several significant differences from the version we know today: the poem began not with a repetition but with the lament "Ay me! ay me! The woods decay and fall"; the "swan," which here dies after many summers was not a swan but a "rose"; and immortality was described as "fatal" rather than "cruel."

The 1833 poem was initially conceived as a pendant, or companion poem, to "Ulysses." "Ulysses" alludes to the danger that fulfillment may bring—"It may be that the gulfs will wash us down"; "Tithonus" represents the realization of this danger. For the character of Tithonus achieves that which Ulysses longs for and finds himself bitterly disappointed: Ulysses wanted to sail "beyond the sunset" because he sensed "how dull it is to pause"; Tithonus, in contrast, questions why any man should want "to pass beyond the goal of ordinance where all should pause" (lines 30-31). "Tithonus" thus serves as an appropriate thematic follow-up to "Ulysses."

This poem was one of a set of four works (also including "Morte d'Arthur," "Ulysses," and "Tiresias") that Tennyson wrote shortly after Arthur Henry Hallam's death in 1833. Whereas Hallam was granted youth without immortality, Tithonus is granted immortality without youth. Tennyson developed the idea for a poem about these themes of age and mortality after hearing a remark by Emily Sellwood, Tennyson's fiancée: Sellwood lamented that unlike the Hallams, "None of the Tennysons ever die." Appropriately, in depicting the futility of eternal life without youth, Tennyson drew upon a timeless figure: the figure of Tithonus is eternally old because he lives on forever as an old man in the popular imagination.

"The Epic"

Summary

This poem describes a gathering of four friends on Christmas Eve: a parson (member of the clergy) named Holmes, a poet named Everard Hall, their host Francis Allen (Frank), and the narrator. After they finish gambling and dismiss the women who were in attendance, they sit around the half-empty bowl of wine and discuss how Christmas is no longer taken seriously as a religious holiday: "All the old honour had from Christmas gone." The narrator is exhausted and soon "falls in a doze." While "half-asleep," he listens to the parson criticize the new science of geology and the internal divisions within the church, which have contributed to "the general decay of faith."

When the poet awakes, he hears the parson lament that there is nothing to depend on in modern times. The host, Francis Allen, suggests that poetry might replace religion as the new source of faith and inspiration. However, upon hearing Frank's tribute to him, the poet Hall remarks sarcastically that he looks for inspiration to the bowl of wine! The narrator, now fully awake, responds that they all remember Hall's fondness for alcohol from their college days. However, he added, they also remember his talent for writing verse, and wonder "What came of that" Before the poet can answer, Frank relates that the poet burnt the twelve books of the epic he had written about King Arthur because he thought that his poetry had nothing new to say. Rushing to his own defence, Hall explains that there was no point in writing poetry that was merely an echo of old times; just as nature cannot restore extinct animals such as the mastodon, the poet should not attempt verse in the classical style that will merely read as "faint Homeric echoes."

Frank informs his friends that he actually salvaged the eleventh of the twelve books in the poet's Arthurian epic, pulling it from the fire before it could burn. The narrator requests that the poet now read aloud from his book, because he remembers the respect Hall enjoyed when they were freshmen in college. Hall reluctantly agrees to share his work with his friends.

After Hall finishes reading, the last light flickers and dies out—but the host and the narrator remain so enraptured by the poet's words that they cannot move. The narrator explains that he is not sure whether "it was the tone in which he read" that made Hall's writing so powerful, or whether the success of his writing can be attributed to "some modern touches here and there," which he added to the classical story. They sit until the cock crows, heralding the arrival of Christmas. The narrator goes to bed and dreams of Arthur: "And so to bed, where yet in sleep I seemed to sail with Arthur." He dreams of a boat carrying Arthur back to the present like a modern gentleman as all the people gather around him to welcome him as the harbinger of peace. Then, the narrator hears the sound of "a hundred bells" and wakes to the church bells on Christmas Morning.

Form

This poem serves as a frame for the twelfth and final book in Tennyson's *Idylls of the King*: the first 51 lines precede the idyll and then lines 324-354 follow it. Its lines are in blank verse, which is a name for unrhymed iambic pentameter. Blank verse, the most common form of counted unrhymed lines, matches the cadences of spoken language more closely than any other form (rather than free-form), and is thus appropriate for a poem chronicling a conversation among four friends. (The entire *Idylls of the King*, too, is written in blank verse.)

Commentary

In 1833, Tennyson proposed to write a long epic about King Arthur, the legendary British leader who resisted the Anglo-Saxon invaders of sixth-century England. By 1838, he had completed one of the twelve books, entitled "Morte d'Arthur," which chronicled the king's death ("morte"). He published this single book in 1842 within the framework of this poem, "The Epic," which consists of 51 lines that precede "Morte d'Arthur" and thirty lines that follow it. "The Epic" provides a modern context for the Arthurian story by casting it as a manuscript read aloud by a poet to three of his friends following their Christmas-Eve revelry. After Tennyson completed all twelve books of *Idylls of the King* in 1869, he discarded this framing poem and retitled "Morte d'Arthur" as "The Passing of Arthur."

Like "The Lady of Shallot," Tennyson's epic poem has its origins in the story of *King Arthur and the Knights of the Round Table*, written by Sir Thomas Malory in 1485. Malory himself had adapted the Arthur story from a variety of 12th-century French romances. However, the literary context of this poem extends back even further, because, as the poet Everard Hall remarks, "These twelve books of mine / Were faint Homeric echoes" (lines 38-39). Like Homer's *Odyssey* and Virgil's *Aeneid,* Tennyson's *Idylls* is a long epic in twelve books chronicling the adventures of a hero. Further, several of the images and references in Tennyson's poem can be traced back to classical sources, and even the term "idylll," which Tennyson used to describe each of the twelve books, refers to a classical genre of poetry consisting of brief but artful representations of contemporary life. The final image in "The Epic;" in which King Arthur sails downstream in a boat until he reaches a waiting crow, which greets him with cheers of "Arthur is come again" (line 347), corresponds to the formula for ending a classical pastoral elegy, in which people gather to lament a death and express faith in the peace-bringing deification of the departed hero. This image also bears a striking resemblance to the final lines of "The Lady of Shallot," in which the lady sails down in her boat to Camelot and is heralded by the people of the town.

However, like "Ulysses," this poem does not stem exclusively from mythology, but also has roots in Tennyson's personal history: his King Arthur is also modeled after his dear friend Arthur Henry Hallam, who died the same year that Tennyson began writing "The Epic." For the rest of Tennyson's life, he retained in his mind an idealized image of his friend, and Arthur's famous characteristics evoke this image: Arthur is renowned for his physical adroitness, insight, penetrating honesty, wisdom, innocence, and nobility of spirit, all of which virtues Tennyson attributed to his departed friend in various other writings.

Moreover, the dissolution of the Round Table alludes to the shock of Hallam's death to his peers in Cambridge, and the closing image in the poem, in which the poet awakes to hear "the clear church bells ring in the Christmas morn," (line 354) references the Christmas bells of Section CVI of "In Memoriam," the poet's elegy for Hallam. In addition, Tennyson's poem has some of the same "modern touches here and there" that his poem's narrator attributes to the poem-within-the-poem (line 329); he uses the Arthurian cycle as a medium for the discussion of contemporary problems, namely the decay of ethical principles that he perceived in commercial, political, and social life.

As in many of Tennyson's poems, this work exhibits a great concern with the scientific developments of his day; the parson mentions geology as one of the sources of the decline in faith in contemporary times (line 16). The science of geology, which suddenly extended the history of the earth back millions of years beyond the standard biblical account, had been formulated by Charles Lyell in his *Principles of Geology* (1830-33). Lyell drew on evidence from fossils found beneath the surface of the earth, and Tennyson's characters, too, rely on fossils as evidence for their arguments. Thus they say, "Why take the style of those heroic times For nature brings not back the mastodon" (lines 35-36): the poet Hall, in arguing that artists must not simply "remodel models," cites as evidence the fact that nature never brings back extinct species such as the mastodon, known only by its fossilized remains. Ironically, then, the poet draws upon fossils as evidence while lamenting the new science that does just this.

"Tears, Idle Tears"

Tears, idle tears, I know not what they mean,
Tears from the depth of some divine despair
Rise in the heart, and gather in the eyes,
In looking on the happy autumn-fields,
And thinking of the days that are no more.
Fresh as the first beam glittering on a sail,
That brings our friends up from the underworld,
Sad as the last which reddens over one
That sinks with all we love below the verge;
So sad, so fresh, the days that are no more.

Ah, sad and strange as in dark summer dawns
The earliest pipe of half-awakened birds
To dying ears, when unto dying eyes
The casement slowly grows a glimmering square;
So sad, so strange, the days that are no more.

Dear as remembered kisses after death,
And sweet as those by hopeless fancy feigned
On lips that are for others; deep as love,
Deep as first love, and wild with all regret;
O Death in Life, the days that are no more!

Summary

The speaker sings of the baseless and inexplicable tears that rise in his heart and pour forth from his eyes when he looks out on the fields in autumn and thinks of the past.

This past, ("the days that are no more") is described as fresh and strange. It is as fresh as the first beam of sunlight that sparkles on the sail of a boat bringing the dead back from the underworld, and it is sad as the last red beam of sunlight that shines on a boat that carries the dead down to this underworld.

The speaker then refers to the past as not "fresh," but "sad" and strange. As such, it resembles the song of the birds on early summer mornings as it sounds to a dead person, who lies watching the "glimmering square" of sunlight as it appears through a square window.

In the final stanza, the speaker declares the past to be dear, sweet, deep, and wild. It is as dear as the memory of the kisses of one who is now dead, and it is as sweet as those kisses that we imagine ourselves bestowing on lovers who actually have loyalties to others. So, too, is the past as deep as "first love" and as wild as the regret that usually follows this experience. The speaker concludes that the past is a "Death in Life."

Form

This poem is written in blank verse, or unrhymed iambic pentameter. It consists of four five-line stanzas, each of which closes with the words "the days that are no more."

Commentary

"Tears, Idle Tears" is part of a larger poem called "The Princess," published in 1847. Tennyson wrote "The Princess" to discuss the relationship between the sexes and to provide an argument for women's rights in higher education. However, the work as a whole does not present a single argument or tell a coherent story. Rather, like so much of Tennyson's poetry, it evokes complex emotions and moods through a mastery of language. "Tears, Idle Tears," a particularly evocative section, is one of several interludes of song in the midst of the poem.

In the opening stanza, the poet describes his tears as "idle," suggesting that they are caused by no immediate, identifiable grief. However, his tears are simultaneously the product of a "divine despair," suggesting that they do indeed have a source: they "rise in the heart" and stem from a profoundly deep and universal cause. This paradox is complicated by the difficulty of understanding the phrase "divine despair": Is it God who is despairing, or is the despair itself divine And how can despair be divine if Christian doctrine considers it a sin

The speaker states that he cries these tears while "looking on the happy autumn-fields." At first, it seems strange that looking at something happy would elicit tears, but the fact that these are fields of autumn suggests that they bear the memories of a spring and summer that have vanished, leaving the poet with nothing to look forward to except the dark and cold of winter. Tennyson explained that the idea for this poem came to him when he was at Tintern Abbey, not far from Hallam's burial place.

"Tintern Abbey" is also the title and subject of a famous poem by William Wordsworth. (See the "Tintern Abbey" section in the SparkNote on Wordsworth's Poetry.) Wordsworth's poem, too, reflects on the passage of time and the loss of the joys of youth. However, whereas Tennyson laments "the days that are no more" and describes the past as a "Death in Life," Wordsworth explicitly states that although the past is no more, he has been compensated for its loss with "other gifts":

> That time is past,
> And all its aching joys are now no more
> And all its dizzy raptures. Not for this
> Faint I, nor mourn nor murmur; other gifts
> Have followed; for such loss, I would believe,
> Abundant recompense.

Thus, although both Wordsworth and Tennyson write poems set at Tintern Abbey about the passage of time, Wordsworth's poem takes on a tone of contentment, whereas Tennyson's languishes in a tone of lament.

"Tears, Idle Tears" is structured by a pattern of unusual adjectives used to describe the memory of the past. In the second stanza, these adjectives are a chiastic "fresh...sad...sad...fresh". The memory of the birth of friendship is "fresh," whereas the loss of these friends is "sad"; thus when the "days that are no more" are described as both "sad" and "fresh," these words have been preemptively loaded with meaning and connotation: our sense of the "sad" and "fresh" past evokes these blossomed and withered friendships. This stanza's image of the boat sailing to and from the underworld recalls Virgil's image of the boatman Charon, who ferries the dead to Hades.

In the third stanza, the memory of the past is described as "sad...strange...sad...strange." The "sad" adjective is introduced in the image of a man on his deathbed who is awake for his very last morning. However, "strangeness" enters in, too, for it is strange to the dying man that as his life is ending, a new day is beginning. To a person hearing the birds' song and knowing he will never hear it again, the twittering will be imbued with an unprecedented significance—the dying man will hear certain melancholy tones for the first time, although, strangely and paradoxically, it is his last.

The final stanza contains a wave of adjectives that rush over us—now no longer confined within a neat chiasmic structure—as the poem reaches its last, climactic lament: "dear...sweet...deep...deep...wild." The repetition of the word "deep" recalls the "depth of some divine despair," which is the source of the tears in the first stanza. However, the speaker is also "wild with all regret" in thinking of the irreclaimable days gone by. The image of a "Death in Life" recalls the dead friends of the second stanza who are like submerged memories that rise to the surface only to sink down once again. This

"Death in Life" also recalls the experience of dying in the midst of the rebirth of life in the morning, described in the third stanza. The poet's climactic exclamation in the final line thus represents a culmination of the images developed in the previous stanzas.

"In Memoriam"

Selected Text

(Summary and Commentary will focus on the following excerpts)

Prologue

Strong Son of God, immortal Love,
Whom we, that have not seen thy face,
By faith, and faith alone, embrace,
Believing where we cannot prove;
Thine are these orbs of light and shade;
Thou madest Life in man and brute;
Thou madest Death; and lo, thy foot
Is on the skull which thou hast made.
Thou wilt not leave us in the dust:
Thou madest man, he knows not why,
He thinks he was not made to die;
And thou hast made him: thou art just.
Thou seemest human and divine,
The highest, holiest manhood, thou.
Our wills are ours, we know not how;
Our wills are ours, to make them thine.
Our little systems have their day;
They have their day and cease to be:
They are but broken lights of thee,
And thou, O Lord, art more than they.
We have but faith: we cannot know;
For knowledge is of things we see
And yet we trust it comes from thee,
A beam in darkness: let it grow.
Let knowledge grow from more to more,
But more of reverence in us dwell;

That mind and soul, according well,
May make one music as before,
But vaster. We are fools and slight;
We mock thee when we do not fear:
But help thy foolish ones to bear;
Help thy vain worlds to bear thy light.
Forgive what seem'd my sin in me;
What seem'd my worth since I began;
For merit lives from man to man,
And not from man, O Lord, to thee.
Forgive my grief for one removed,
Thy creature, whom I found so fair.
I trust he lives in thee, and there
I find him worthier to be loved.
Forgive these wild and wandering cries,
Confusions of a wasted youth;
Forgive them where they fail in truth,
And in thy wisdom make me wise.

XXVII

Thou comest, much wept for: such a breeze
Compell'd thy canvas, and my prayer
Was as the whisper of an air
To breathe thee over lonely seas.
For I in spirit saw thee move
Thro' circles of the bounding sky,
Week after week: the days go by:
Come quick, thou bringest all I love.
Henceforth, wherever thou may'st roam,
My blessing, like a line of light,
Is on the waters day and night,
And like a beacon guards thee home.
So may whatever tempest mars
Mid-ocean, spare thee, sacred bark;
And balmy drops in summer dark
Slide from the bosom of the stars.
So kind an office hath been done,

Such precious relics brought by thee;
The dust of him I shall not see
Till all my widow'd race be run.

LVI

'So careful of the type' but no.
From scarped cliff and quarried stone
She cries, 'A thousand types are gone:
I care for nothing, all shall go.
'Thou makest thine appeal to me:
I bring to life, I bring to death:
The spirit does but mean the breath:
I know no more.' And he, shall he,
Man, her last work, who seem'd so fair,
Such splendid purpose in his eyes,
Who roll'd the psalm to wintry skies,
Who built him fanes of fruitless prayer,
Who trusted God was love indeed
And love Creation's final law-
Tho' Nature, red in tooth and claw
With ravine, shriek'd against his creed-
Who loved, who suffer'd countless ills,
Who battled for the True, the Just,
Be blown about the desert dust,
Or seal'd within the iron hills
No more A monster then, a dream,
A discord. Dragons of the prime,
That tare each other in their slime,
Were mellow music match'd with him.
O life as futile, then, as frail!
O for thy voice to soothe and bless!
What hope of answer, or redress
Behind the veil, behind the veil.

Summary

***Prologue*:**

The poem begins as a tribute to and invocation of the "Strong Son of God." Since man, never having seen God's face, has no proof of His existence, he can only reach God through faith. The poet attributes the sun and moon ("these orbs or light and shade") to God, and acknowledges Him as the creator of life and death in both man and animals. Man cannot understand why he was created, but he must believe that he was not made simply to die.

The Son of God seems both human and divine. Man has control of his own will, but this is only so that he might exert himself to do God's will. All of man's constructed systems of religion and philosophy seem solid but are merely temporal, in comparison to the eternal God; and yet while man can have knowledge of these systems, he cannot have knowledge of God. The speaker expresses the hope that "knowledge [will] grow from more to more," but this should also be accompanied by a reverence for that which we cannot know.

The speaker asks that God help foolish people to see His light. He repeatedly asks for God to forgive his grief for "thy [God's] creature, whom I found so fair." The speaker has faith that this departed fair friend lives on in God, and asks God to make his friend wise.

XXVII

Here the speaker states that he feels no jealousy for the man who is captured and does not know what it means to feel true rage, or for the bird that is born with in a cage and has never spent time outside in the "summer woods." Likewise, he feels no envy for beasts that have no sense of the passage of time and no conscience to check their behaviour. He also does not envy those who have never felt pain ("the heart that never plighted troth") or those who complacently enjoy a leisure that they do not rightfully deserve. Even when he is in the greatest pain, he still realises that "'Tis better to have loved and lost / Than never to have loved at all."

LVI

After having asserted in Section LV that Nature cares only for the survival of species ("so careful of the type") and not for the survival of individual lives, the speaker now questions whether Nature even cares for the species. He quotes a personified, feminine Nature asserting that she does not attend to the survival of the species, but arbitrarily bestows life or death on all creatures. For Nature, the notion of the "spirit" does not refer to any divine, unearthly element, but rather to the simple act of breathing.

The poet questions whether Man, who prays and trusts in God's love in spite of the evidence of Nature's brutality ("Nature, red in tooth and claw"), will eventually be reduced to dust or end up preserved like fossils in rock: "And he, shall he, Man...Be blown about the desert dust, Or sealed within the iron hills" The thought of this evokes a notion of the human condition as monstrous and more terrifying to contemplate than the fate of prehistoric "dragons of the prime." The speaker declares that life is futile and longs for his departed friend's voice to soothe him and mitigate the effect of Nature's callousness.

Form

"In Memoriam" consists of 131 smaller poems of varying length. Each short poem is comprised of isometric stanzas. The stanzas are iambic tetrameter quatrains with the rhyme scheme *ABBA,* a form that has since become known as the "In Memoriam Stanza." (Of course, Tennyson did not invent the form—it appears in earlier works such as Shakespeare's "The Phoenix and the Turtle"—but he did produce an enduring and memorable example of it.) With the *ABBA* rhyme scheme, the poem resolves itself in each quatrain; it cannot propel itself forward: each stanza seems complete, closed. Thus to move from one stanza to the next is a motion that does not come automatically to us by virtue of the rhyme scheme; rather, we must will it ourselves; this force of will symbolizes the poet's difficulty in moving on after the loss of his beloved friend Arthur Henry Hallam.

Commentary

Tennyson wrote "In Memoriam" after he learned that his beloved friend Arthur Henry Hallam had died suddenly and unexpectedly of a fever at the age of 22. Hallam was not only the poet's closest friend and confidante, but also the fiancée of his sister. After learning of Hallam's death, Tennyson was overwhelmed with doubts about the meaning of life and the significance of man's existence. He composed the short poems that comprise "In Memoriam" over the course of seventeen years (1833-1849) with no intention of weaving them together, though he ultimately published them as a single lengthy poem in 1850.

T.S. Eliot called this poem "the most unapproachable of all his [Tennyson's] poems," and indeed, the sheer length of this work encumbers one's ability to read and study it. Moreover, the poem contains no single unifying theme, and its ideas do not unfold in any particular order. It is loosely organized around three Christmas sections (28, 78, and 104), each of which marks another year that the poet must endure after the loss of Hallam. The climax of the poem is generally considered to be Section 95, which is based on a mystical trance Tennyson had in which he communed with the dead spirit of Hallam late at night on the lawn at his home at Somersby.

"In Memoriam" was intended as an elegy, or a poem in memory and praise of one who has died. As such, it contains all of the elements of a traditional pastoral elegy such as Milton's "Lycidas," including ceremonial mourning for the dead, praise of his virtues, and consolation for his loss. Moreover, all statements by the speaker can be understood as personal statements by the poet himself. Like most elegies, the "In Memoriam" poem begins with expressions of sorrow and grief, followed by the poet's recollection of a happy past spent with the individual he is now mourning.

These fond recollections lead the poet to question the powers in the universe that could allow a good person to die, which gives way to more general reflections on the meaning of life. Eventually, the poet's attitude shifts from grief to resignation. Finally, in the climax, he realises that his friend is not lost forever but survives in another, higher form. The poem closes with a celebration of this transcendent survival.

"In Memoriam" ends with an epithalamion, or wedding poem, celebrating the marriage of Tennyson's sister Cecilia to Edmund Lushington in 1842. The poet suggests that their marriage will lead to the birth of a child who will serve as a closer link between Tennyson's generation and the "crowning race." This birth also represents new life after the death of Hallam, and hints at a greater, cosmic purpose, which Tennyson vaguely describes as "One far-off divine event / To which the whole creation moves."

Not just an elegy and an epithalamion, the poem is also a deeply philosophical reflection on religion, science, and the promise of immortality. Tennyson was deeply troubled by the proliferation of scientific knowledge about the origins of life and human progress: while he was writing this poem, Sir Charles Lyell published his *Principles of Geology*, which undermined the biblical creation story, and Robert Chambers published his early evolutionary tract, *Vestiges of the Natural History of Creation*. In "In Memoriam," Tennyson insisted that we hold fast to our faith in a higher power in spite of our inability to prove God's existence:

"Believing where we cannot prove." He reflects early evolutionary theories in his faith that man, through a process lasting millions of years, is developing into something greater. In the end, Tennyson replaces the doctrine of the immortality of the soul with the immortality of mankind through evolution, thereby achieving a synthesis between his profound religious faith and the new scientific ideas of his day.

"The Charge of the Light Brigade"

Complete Text
Half a league, half a league,
Half a league onward,
All in the valley of Death
Rode the six hundred.
'Forward, the Light Brigade!
Charge for the guns!' he said:
Into the valley of Death

Rode the six hundred.
'Forward, the Light Brigade!'
Was there a man dismay'd
Not tho' the soldier knew
Someone had blunder'd:
Their's not to make reply,
Their's not to reason why,
Their's but to do and die:
Into the valley of Death
Rode the six hundred.
Cannon to right of them,
Cannon to left of them,
Cannon in front of them
Volley'd and thunder'd;
Storm'd at with shot and shell,
Boldly they rode and well,
Into the jaws of Death,
Into the mouth of Hell
Rode the six hundred.
Flash'd all their sabres bare,
Flash'd as they turn'd in air
Sabring the gunners there,
Charging an army, while
All the world wonder'd:
Plunged in the battery-smoke
Right thro' the line they broke;
Cossack and Russian
Reel'd from the sabre-stroke
Shatter'd and sunder'd.
Then they rode back, but not
Not the six hundred.
Cannon to right of them,
Cannon to left of them,
Cannon behind them
Volley'd and thunder'd;
Storm'd at with shot and shell,
While horse and hero fell,

They that had fought so well
Came thro' the jaws of Death,
Back from the mouth of Hell,
All that was left of them,
Left of six hundred.
When can their glory fade
O the wild charge they made!
All the world wonder'd.
Honour the charge they made!
Honour the Light Brigade,
Noble six hundred!

Summary

The poem tells the story of a brigade consisting of 600 soldiers who rode on horseback into the "valley of death" for half a league (about one and a half miles). They were obeying a command to charge the enemy forces that had been seizing their guns.

Not a single soldier was discouraged or distressed by the command to charge forward, even though all the soldiers realised that their commander had made a terrible mistake: "Someone had blundered." The role of the soldier is to obey and "not to make reply...not to reason why," so they followed orders and rode into the "valley of death."

The 600 soldiers were assaulted by the shots of shells of canons in front and on both sides of them. Still, they rode courageously forward toward their own deaths: "Into the jaws of Death / Into the mouth of hell / Rode the six hundred."

The soldiers struck the enemy gunners with their unsheathed swords ("sabres bare") and charged at the enemy army while the rest of the world looked on in wonder. They rode into the artillery smoke and broke through the enemy line, destroying their Cossack and Russian opponents. Then they rode back from the offensive, but they had lost many men so they were "not the six hundred" any more.

Canons behind and on both sides of the soldiers now assaulted them with shots and shells. As the brigade rode "back from the mouth of hell," soldiers and horses collapsed; few remained to make the journey back.

The world marveled at the courage of the soldiers; indeed, their glory is undying: the poem states these noble 600 men remain worthy of honour and tribute today.

Form

This poem is comprised of six numbered stanzas varying in length from six to twelve lines. Each line is in diameter, which means it has two stressed syllables; moreover, each stressed syllable is followed by two unstressed syllables, making the rhythm dactylic. The use of "falling" rhythm, in which the stress is on the first beat of each metrical unit, and then "falls off" for the rest of the length of the meter, is appropriate in a poem about the devastating fall of the British brigade.

The rhyme scheme varies with each stanza. Often, Tennyson uses the same rhyme (and occasionally even the same final word) for several consecutive lines: "Flashed all their sabres bare / Flashed as they turned in air / Sab'ring the gunners there." The poem also makes use of anaphora, in which the same word is repeated at the beginning of several consecutive lines: "Cannon to right of them / Cannon to left of them / Cannon in front of them." Here the method creates a sense of unrelenting assault; at each line our eyes meet the word "cannon," just as the soldiers meet their flying shells at each turn.

Commentary

"The Charge of the Light Brigade" recalls a disastrous historical military engagement that took place during the initial phase of the Crimean War fought between Turkey and Russia (1854-56). Under the command of Lord Raglan, British forces entered the war in September 1854 to prevent the Russians from obtaining control of the important sea routes through the Dardanelles. From the beginning, the war was plagued by a series of misunderstandings and tactical blunders, one of which serves as the subject of this poem: on October 25, 1854, as the Russians were seizing guns from British soldiers, Lord Raglan sent desperate orders to his Light

Cavalry Brigade to fend off the Russians. Finally, one of his orders was acted upon, and the brigade began charging—but in the wrong direction! Over 650 men rushed forward, and well over 100 died within the next few minutes. As a result of the battle, Britain lost possession of the majority of its forward defences and the only metaled road in the area.

In the 21st century, the British involvement in the Crimean War is dismissed as an instance of military incompetence; we remember it only for the heroism displayed in it by Florence Nightingale, the famous nurse. However, for Tennyson and most of his contemporaries, the war seemed necessary and just. He wrote this poem as a celebration of the heroic soldiers in the Light Brigade who fell in service to their commander and their cause. The poem glorifies war and courage, even in cases of complete inefficiency and waste.

Unlike the medieval and mythical subject of "The Lady of Shallot" or the deeply personal grief of "Tears, Idle Tears," this poem instead deals with an important political development in Tennyson's day. As such, it is part of a sequence of political and military poems that Tennyson wrote after he became Poet Laureate of England in 1850, including "Ode on the Death of the Duke of Wellington" (1852) and "Riflemen, Form" (1859). These poems reflect Tennyson's emerging national consciousness and his sense of compulsion to express his political views.

This poem is effective largely because of the way it conveys the movement and sound of the charge via a strong, repetitive falling meter: "Half a league, half a league / half a league onward." The plodding pace of the repetitions seems to subsume all individual impulsiveness in ponderous collective action. The poem does not speak of individual troops but rather of "the six hundred" and then "all that was left of them." Even Lord Raglan, who played such an important role in the battle, is only vaguely referred to in the line "someone had blundered." Interestingly, Tennyson omitted this critical and somewhat subversive line in the 1855 version of this poem, but the writer John Ruskin later convinced him to restore it for the sake of the poem's artistry. Although it underwent several revisions following its initial publication in 1854, the poem as it stands today is a moving tribute to courage and heroism in the face of devastating defeat.

[SH] "Crossing the Bar"

Complete Text

Sunset and evening star
And one clear call for me!
And may there be no moaning of the bar,
When I put out to sea,
But such a tide as moving seems asleep,
Too full for sound and foam,
When that which drew from out the boundless deep
Turns again home.
Twilight and evening bell,
And after that the dark!
And may there be no sadness of farewell,
When I embark;
For though from out our bourne of Time and Place
The flood may bear me far,
I hope to see my Pilot face to face
When I have crossed the bar.

Summary

The speaker heralds the setting of the sun and the rise of the evening star, and hears that he is being called. He hopes that the ocean will not make the mournful sound of waves beating against a sand bar when he sets out to sea. Rather, he wishes for a tide that is so full that it cannot contain sound or foam and therefore seems asleep when all that has been carried from the boundless depths of the ocean returns back out to the depths.

The speaker announces the close of the day and the evening bell, which will be followed by darkness. He hopes that no one will cry when he departs, because although he may be carried beyond the limits of time and space as we know them, he retains the hope that he will look upon the face of his "Pilot" when he has crossed the sand bar.

Form

This poem consists of four quatrain stanzas rhyming *ABAB*. The first and third lines of each stanza are always a couple of beats longer than the second and fourth lines, although the line lengths vary among the stanzas.

Commentary

Tennyson wrote "Crossing the Bar" in 1889, three years before he died. The poem describes his placid and accepting attitude toward death. Although he followed this work with subsequent poems, he requested that "Crossing the Bar" appear as the final poem in all collections of his work.

Tennyson uses the metaphor of a sand bar to describe the barrier between life and death. A sandbar is a ridge of sand built up by currents along a shore. In order to reach the shore, the waves must crash against the sandbar, creating a sound that Tennyson describes as the "moaning of the bar." The bar is one of several images of liminality in Tennyson's poetry: in "Ulysses," the hero desires "to sail beyond the sunset"; in "Tithonus", the main character finds himself at the "quiet limit of the world," and regrets that he has asked to "pass beyond the goal of ordinance."

The other important image in the poem is one of "crossing," suggesting Christian connotations: "crossing" refers both to "crossing over" into the next world, and to the act of "crossing" oneself in the classic Catholic gesture of religious faith and devotion. The religious significance of crossing was clearly familiar to Tennyson, for in an earlier poem of his, the knights and lords of Camelot "crossed themselves for fear" when they saw the Lady of Shallot lying dead in her boat. The cross was also where Jesus died; now as Tennyson himself dies, he evokes the image again. So, too, does he hope to complement this metaphorical link with a spiritual one: he hopes that he will "see his Pilot face to face."

The *ABAB* rhyme scheme of the poem echoes the stanzas' thematic patterning: the first and third stanzas are linked to one another as are the second and fourth. Both the first and third stanzas begin with two symbols of the onset of night:

"sunset and evening star" and "twilight and evening bell." The second line of each of these stanzas begins with "and," conjoining another item that does not fit together as straightforwardly as the first two: "one clear call for me" and "after that the dark!" Each of these lines is followed by an exclamation point, as the poet expresses alarm at realizing what death will entail. These stanzas then conclude with a wish that is stated metaphorically in the first stanza: "may there be no moaning of the bar / When I put out to sea"; and more literally in the third stanza: "And may there be no sadness of farewell / When I embark." Yet the wish is the same in both stanzas: the poet does not want his relatives and friends to cry for him after he dies. Neither of these stanzas concludes with a period, suggesting that each is intimately linked to the one that follows.

The second and fourth stanzas are linked because they both begin with a qualifier: "but" in the second stanza, and "for though" in the fourth. In addition, the second lines of both stanzas connote excess, whether it be a tide "too full for sound and foam" or the "far" distance that the poet will be transported in death.

Chapter 8

Study Questions

Q. Give the critical analysis of Alfred Tennyson's "Ulysses" ?

Or

Q. Discuss about the environment of the land in which they rested ?

Or

Q. Briefly describe about the nature of the land and its inhabitants ?

Ans. Alfred Tennyson's 'Ulysses' is both a lament and an inspiring poem. Even modern readers who are not so familiar with the classics, can visualize the heroic legend of Ulysses, and so is not prepared for what he finds in the poem—not Ulysses the hero but Ulysses the man. Tennyson brings out the agony felt by Ulysses at his old age, The influence of the Industrial age can be seen in Tennyson's usage of the word 'profits' in the very first line. The character calls himself 'idle' showing his disillusionment at this ripe stage of life.

The "still hearth" and "the barren crags" symbolize death. He continues complaining about his hapless state and the reader begins to detect the shallowness of character of this otherwise larger than life legend. He is so self-centreed and full of self pity that he shows scant respect for those close to him and those that he rules as seen in lines 4-5. His pride keeps him from calling himself old, in that many words; He has to allude to his wife's age to let the reader in on his own advanced years.

The wisdom and grace of old age seem to elude him completely as he metaphorically claims, "I will drink life to the lees."Tennyson uses vivid imagery in lines 10 - 11, the "rainy Hyades"again bringing out the fear of death in the narrator. The lines "I am become a name", and "myself not least, but honoured them all" reflects the awareness Ulysses has of his legendry fame. The reader begins to identify with the character as he seems fraught with the same faults that afflict normal men.

"A hungry heart' is a personification used to highlight the character's insatiable desire to travel and explore " I am part of all that I met ", portray the swelling pride of one who knows he is a legend. In lines 22-25 the character laments at having to, 'pause' and "to make an end" symbolizing imminent death. He hates his infirm state as can be seen in lines 24- 30."For some three suns "is a connotation suggesting he has been in bed for three days, which for him is the most demeaning of all. Ulysses can see death at his doorstep, yet feels every hour can be used for the unending quest for knowledge.

Tennyson uses a powerful simile in line 31 equating 'knowledge ' to 'the sinking star' which is the most elusive and the most difficult to discern in the sky. In line 32 he uses a hyperbole to dramatize the extent of the character's desire for the unknown and the unexplored. The second part of the poem, lines 33-43 are devoted to the contrast between father and son, one can feel the heavy sarcasm in the words " slow prudence" "blamelessness" and "decency" of his son. He is contemptuous of these traits, which maybe harmless and noble, yet are hardly worthy of a great king.

Ulysses' wandering spirit looks upon any kind of softness as a failing. He sneers at the more 'centreed' personality of his son who governs his people in a mild and orderly manner.In lines 37-38 he reveals his paradoxical personality as he feels soft handling is a form of subjugation that " subdues them to the useful and the good". Here the reader can peer into the maverick character of Ulysses and his complete disregard of anything normal and routine. Another character trait that shows through in lines 41- 42 is that of an agnostic or to put it less strongly, he shows a "jovial agnosticism". (Landow).The poem is a dramatic representation of a man who has faith neither in the gods nor in the necessity of preserving order in his kingdom and his own life (Landow). Just as the reader is wearing down under the relentless spate of negative traits of Ulysses, Tennyson brings respite in the third stanza reminding one of the past glories of this fabled soldier of the Trojan war.

With rich usage of symbols and visual imagery, he manages to finally make a connection between the character and the reader. The last stanza is directed to his mariners as also to the readers who after visiting upon all the negative traits of his character realised that he too was human like them. He calls upon them, "souls that have toiled, and wrought, and thought with me" (46), immediately connecting them to his struggle. Tennyson uses symbolism all through this last stanza."

The port" symbolizes the final place (44), the "vessel puffs her sail" symbolizes the soul ready to leave." There gloom the dark, broad seas" (45) denote the unknown nature of the final journey. Ulysses calls upon his friends to take up the challenge in the face of death and like a true soldier, to fight until the end. He refuses to give in to the vagaries of old age and extols the readers to join him in the final battle. "this open invitation to join Ulysses in his last heroic attempt seals the bond between reader and speaker".The hero in us rises to the fore as he implores us with his appeal in line 56-57 "come, my friends.'Tis not too late to seek a newer world".

In lines 60 - 65 Ulysses is not certain where death will take him. "Maybe that the gulf will wash us down"(62) symbolizes the possibility of hell but "Happy Isles" (63) stand for heaven where he feels he will be greeted by his old friends like Achilles.In line 67 Tennyson uses the hyperbolic expression "Moved earth and heaven", to highlight the legendry strength of Ulysses. "That which we are, we are", indicate the coming to terms with life or maybe it could even mean the final realization that the soul is more powerful that the body.

In the end there is a strong message for the reader - more than a message it is a model to base ones life on -"Made weak by time and fate, but strong in will.To strive, to seek, to find, and not to yield. (66-70).As the last lines unfold a realization far beyond what is apparent starts emerging. In the initial stanzas of the poem was Ulysses lamenting at his sorry state because he couldn't gracefully accept old age or was it an appeal to those who pod along, "That hoard, and sleep, and feed" to take notice of life. In that light Ulysses seems to be an enlightened soul, who saw far ahead of the normal people. His quest for knowledge like a 'sinking star' was unquenchable.

Was he seeking the higher truth? Did he know something that the others were not aware of "Beyond the utmost bound of human thought" (32). He was seeking something beyond death is evident in "for my purpose holds.To sail beyond sunset." What does he mean by "seek a newer world" (57). When we see Ulysses in this light we realise that the faults we sought in him in the initial stages of the poem are failings only as perceived by a society "centreed in the sphere of common duties" (39). Otherwise, they were not faults but relentless endeavors of a restless soul to seek that, which is beyond the realms of human thought.

Tears, Ay, Dull Tears: Tennyson's Idle Idol-Idyll

As when we dwell upon a word we know,
Repeating, till the word we know so well
Becomes a wonder, and we know not why...
—"Lancelot and Elaine"

The noted critic and editor of the most important collection of Tennyson's poetry makes an unimportant but suggestive tiny slip in his fine study of the poet's life and works. In a discussion of the 1855 publication, Maud, Christopher Ricks writes that "Tennyson at this stage of his life was haunted by the feeling that the dead are all too intimidating alive"; and, lending the poet the words of Maud's narrator, Ricks continues: "He remembers his dead mother— `And that dead man at her heart and mine'". In fact, however, Alfred Tennyson's mother, Elizabeth, was to live for ten years following Maud. Can the living be intimidating dead Ricks' elision of Tennyson's mother is the more curious since he chooses as the epigraph for his first chapter these lines from "The Coming of Arthur":

Moreover, always in my mind I hear
A cry from out the dawning of my life,
A mother weeping and writes that this cry and weeping "was the core of his childhood and youth." But that first chapter, titled "Tennyson and his father till 1827", is after more dramatic and accessible material than the "good and kind" mother, and we soon read that what Tennyson "deeply and experimentally felt from his earlier years" was "the plight of his father". Certainly growing up as a younger son of an epileptic dipsomaniac locked in a struggle with his rejecting father ("the old man of the wolds") offers ample occasion for psychic traumata."

When the Rector's moods were at their worst, Alfred would run through the night to the churchyard and throw himself prostrate among the graves, wishing that he were dead". Such a problematic paternal model might well lend a greater prominence to the mother's role in shaping the son's sensibilities. Tennyson, more than most, insists on our keeping in mind the inaccessibly complex interactions of genetic endowment (the all-too-evident "black blood" of the Tennyson) and family conflict across generations and bloodlines, not to mention intimate family dynamics.

Tennyson's few comments about his mother suggest some post-adolescent idealization. In a letter written when he was twenty-three, he refers to her as "one of the most angelic natures on God's earth, always doing good as it were by a sort of intuition". At her funeral, he told the officiating clergyman, rather fulsomely, "`I hope you will not think that I have spoken in exaggerated terms of my beloved mother, but indeed she was most beautiful thing God Almighty ever did make'.

These descriptions sit a bit awkwardly with the ludicrous picture a thirty-nine year old Tennyson relates of his mother "grovelling on the floor in an extremity of fear" during a thunderstorm, and his following comment that "My mother is afraid if I go to town even for a night; how could they get on without me for months". So the narrator of Maud recalls... my dark-dawning youth,

Darkened watching a mother decline
And that dead man at her heart and mine:
For who was left to watch but I
Yet so did I let my freshness die.

Alan Ker, one of the poet's in-laws, reported for Hallam Tennyson's memoir of his father that Elizabeth Tennyson was "so sensitive that touch her feelings ever so lightly and the tears rushed to her eyes". This account continues with the remarkable information that, "Then it was we used to hear your father say, `Dam your eyes, mother, dam your eyes!' and then she smiled and applied the white pocket-handkerchief and shook her head at her son" (220). However improbable the suggestion of the poet's punning on the abusive expression "damn your eyes!," the description seems drawn from life—or if not, adds strikingly to Ker's recollection of Maud and the narrator's memory of his mother:

For how often I caught her with eyes all wet,
Shaking her head at her son and sighing
A world of trouble within!

These teary mother's eyes are far from those the poet earlier fantasized for the "trustful infant" who knows "Nothing beyond his mother's eyes. / They comfort him by night and day" ("Supposed Confession of a Second-Rate Sensitive Mind". These "mild deep eyes upraised" may manifest "The beauty and repose of faith, / And the clear spirit shining through", but in realizing that her faith is not faith in him the boy soon experiences cognitive dissonance and ambivalence.

The piety of Tennyson's mother can be gauged from one of her few letters to him which survive, albeit one written when she was near eighty and her "Dearest Ally" fifty. "It does indeed" give her "the purest satisfaction," she writes, "to notice that a spirit of Christianity is perceptible" through her son's latest volume (Idylls of the King):

O dearest Ally, how fervently have I prayed for years that our merciful Redeemer would intercede with our Heavenly Father, to grant thee His Holy Spirit to urge thee to employ the talents He has given thee, by taking every opportunity of endeavoring to impress the precepts of His Holy Word on the minds of others. My beloved son, words are too feeble to express the joy of my heart in perceiving that thou art earnestly endeavouring to do so. Dearest Ally, there is nothing for a moment to be compared to the favour of God: I need not ask thee if thou art of the same opinion. The writings are a convincing proof that thou art.

My beloved child, when our Heavenly Father summons us hence, may we meet, and all that are dear to us, in that blessed state where sorrow is unknown, never more to be separated. Her son's contention that "There lives more faith in honest doubt, / Believe me, than in half the creeds" (In Memoriam) evidently didn't warrant concern (Tennyson's feelings about religion included his punning "Te Deum" into "tedium" .

But for Tennyson, the disjuncture between his doubts and his mother's faith pointed to something more serious, and at twenty, his "Supposed Confessions of a Second-Rate Sensitive Mind" wonders "wherefore do we grow awry", and

What Devil had the heart to scathe
Flowers thou hadst reared—to brush the dew
From thine own lily, when thy grave
Was deep, my mother, in the clay
Myself Is it thus Myself Had I
So little love for thee But why
Prevailed not thy pure prayers

As speaker moves to conclude his confession, he expresses his fear that "everywhere / Some must clasp Idols." "Yet, my God," he wonders, "Whom call I Idol". Devotion to what Tennyson called "mein liebes Ich" is the desperate defence against the second-rate sensitivity bequeathed by the mother:

- Weary life!
- Weary death!
- Spirit and heart made desolate!
- Damnéd vacillating state!

"Perdidi Diem," whose title invokes the Emperor Titus's lament for a day lost to good action, is another early poem that suggests pre-oedipal fantasies. Here the speaker reports that

I must needs pore upon the mysteries
Of my own infinite Nature and torment
My spirit with a fruitless discontent

This self-wasting idleness is glossed by the ensuing extended simile that tells of "Young ravens fallen from their cherishing nest". Though they cry continually and "trail and spoil / Their new plumes on the misty soil," still "not the more for this / Shall the loved mother minister" to them nor win them to their wonted rest "With sleep-compelling down of her most glossy breast":

In chill discomfort they cry:
What is the death of life if this be not to die

Once again "trustful infancy" with "no care of life or death" drops into hyper- consciousness of that opposition and attempts to escape in idle poring upon the self-idol and the idle—ineffectual for real change—outpouring of writing.

Tennyson's disciple and the famed anthologist of The Golden Treasury F. T. Palgrave reported the poet as saying, more than once, "`that his poems sprang from a "nucleus," some one word, may be, or brief melodious phrase which had floated through the brain, as it were unbidden'". The most celebrated instance of this is Hallam Tennyson's story of how his father "wrote `The Charge of the Light Brigade' in a few minutes, after reading the description in the Times in which occurred the phrase `some one had blundered,' and this was the origin of the metre of his poem" (320).

Edgar Shannon and Christopher Ricks make this account still more interesting by pointing out that the actual source phrase read "some hideous blunder" and that it appeared in the Times three weeks before the poem's composition. "Far—Far—Away," written when Tennyson was seventy-nine offers another example, the title (and refrain) being words that "had always a strange charm" for him. One wonders if the charm of the phrase owed anything to a context where Tennyson may have met (or re-met) it and which it then served to condense: for in Coleridge's Zapolya, published in 1817, he would have read that "Love's dreams prove seldom true" and hence, "We must away; / Far, far away!"

As it happens, the single word "idle" of the quintessentially Tennysonian lyric known by its incipit "Tears, idle tears" revises an earlier "foolish" ("Tears, foolish tears"), but the exponential increase in meaning that the revision achieves reveals an aural matrix of idols, idylls, and idleness, not to mention the repetition compulsion now incipient in the sounds ("Tears, idle tears, I..."). "Idle," "idol," and "idyll" each represents a different emphasis or interpretation or hearing of the poem; each reflects a different drive motivating the text.

The poem presents a particularly successful compromise between the different voices that would claim it—that want to speak through it as a single voice. In the unconscious ongoing negotiation of composition and revising the seemingly unbidden, floating phonemes of the poem's "charged word," "idle", come together as a kind of Knotenpunkt or nodal point that binds up the text, ensuring that each conflicting, constituting element has the possibility of a hearing.

The identical sound of the semes facilitates the plurality of themes. "Idle" can be imagined as first the catalyst and lastly the precipitate of the mix making up the text's authority, the trace of tension in whatever intention one imputes to the author.

The poem is not a hostage to language, to be liberated by deconstruction, but a new moment and monument of Tennyson's language, his mother tongue, participating in an orbit of associations the ideal display of which would show something like the terms and structure of Tennyson's unconscious. As Ricks observes, "No poem of Tennyson compacts more of his deepest feelings with a more graceful fluency". Hearing the different meanings broached by the mother word requires a sense of parallel (rather than serial) mental processing with which one will probably never be entirely at ease. The sound of the poem's second word, at any rate, activates several channels: the OED pronounces "idle," "idol," and "idyll" as [id'l], [i d'l], and [i dil], while Daniel Jones's English Pronouncing Dictionary (12th ed., 1964) suggests ['aid l], ['aidl], and ['idil] or ['aid-l].

'Tears, idle tears, I know not what they mean,
Tears from the depth of some divine despair
Rise in the heart, and gather to the eyes,
In looking on the happy Autumn-fields,
And thinking of the days that are no more.
'Fresh as the first beam glittering on a sail,
That brings our friends up from the underworld,
Sad as the last which reddens over one
That sinks with all we love below the verge;
So sad, so fresh, the days that are no more.
'Ah, sad and strange as in dark summer dawns
The earliest pipe of half-awakened birds
To dying ears, when unto dying eyes
The casement slowly grows a glimmering square;
So sad, so strange, the days that are no more.
'Dear as remembered kisses after death,
And sweet as those by hopeless fancy feigned
On lips that are for others; deep as love,
Deep as first love, and wild with all regret;
O Death in Life, the days that are no more.'

The poem's conflicting voices come closest to the surface with the image of friends brought "up from the underworld." An audience concerned with physical reality and its mimesis might construe "the underworld" as "the Antipodes" or Australia ("down under"), and for this sense— as the first instance—the OED cites this passage. But since the publication of The Well Wrought Urn in 1947 readers have had the benefit of Cleanth Brooks's sense that the word would "necessarily suggest the underworld of Greek mythology",—an argument for Tennysonian "paradox and ambiguity" now thoroughly assimilated. In "Ulysses," Tennyson joins Homer's account of Odysseus' sailing to the entrance of the underworld with Dante's vision of Ulysses' sea-voyage to Purgatory, so that Tennyson's old wanderer says:

It may be that the gulfs will wash us down,
It may be we shall touch the Happy Isles,
And see the great Achilles, whom we knew.
(62- 64)

But the hero of the Odyssey, as Tennyson could expect his readers to know, meets Achilles not in any "Happy Isles" or Elysian "happy Autumn-fields," but in the land of the dead, where dwell the "mere imitations of perished mortals": "broton eidola kamonton". These dead are idols (eidola—images, literally, "things seen"), as, in turn, some readers suspect Tennyson's Ulysses himself to be, an "idle king" speaking in a kind of afterlife as a "gray spirit" to his "mariners, souls" who, according to the Odyssey, at least, have long since died. The big tears ("thalaron dakru," Od.) which Homer's dead share with mortal Odysseus are, literally, idol tears; Tennyson, too, can imagine "phantasms weeping tears" ("The Palace of Art,").

Still more common are mortal tears shed for the idol or image of a loved one, like those of Odysseus for his dead mother—an "idoll" in Chapman's 1616 translation—or Aeneas for the "imago" of his wife the image becomes a commonplace). As the OED notes, "idol" functions as subjective and objective genitive, permitting "idol tears" that are both "tears of an idol" and "tears for an idol."

Odysseus' lament following the underworld interview with his mother—that embodiment of "first love"—can shade into that of the speaker of "Tears, Idle Tears" who ends "wild with all regret." Odysseus strives to embrace his mother's image, but, in the translation of Pope which young Tennyson often imitated,

Thrice through my arms she slipp'd like empty wind,
Or dreams, the vain illusions of the mind.
Wild with despair, I shed a copious tide
Of flowing tears...

Similarly, in In Memoriam:

Tears of the widower, when he sees
A late-lost form that sleep reveals,
And moves his doubtful arms, and feels
Her place is empty, fall like these.

So, also, section ten of In Memoriam imagines the sailing ship conveying Arthur Hallam's body as bearing "dark freight, a vanish'd life" and comments, "we have idle dreams... home-bred fancies." The frequent collocation in English of "idle" and "fancy" must be in part encouraged by the semantic identity of "idol" (eidolon) and "phantom", a power of association evident in a somewhat different way when Tennyson writes how, looking in a stream "With idle care... I saw your troubled image there" ("The Miller's Daughter" [1832 version]. But "vanity"—the quality of being (in) vain—seems to be the underlying sense joining idol ("late-lost form") and idle ("empty"): Swift, for example, writes of "vain, idle, visionary thoughts" ("A Modest Proposal"), while Pope, in a poem partly memorized by Tennyson, describes Dulness's created image of "A Poet's form" (gifted with "empty words") as an "Idol void and vain!". Blake, similarly, punningly mocks the vain, in vain "Idol Virtues of the Natural Heart". And Joyce's "Araby" (Dubliners), has the narrator recall how, owing to his idolizing "adoration" of his first love, "My eyes were often full of tears (I could not tell why)"; at night and by day "her image came between me and the page," he relates, and the punning outcome is that his schoolmaster criticizes him for beginning "to idle."

Eidola, according to Cicero, figure in the system of Epicurus as the films given off by any object and conveying an impression to the eye: the exterior eidola give rise to interior phantasia, fancy or mental vision. Lucretius develops this idea in De Rerum Natura, Book 4, and, in Tennyson's poem about him, wonders, as he despairs of his "death-in-life," how he can be troubled by unbidden mental images: "'How should the mind, except it loves them, clasp / These idols to herself'". So, "in looking," the image-films, the idol tears are torn from their source and, like the image of the happy Autumn-fields, "gather to the eyes" in some way that implicates "I". The poem, Tennyson said, "was written in the yellowing autumn-tide at Tintern Abbey, full for me of its bygone memories". Those memories included Wordsworth's "Lines written a few miles above Tintern Abbey," and, more powerful for Tennyson, Keats's "To Autumn." But as Herbert F. Tucker notes, it is precisely at his greatest idol's most personal and self-referential moment that Tennyson tears away into his own inner space.Keats asks "Where are the songs of Spring Ay, where are they", only to enjoin, "Think not of them, thou hast thy music too". Tennyson's music, however, rises in "thinking of the days that are no more," and is finally unconcerned whether Autumn or Summer waits outside.

The emphatic source of the eye-dulling tears echoes though the poem in the vocal signature carried by the shifting first-person i sounds: "idle," "I," "rise," "eyes," "pipe," "dying," "wild," "Life." The speaker gives rise to the tears; indeed, "I" doles them out (like Tennyson's Ulysses, "an idle king... I mete and dole") as dole (as when Elaine dies and "there was dole in Astolat"). In doling out his condition the speaker makes the poem, like so many others of Tennyson's, an elegiac idyll and one, moreover, evoking a recurrent theme of the 1842 Poems (initially titled Morte d'Arthur; Dora, and other Idylls): "recollections of older men recalling their youth, in which the beloved had died".

"Tears, Idle Tears" appears as a song in the volume which followed those idylls in 1847, The Princess (given Tennyson's habits of revision, publication dates give little indication as to compositional chronology; The Princess was begun, evidently, in 1839, and "Tears, Idle Tears" perhaps dates from 1834. When The Princess appeared, Tennyson was already strongly associated with the word "idyll"; contemporary reviews remarked the volume's "idylllic manner," and later critics call it "a series of idylls," "a poem that seeks to evolve the idylll beyond its previous Tennysonian limits". William Allingham reports Tennyson using a curiously possessive turn of phrase to express displeasure over the title of Browning's Dramatic Idylls: "I wish Browning had not taken my word Idylll" (291). After his name, then, "idyll" would perhaps best qualify as "The word that is the symbol of myself" ("The Ancient Sage" goes on to say that "idle gleams to thee are light to me").

In the framing context of The Princess, the "mournful song" of "Tears, Idle Tears" is sung by "a maid... with such passion that the tear, / She sang of, shook and fell". The Princess, however, condemns the song, using an association already noted to argue that women should stop their ears to such a siren song of "fancies hatched / In silken-folded idleness". Following a revealing line of association, she urges that women "let the past be past" and not care though "the wild figtree split / [Men's] monstrous idols". Tennyson names the Princess "Ida," and at one point permutates the name in the space of fifty-five lines from "Sweet Ida" to "Sweet dream" to another "Sweet Idyll" set within the text. For Tennyson, the name "Ida" powerfully associates with the idea of "mother" and death of the "I" through the story and obsessive refrain of "Oenone" (first published in 1832):

My eyes are full of tears, my heart of love,
My heart is breaking, and my eyes are dim,
And I am all aweary of my life.
'O mother Ida, many-fountained Ida,
Dear mother Ida, hearken ere I die.

The male protagonist of The Princess, whose presence in effect occasions "Tears, Idle Tears," is himself a kind of eidolon, as Tennyson made clear in revising the poem. Subject to recurrent "weird seizures," the Prince often seems "to move among a world of ghosts," himself "the shadow of a dream" some half-century later, "Akbar's Dream" will feature "'The Shadow of a dream—an idle one'. Given the old proverb "after wyrd comes weird" and the poet's being possessed by "some one word, may be, or brief melodious phrase," one wonders whether the Prince's trances might not be "seizures" by "words, / Themselves but shadows of a shadow-world". Towards the end of The Princess, the action of which revolves around the Prince's attempt to make Ida his own, the Prince, near defeat, gives himself up to tears "all for langour and self-pity" and asks Ida only "to kiss me ere I die".

As the conclusion unfolds, the Prince argues for a kind of mutual marriage—"The two-celled heart beating, with one full stroke" and Ida asks him from what woman he learned that idea. The response is a long encomium on his mother, concerning which the poet once evasively assented that it was indeed based on Elizabeth Tennyson:

> No Angel, but a dearer being, all dipt
> In Angel instincts, breathing Paradise,
> Interpreter between the Gods and men,
> Who looked all native to her place, and yet
> On tiptoe seemed to touch a sphere
> To gross to tread, and all male minds perforce
> Swayed to her from their orbits as they moved,
> And girdled her with music. Happy he
> With such a mother! faith in womankind
> Beats with his blood, and trust in all things high
> Comes easy to him, and though he trip and fall
> He shall not blind his soul with clay.

Despite such praise and professed importance of his mother, it is oddly "never clear whether she is alive or dead". Princess Ida immediately notes that this idealization doesn't suit her and marks her distance from it:

> It seems you love to cheat yourself with words:
> This mother is your model. I have heard
> Of your strange doubts....

But the Prince, swept up in his projection, denigrates his doubts with what for Tennyson would be a most fantastic possibility: "the past / Melts mist-like into this bright hour, and this / Is morn to more". According to its author, "Tears, Idle Tears" expresses "the passion of the past, the abiding in the transient", which suggests that one might see its speaker as weeping over the little picture (eidullion, idyll) of his self-idolizing or idolizing. Tennyson refers not to some antique passion for the past but raises the suggestion of a past suffering on in his present: suffering on and being suffered (passus, whence "passion," is the perfect participle of patior, "I suffer").

The speaker of "Tears, Idle Tears" might in this case be heard to recognize that the action in which he is engaged (idyll making) is potentially "idle"—that his very poetic spinning of wheels prevents the authentic experience of a different, transformed reality which is, at least on one level, desired. If the speaker knows he doesn't know what his tears mean and thus what he himself means and is ("Tears, idle tears, I know not what I mean"), then he is in one way admitting to "idle chatter" in the face of the gospel that "every idle word that men shall speak, they shall give an account thereof in the day of judgment". That Day, says Revelation, "there should be time no longer", or, as Tennyson preferred to translate it, "time should be no more".

The ultimate dissatisfaction of "Tears, Idle Tears," then, is with "days that are no more" than a meaningless, inauthentic "Death in Life,"—with, finally, itself. The poem cannot escape Shelley's earlier insight in The Revolt of Islam that

It is the dark idolatry of self,
Which, when our thoughts and actions once are gone,
Demands that man should weep, and bleed, and groan;
O vacant expiation!

Grounds for the narcissistic avoidance of the reality-principle inherent in labouring such idleness (as well as in the long tradition of English literary melancholy) can be seen in George Meredith's dissection of Sir Willoughby Patterne's I-doll in The Egoist (1879). There, Patterne's "hatred of the world" stems from "an appalling fear on behalf of his naked eidolon, the tender infant self swaddled in his name before the world, for which he felt as the most highly civilized of men alone can feel, and which it was impossible for him to stretch out his hands to protect the self-idol or self-hood is that state the individual enters as he or she grows, losing touch with an imagined original eidos or form: " I am not what see/ And other than the things touch (In Memoriam)."I," in this reading, originates in the separation of "the baby" from "the circle of the breast", and despair over such un-pairing seems the source of "Tears, Idle Tears" and much of Tennyson's work.

Despair is the active link to that ancient break, hence "divine" or idolized in order that, as Odysseus says to the image of his mother, "we may delight ourselves with sorrow". The holding on to sorrow occurs unconsciously for the most part, following a dynamic Tennyson identified in dedicating his Arthurian cycle to the memory of the Prince Consort: "since he held them dear, / Perchance as finding there unconsciously / Some image of himself" (so, he continues, "I dedicate, I consecrate with tears— / These Idylls".

But the last half of "Tears, Idle Tears" offers the possibility of breaking the idle idol-idyll by dying to this world, not necessarily by physical death, since the poet proposes in the first section of In Memoriam that "men may rise on stepping stones / Of their dead selves". The third stanza of "Tears, Idle Tears" calls up mythic imagery to set the scene for this death of the self. As the body "dies," the birds awaken, and the spirit awakens to join them, like the soul of the speaker in Andrew Marvell's "The Garden". The birds are, perhaps, a new form of the idols, "our friends," recognized as we change form of being. Here again, In Memoriam, section thirteen, supplies an apposite comment:

For now so strange do these things seem,
Mine eyes have leisure for their tears;
My fancies time to rise on wing,
And glance about the approaching sails.

The "fancies," or phantoms, idols, rise—like tears to the eyes and friends from the underworld—and take wing in bird-form. In Tennyson's early "Remorse" the speaker feels himself condemned by "shadowy forms of guilt" to "living death" and proposes that his "soul shall wing her weary way" to underworld depths where "glow / The glimmerings of the boundless flame".

The casement that slowly turns into a glimmering square of window invokes one of Tennyson's favourite images in Keats, the "Charm'd magic casements, opening on the foam / Of perilous seas, in faery lands forlorn" of "Ode to a Nightingale" Allingham records two instances of Tennyson's quoting this. As in Keats, the glimmering threshold—the "square of text," the "arch where through / Gleams that untraveled world" is no sooner formulated than (and in consequence) the speaker is thrown back to his burden of loss, solitude, desperation, and his attempt to write a passage out of the world rendered idle:

> There he sat down gazing on all below;
> There did a thousand memories roll upon him,
> Unspeakable for sadness. By and by
> The ruddy square of comfortable light,
> Far-blazing from the rear of Philip's house,
> Allured him, as the beacon-blaze allures
> The bird of passage, till he madly strikes
> Against it, and beats out his weary life.
> ("Enoch Arden" 719-26, 2.644)

The polysemous line, which opens the final stanza of "Tears, Idle Tears", establishes the possibility that the speaker himself is among the dead (remembering kisses during life), so confirming the silent presence of the poem's "idol" and giving one reason for its tears. "Hopeless fancy" can thus offer an instance of one idol's idle idyll hopes. The lack of such surplus of meaning in the words prompts the text's lament that there is "no more," but the "sweetness" attributed to "feigned"—imaginary—kisses reveals that real contact with "others" is not the surface speaker's only desire.

"Hopeless" brings up its Latin equivalent from line two, "despair" (desperare), and evidently both "hopeless fancy" and "divine despair" offer the speaker a certain pleasurable melancholy. Fancy and despair are false others, spurious formulations of the speaker's ground which in reality permit a narcissistic avoidance of the encounter with the other, particularly that other the self may become through change. Instead of a poem bemoaning inconsolable loss, we begin to see the outline of one which, like a young Rasselas, turns inward to lament its own regret (and regression).

The succeeding charac- terization, "deep as first love," adds to this impression. First love, rooted in the pre-oedipal relation to the mother, is but another form of self-love, the intrinsic self-regard arising in infancy and then projected on to another. The artist-narrator of "The Gardener's Daughter" literally defines himself through the eidolon he has painted to keep his past before him; at the poem's climax he raises the veil from the picture of

My first, last love; the idol of my youth,
The darling of my manhood, and alas!
Now the most blessed memory of mine age.

Here again the "idol" is a function of present memory, and the speaker's "first, last love" equates in effect with the self-imaged "memory of mine."

The speaker of "The Miller's Daughter" manifests a slightly less idolizing attitude toward the object of his memory as he recalls a song occasioned by a "blue Forget-me- not" and which recognizes the possibility that

Love is made a vague regret.
Eyes with idle tears are wet.
Idle habit links us yet.

This same speaker as much as confesses to an earlier idle idol-idyll as he remembers lines from his "long and listless" youth which "haunted me, the morning long, / With weary sameness in the rhymes, / The phantom of a silent song". Wordsworth's Matthew, somewhat similarly, finds

My eyes are dim with childish tears,
My heart is idly stirred,
For the same sound is in my ears
As in those days I heard. ("The Fountain," 29-32)

But in "Tears, Idle Tears," the speaker's wild emotions stem from the realization, as one critic observes of the (again, evidently male) speaker of Tennyson's "Break, Break, Break," that "not only will his friend never come back, but he will never be able to recapture his presence in memory". In "Tears, Idle Tears," the presence that cannot be recaptured is that of the speaker himself, who in the very act of articulation begins to slip away from, to tear himself from—and so, know more about—the days that are no more. We verge here on the poem's desperate yet trance- like, obsessive refrain and injunction, no mor. But the speaker's superficial hope for no mortality, Revelation's promise of "no more death", founders on an inability to accept that "the former things are passed away" (idem). Tennyson's concern with the repeated phrase appears in a short poem written when he was seventeen and evidently the germ for "Tears, Idle Tears":

Oh sad No More! Oh sweet No More!
Oh strange No More!
By a mossed brookbank on a stone
I smelt a wildweed-flower alone;
There was a ringing in my ears,
And both my eyes gushed out with tears.
Surely all pleasant things had gone before,
Lowburied fathomdeep beneath with thee, NO MORE!

The self-idol or self-hood is that state the individual enters as he or she grows, losing touch with an imagined original eidos or form: "I am not what see/ And other than the things I touch." Memory (me-moriso to speak) is form of Death in Life idol past though present poem (as real time) even that dying. Single concluding exclamation mark inserted by some editors days are no more!" may serve to mark the sense (or hope!) that the speaker is entering into his future, a critical experience of self-awareness and the realization of change. At the same time that he is filled with wild regret for the days past, he experiences anxious agitation that his days are no more than a memory- filled Death in Life. At the same time that he would fain live a fuller life to relieve the pressure of loss, he weeps for the impending change in psychic investment which such a fuller life implies ("O last regret, regret can die!".

So one might argue, as does Leo Spitzer, that the poem offers "two protagonists"; but while Spitzer limits these to "the poet who sheds idle tears" and a god named Death-in-Life, "wrapped in idle despair," his discussion suggests another possibility. The "impersonal supernal power" of which Spitzer sees the poet becoming aware at the end, "in a manner reminiscent of ancient tragedy" is not despair but consciousness itself, a textual "I" verging on the "the place where that was". But like a belated Peter Pan—like so many of Tennyson's characters young and old—the speaker suggests a powerful drive never to grow up, change, shift, or become conscious. "Memory [feeds] the soul of Love with tears," we learn in "The Lover's Tale", which is to say that memory, that fancy word for phantasized reconstruction of the past, offers an easy defence against the pain for what never was.

According to Tennyson, "Tears, Idle Tears" did not express real woe, but "rather the yearning that young people occasionally experience for that which seems to have passed away from them for ever". Yet one might well wonder if this is only another one of Tennyson's "two voices," here defensively passing the poem off as "not real woe." Section VI of The Princess, for instance, looks back to describe "Tears, Idle Tears," as "the mournful song" and also tells, for the first time, that it was sung by someone named "Violet". In the 1832 song, "Who can say," Tennyson finds that "The violet, recalls the dewy prime / Of youth and buried time". Similarly the speaker of "A Dream of Fair Women" (1832), familiar with the "tearful glimmer of the languid dawn", reports that "the smell of violets" pours

... back into my empty soul and frame
The times when I remember to have been
Joyful and free from blame.

Here, then, are "the days that are no more" and the attraction of a life free from guilt. "A Dream of Fair Women" concludes with an image of inviolate memory which belies the "not real woe" and "occasional yearning" that the author used to characterize his "Tears, Idle Tears":

As when a soul laments, which hath been blest,
Desiring what is mingled with past years,
In yearnings that can never be exprest
By signs or groans or tears;
Because all words, though culled with choicest art,
Failing to give the bitter of the sweet,
Wither beneath the palate, and the heart
Faints, faded by its heat.

"Melancholia" seems the appropriate description of this condition, which, as Freud defines it, "borrows some of its features from mourning, and others from the process of regression... to narcissism" ("Mourning and Melancholia" 250).

Still, one might claim for the poem the insight that, despite the narcissistic opposition of the surface speaker, the dying of the old self through change and growth is already underway. at the dynamic of "Tears, Idle Tears" connects with the "one basic action" Donald S. Hair identifies in his study of Tennyson's idylls, the process of "dying out of an unsatisfactory life and... a birth into a new and better one" (103, 104). As the speaker is dis- paired (tears tear him away) from the old days, from the dead, from idle language and "Melancholy's idol dreams", so the poem begins painfully to divine—"rounds he to a separate mind... / His isolation grows defined" (In Memoriam). Like the melancholic in Freud's analysis, the speaker begins to feels that "he himself has willed [the condition]" and so feel anxiety as guilt.

Guilt, here, for the idleness he has willed by wallowing in the continually asserted "fresh" and "so sad" quality of his emotions, "emotion" (as F. R. Leavis objected) "for its own sake without a justifying situation". In such a case, the speaker "wild with all regret" would be only a few steps from "no longer caring to embalm / In dying songs a dead regret" (In Memoriam, "Epilogue").

But the immediate and nearly universal affect-effect of the poem on readers testifies that an idylllic appeal to our narcissistic identification, our idol, is its own justification—however guilty our complicity in that idle thrill, whatever the account to be required in the day of judgment.

Ricks points out that the "idle tears" can be compared with those Aeneas weeps on leaving Carthage and Dido: Mens immota manet; lacrimae volvuntur inanes (Aeneid 4.449).

Many critics have noticed Virgilian parallels and sentiment in Tennyson's work, and one commentator even describes "Tears, Idle Tears" as "the century's most intense lyric distillation of the Vergilian `tears of things'". But where Aeneas serves the impersonal power of history, Tennyson's speaker is but a man emoting. The speaker himself is the victim, caught (mens immota) between the conflicting drives of an Other-seeking Eros and a narcissistic, stasis-seeking Thanatos. As the product of merely one moment of equilibrium in the history of those drives, the text has, finally, no one speaker, no "I" at all—at least, we know not what its "I" means (even arguing that whatever it meant it means no more). If we credit the presence of such unconscious authority, perhaps it is not surprising to find one of the central terms behind the poem, "idol," making a cryptographic appearance in the variously identified "tortured cry," "loose appositive," or (and) "vocative" address of the poem's concluding line:

Death in Life, the days that are no more

So as to subjoin, "Idol, the days that are know more.". As Blake has it, "the ratio of all we have already known. is not the same that it shall be when we know more" ("There is No Natural Religion"). The "I" that comes to know more is that "I" no more, just as the "I" that grasps "no more," even unto "Death in Life," is an "I" that comes to know more. So, does Tennyson's idle idol-idyll rise in the hearing as we gather in its "I"s.

Q. Illustrate "The Lady of Shallot" as the conflict of Men vs. Women

Or

Q. What was the curse beckoned upon the Lady of Shallot?

Or

Q. What is the theme behind calling the woman as follows?

The Pre-Raphaelites, a group of artists in the mid-nineteenth century, challenged the artistic conventions of their day as they sought to return art to a truer state. Rebelling against the teachings of the Royal Academy schools, which emphasized pyramidal compositions of figures, imbalanced lighting, and the prominence of tone and shadow at the expense of colour, the Pre-Raphaelite Brotherhood formed in 1849. Its members included William Holman Hunt, Dante Gabriel Rossetti, and Sir John Everett Millais. From the Pre-Raphaelite Brotherhood arose a larger circle of artists who formed the movement known as Pre-Raphaelitism. Bright colours, even lighting, and flat figures marked the Pre-Raphaelites' paintings as they aimed to achieve photographic realism in their art, particularly in their representations of nature.

"The Lady of Shallot", one of Tennyson's most well-known poems, inspired a number of Pre-Raphaelite artists. The poem appealed to these artists because of its eroticized medieval setting and tragic subject, popular themes in Pre-Raphaelite art. Artists such as Hunt, Rossetti, John William Waterhouse, Sidney Harold Meteyard, and John Liston Byam Shaw painted various scenes from the poem, capturing their fascination with themes of tragic love, the beautiful, imprisoned woman figure, and the conflicted role of the artist. While these well-established male artists illustrated Pre-Raphaelite ideals in their renditions of "The Lady of Shallot", the poem also inspired some lesser-known female artists of the period, such as Elizabeth Siddal, Inez Warry, and Florence Rutland. As a whole, these women's illustrations dramatized, romanticized, and sexualized the subject to a lesser extent than men's illustrations did.

The Poem

Tennyson's "The Lady of Shallot", a poem in four parts, tells the story of a cursed Lady imprisoned on the island of Shallot. Forbidden even a single glance out of her window, she sits each day weaving a tapestry that illustrates the outside world — which she may glimpse only through her mirror's reflections.

One day, however, the Lady hears the voice of Sir Lancelot as he rides by outside, and she catches sight of his reflection in her mirror. Captivated, she steps away from her loom and looks out the window to see him, and thus doomed by her love, the Lady leaves the island on a boat, in which she dies.

An atmosphere of mystery pervades the poem, one of the reasons it so intrigued Pre-Raphaelite artists, who were eager to express the images of their imaginations. Tennyson opens the poem with descriptions of the beautiful island on which the Lady is imprisoned, rather than explaining anything about the Lady herself. He finally mentions her in the last line of the second stanza, and even then, only briefly.

Willows whiten, aspens quiver,
Little breezes dusk and shiver
Through the wave that runs forever
By the island in the river
Flowing down to Camelot.
Four gray walls, and four gray towers,
Overlook a space of flowers,
And the silent isle imbowers
The Lady of Shallot.

The vibrancy of the outside world contrasts with the Lady's prison of "gray" walls and towers, asserting her isolation from the activity of life. Yet although Tennyson introduces the Lady in this stanza, the poem's sense of mystery continues. Throughout the poem, Tennyson thoroughly details the outside world, while the Lady remains a woman of mystery. Tennyson does not explain what the Lady looks like, why the Lady is cursed, or her inner state of mind. One of the only times the Lady speaks during the poem, and one of the only times Tennyson alludes to her thoughts or emotions, occurs in the eighth stanza.

But in her web she still delights
To weave the mirror's magic sights,
For often through the silent nights
A funeral, with plumes and lights
And music, went to Camelot:

Or when the moon was overhead,
Came two young lovers lately wed;
"I am half-sick of shadows, " said
The Lady of Shallot.

Tennyson considered this declaration the poem's most crucial moment. Although at first the Lady seemed content to remain isolated from the darkness and sadness of the world outside, another aspect of that life appealed to her: seeing the "two young lovers lately wed" made her yearn for a lover of her own. Tennyson's use of contrasts within the poem highlight this conflict. As mentioned before, Tennyson juxtaposes descriptions of the lively outside world with the Lady's stark, static existence in her room. Although the Lady might be satisfied with safely weaving her tapestry from a distance, removed from the pain the world outside could offer, her admission in this stanza proves that she is not content. This discontent causes the Lady's fateful actions in the thirteenth stanza.

She left the web, she left the loom,
She made three paces through the room,
She saw the water-lily bloom,
She saw the helmet and the plume,
She looked down to Camelot.
Out flew the web and floated wide;
The mirror cracked from side to side;
"The curse is come upon me, " cried
The Lady of Shallot.

The Lady at last sees the outside world directly, and she must now die. The image of the blooming water-lily, the first bit of life the Lady directly gazes upon out her window, may represent the Lady herself, interacting with the natural world for the first time. However, the cursed Lady cannot exist as a part of this life. Getting into a boat, upon which she carves her name, the dying Lady leaves her island. The boat floats towards Camelot, where in the last stanza Lancelot finds the Lady dead.

Who is this and what is here
And in the lighted palace near

Died the sound of royal cheer;
And they crossed themselves for fear,
All the knights at Camelot:
But Lancelot mused a little space;
He said, "She has a lovely face;
God in his mercy lend her grace,
The Lady of Shallot. "

Lancelot cannot know that the Lady's love for him caused her death, that she sacrificed everything so that she might experience his love. Adding to the irony of the scene, the Lady has in fact finally joined Lancelot's physical world, as he stands before her body, but she nevertheless cannot share her love with him. Together in the outside world, the Lady and Lancelot still exist separately, one living and the other dead, and the Lady never achieves what she desired — she remains forever alone.

Q. Do u agree that the illustrations of Tennyson's poetry were driven from ancient literature?

Pre-Raphaelite artists often drew from literary sources in their artwork, using subjects of literary narration to portray individualized emotional conflicts. These personal, internal states stood as metaphors for the common condition of humanity as a whole. It thus follows that the most popular scenes, which artists illustrated from "The Lady of Shallot", expressed the Lady's emotional turmoil, showing the imprisoned Lady, "half-sick of shadows"; the Lady looking out her window at Lancelot; the Lady leaving the island; the dying Lady in her boat; and the dead Lady in her boat (Nelson 6). However, the same artists drawn to the intense conflicts within "The Lady of Shallot" often did not remain faithful to the poem's explanations of events.

Tennyson's sparse descriptions of the Lady allowed artists a great deal of freedom in illustrating the poem, yet these artists often did not remain faithful to what little details were given to them.

According to John Ruskin, the young artists' departures from the poem expressed their artistic visions and goals. Ruskin stated in a letter to Tennyson regarding the illustrations of the Moxon

Tennyson, "Many of the plates are very noble things, though not, it seems to me, illustrations of your poems. I believe, in fact, that good pictures never can be; they are always another poem, subordinate but wholly different from the poet's conception, and serve chiefly to show the reader how variously the same verses may affect various minds". This explanation, however, did not satisfy Tennyson, who expressed dissatisfaction with the artists' unfaithful renderings.

William Holman Hunt's two versions of The Lady of Shallot: His woodblock illustration from the Moxon Tennyson at left and the painting he finished four decades afterward at the right.

In particular, Tennyson complained about Hunt's interpretation in his The Lady of Shallot, which detailed the scene in which the Lady looks out her window and realises her fate. Hunt's painting, very similar to his Moxon Tennyson version of the scene, depicts the Lady in elabourate surroundings, unlike the stark room described in the poem. Hunt also takes the liberty of representing the Lady tangled in her tapestry's threads, a detail not included in the poem and of which Tennyson did not approve.

However, Hunt had a purpose in straying from certain elements of the poem. For example, the ornate decoration of the Lady's room served to communicate concepts such as the conflict between pure love and romantic, passionate love, a tension represented by the image of the Virgin and Child on the left side of the painting and the image of Hercules taking the golden apples of Hesperides on the right side of the painting.

Other elabourations of the poem, such as the details of the Lady's hair blowing violently about her and the threads of the Lady's tapestry entangling her, reinforce Hunt's rendition of a wild emotional state. These deviations do not detract from viewers' recognition of the subject matter. For example, Hunt includes the Lady's loom and the cracked mirror with Lancelot's reflection, which identify the painting as the climactic scene from Tennyson's poem.

Similar variations occur in Rutland's The Lady of Shallot, an illustration of the same scene. Rutland, like Hunt, portrays the intense emotion of the moment, in this version through the Lady's aghast facial expression and the way her tapestry's threads reach around her body. Also like Hunt, Rutland includes the identifying loom and cracked mirror. However, Rutland details the Lady's room as decorated with religious images upon the walls and furniture.

These details, not found in the poem, give the illustration a symbolic depth that suggests the Lady's purity and asserts her sacrifice. As with Hunt's painting, in order for a viewer to fully comprehend Rutland's illustration, the viewer requires knowledge of Tennyson's poem. However, Hunt's and Rutland's depictions of intense psychological states allow the illustrations to remain powerful nevertheless.

Perhaps, in fact, these illustrations would not produce the same emotional effects were the Lady not tangled in her own tapestry, her facial expression not one of horror, or her hair not blowing forcefully about her. Perhaps in order to achieve the power of the written scene, Hunt and Rutland found it necessary to rearrange and reconstruct elements of their visual representations.

Siddal's drawing of the scene, The Lady of Shallot at her loom, is perhaps the most faithful illustration to the poem, yet it lacks the intensity of Hunt's and Rutland's versions. Siddal accurately illustrates the starkness of the Lady's surroundings, seating the Lady appropriately at her loom, with Lancelot's reflection in the cracked mirror. Compared to the illustrations by Hunt and Rutland, Siddal's appears simple and unembellished.

Siddal's drawing departs from the poem only in its inclusion of a crucifix in front of the window, an image that adds symbolic meaning to the illustration in the same way Rutland's religious ornamentations suggested purity and sacrifice. However, Siddal's much more straightforward construction of the scene lacks the emotional intensity of Hunt's and Rutland's illustrations. By remaining faithful to Tennyson's staging of the scene, Siddal in fact betrays the poem in another way — her Lady seems quietly calm, rather than appropriately frenzied and passionate.

Warry, in contrast, renders the Lady more inaccurately than Hunt, Rutland, or Siddal, and for different reasons entirely. Warry's The Lady of Shallot illustrates the Lady very early in the poem, before the Lady's announcement that she has grown tired of shadows.

Yet Warry's Lady does not weave at a loom, nor does she appear imprisoned in a room with a mirror or window. Instead, Warry depicts a dignified Lady seated on a cushioned stool, contentedly embroidering. These drastic alterations reveal Warry's goal of presenting the Lady not as a powerful, tragic figure, but as a respectable upper-class Victorian woman. In this version, in fact, there are no signs, other than the title, that this image illustrates "The Lady of Shallot". By removing all visual links to its literary source, Warry created a generalized image whose connection to the poem remains only in its title.

Q. Can the poem be called as a "Tragic Love" Story? Discuss. ?

"The Lady of Shallot" attracted various Pre-Raphaelite artists through its theme of tragic love. The poem's demonstration of the melancholy aspects of love, and the spiritual state of suffering for love, fascinated the Pre-Raphaelites. The poem dealt with the popular topic of unrequited love, and the Lady of Shallot exemplified the unattainable woman, the cursed woman, and the woman sacrificing everything for a doomed love (Nelson 6). Artists such as Hunt, Waterhouse, and Shaw emphasized these themes by illustrating the most tragic scenes of the poem. They concentrated on those moments which best portrayed the Lady's suffering, and they affirmed her suffering in their dramatic renderings of her.

Both Shaw and Waterhouse illustrate the Lady dying. In his The Lady of Shallot, Shaw paints the Lady inscribing her name along the side of the boat in which she will die. She rests dramatically on her knees, her head tilted to the side with an expression of deep sorrow. Dead leaves fall about her, symbolizing her own oncoming death. Waterhouse's The Lady of Shallot takes place moments later, as the Lady frees herself from the island of her imprisonment.

She sits upon her tapestry in the boat, and she holds the chain in her right hand. Waterhouse asserts the Lady's emotional distress through her facial expression: her eyes stare forward in trancelike grief, and her mouth has dropped open slightly. Waterhouse places three candles and a crucifix at the front of the boat, again affirming the Lady's sacrifice through religious symbols, which in this scene also suggest a funeral-like mood. A single, dead leaf has fallen onto the Lady's lap, foreshadowing her fate, as in Shaw's illustration.

The portrayals by Siddal and Warry, however, did not display an equal fixation with the concept of tragic love. Although Siddal's drawing illustrates the moment at which the Lady turns from her loom to look at Lancelot directly, she shows no recognition.of her fate. The Lady's expression is not horrified; she shows no signs of distress. Instead, the Lady appears entirely composed. Warry's depiction shares this sense of calm. In this illustration, the Lady has not yet heard Lancelot's voice or declared herself "half-sick of shadows". While Siddal expresses the poem's climax as an emotionless moment, Warry actually illustrates the poem's most emotionless moment, as the Lady shows no yearnings or inner turmoil whatsoever at this point.

It thus seems that Siddal and Warry did not share the Pre-Raphaelite goal of displaying love at its most tragic. Instead, Siddal illustrated the poem at a purely visual level: she placed the figures and objects precisely as she read them to be placed, ignoring the poem's emotional plane altogether. Warry, meanwhile, could not have exhibited the tragic aspect of the Lady's story and simultaneously achieved her goal of presenting the Lady as a dignified Victorian woman, so it seems she chose the latter objective.

Rutland's illustration, though displaying a state of emotional distress, nevertheless does not appear quite as tragic or dramatic as the illustrations by male artists. Rutland does not illustrate the Lady at her most tragic, dying or dead, but she does interpret the poem's climactic moment as a moment of emotional turmoil. The Lady, realizing her doom, steps forward, her body hunched as though weak with alarm. One hand grips the small table beside her, and she presses her other hand against the side of her head. She has a horrified facial expression, and the threads of her tapestry have blown forward, some snaking between her arm and waist. Rutland's illustration displays much more emotional intensity than those of Siddal and Warry, and in fact shows many similarities to the images of the same scene by Waterhouse and Hunt. The pose of Rutland's Lady seems to mimic that of Waterhouse's The Lady of Shallot, as she steps forward in the same hunched position.

Rutland's illustration resembles Hunt's painting in the detail of the threads blowing about the room. However, Hunt's illustration appears much more frenzied and chaotic, showing his Lady actually tangled in the threads, her hair blowing wildly about her to symbolize her inner turmoil. Thus while Rutland's illustration presented the Lady as a more tragic figure than did Siddal or Warry, it seems that overall, male artists such as Waterhouse, Shaw, and Hunt displayed a greater fascination with the tragic aspects of love.

Q. Does this define "The Lady of Shallot as an Object of Desire"?

Although Victorian attitudes towards women were highly complex, the most striking difference between male artists' representations of the Lady of Shallot and female artists' representations occurred in the artists' attitudes towards the Lady as a woman. Male artists stressed the Lady's position as an object of desire, depicting her as an idealized, sensual woman: beautiful, mysterious, pure, and above all, unattainable. These characteristics of the Lady contributed to her supreme desirability, which was emphasized in illustrations by artists such as Meteyard, Hunt, and Rossetti.

In "I Am Half-Sick of Shadows," Said the Lady of Shallot, Meteyard painted the moment at which the Lady declared the famous line. However, the emphasis of the painting does not seem to be upon the Lady's emotional distress, but rather on the Lady as a beautiful, sensual woman. The Lady reclines erotically in her seat, the thin, soft fabrics of her dress accentuating the shape of her body.

Her head leans to one side, revealing the delicate white skin of her neck, intensified in contrast to the darker shades of the painting. Flowers surround the Lady; like her, they are delicately soft and pale. The Lady's eyes are closed as though she is lost in a dream, and this position highlights her situation as a vulnerable object: she cannot see anything, but anyone may stare at her, as her sensual pose invites viewers to do.

Hunt painted a different type of woman, less overtly sexualized, yet nevertheless the typical Pre-Raphaelite woman of ideal form. Hunt's Lady of Shallot resembled the idealized Rossettian woman, with strong facial features, full lips, and bright red hair. Hunt punctuates her physical beauty by leaving her thick hair loose, the wind drawing additional attention to this feature by spreading it upwards in the air. Hunt also leaves the Lady's feet bare, revealing her skin as they peek out from beneath her dress, which the wind has lifted to expose her undergarments. The decorations of the Lady's room further her desirability.

The image of the Virgin and Child suggests the Lady's purity, while the image of Hercules suggests romantic passion: Hunt has achieved a Lady who is at once pure and erotic. In addition, the inclusion of exotic objects, such as the teapot and sandals, add to the Lady's alluring mystery.

Rossetti's illustration The Lady of Shallot depicts the moment at which Lancelot gazes upon the dead Lady, remarking that she "has a lovely face." In this illustration, Rossetti presents the Lady as a pure woman, her garments fully covering her body, yet this representation may also most blatantly render the Lady an object. She lies limply at the bottom of the frame, while Lancelot, stooping down to stare at her, takes up the majority of the space. Lancelot, towering over the Lady, appears strong and powerful, while she appears defenceless, vulnerable to his gaze as he judges her beauty. The figures' poses assert Lancelot's position of power, as he stands firmly, in contrast to the Lady's position as a mere object, lying in her boat.

Illustrations by female artists, however, did not reduce the Lady of Shallot to an object of desire. Instead, the illustrations by Siddal and Warry define the Lady by her position, either in relation to her surroundings and situation of imprisonment, or in relation to her status in society. These portrayals do not emphasize the Lady's sensuality. Siddal's illustration shows little attention to details of the Lady's body. She wears a plain, loose-fitting gown, and her body has a very simple form.

This illustration does not focus on the Lady's beauty, as Siddal draws her plainly. There is nothing sensual about the Lady's pose; she simply sits before her loom, head turned toward the window. In fact, it does not seem that this drawing focuses on the Lady as a woman, but on the Lady as a figure seated before a loom — the Lady is an element of a larger scene, and therefore the scene, not her appearance, defines her. This scene underscores the Lady's situation of imprisonment. The walls are bare, and there is no sign of a door. She sits in the centre of the rather small room, alone in her sparse surroundings. Here, the Lady is a figure of imprisonment, not a sensual being.

Warry's version does concentrate on the Lady herself, but it does not present her sensually. Although Warry emphasizes the Lady's appearance, she wears clothing that covers all but her hands, neck, and face. Her hair is modestly pinned up, and she even wears a hat with a long veil. She does not pose sensually; she sits and embroiders. This illustration portrays the Lady as a refined woman, not as an object of desire. Warry defines her Lady by her place in society, as an upper-class Victorian woman. Rather than engaging in weaving, which was normally left to the lower classes, she daintily embroiders. It is not even clear from this illustration that the Lady is imprisoned, cursed, or doomed; she displays none of the characteristics that would identify her as an object of desire to Pre-Raphaelite artists.

Rutland's illustration brings an aspect of sensuality to the scene that does not appear in the illustrations by Siddal and Warry, but in this illustration the Lady does not appear vulnerable or defenceless. The Lady's hair is loose and flowing, and she has the bold facial features of a typical Pre-Raphaelite woman of beauty. Her curved stance draws attention to her physicality, lending her figure a weight not seen in the depictions by Siddal and Warry.

She is both the imprisoned woman and the mysterious woman here: her elabourate dress and the decorations of her chamber accentuate the air of mysterious beauty surrounding her. Yet Rutland gives her Lady a sort of power. Stepping forward, gazing out at the viewer, there is a challenge to her look. The Lady may be sensual and beautiful, but Rutland empowers her by allowing her to stare back at those who stare at her.

Q. Does this poem reflect "The Artist's Conflict"?

The Lady of Shallot was an attractive subject to the Pre-Raphaelites also because she could represent the artist, and her fate could represent the destruction of the artist by the necessity of interacting directly with the world. The poem places the Lady in a state of isolation, torn between the outside world and her necessary confinement, lost in a world of shadows. In fact, this world of shadows in which the Lady lives highlights her role as an artist figure, as it affirms her distance from the reality of nature. She weaves images from reflections, not even from any actual life she might see outside her window. The conflicts between the Lady's interior and exterior worlds exemplify the tension between the artist's function of creating his or her own interpretation of nature and the simultaneous necessity of directly experiencing the natural world. The Pre-Raphaelites' explorations of these conflicts appear in their illustrations through their use of symbols, particularly the Lady's mirror.

For example, Hunt's painting emphasizes the large mirror in the background, upon which the image of Lancelot riding away in the fields appears somewhat faded compared to the vibrant colours elsewhere in the painting, asserting the reflection's place as a mere shadow of life. Hunt also portrays the Lady in darkness, while sunlight from the window, the world outside, falls across the floor and her legs, representing her first steps into this livelier world. Hunt further clarifies the Lady's position as an artist figure by tangling her in her own creation, the threads of her tapestry.

Meteyard's illustration, which details the moment at which the Lady declares her dissatisfaction with the world of shadows, places emphasis on the Lady's internal state. The mirror behind her does not actually reflect the outside world at all. It appears mostly dark, except for the small image of two lovers at its centre. Here, the mirror seems to reflect the Lady's thoughts and dreams.

The flowers, symbols of fleeting, fragile life, contrast the Lady's creation, her tapestry, which is long-lasting but not alive in the same way. Instead, her tapestry diminishes to a shadow of a shadow, woven from a reflection. The Lady even turns her head away from the flowers, representing her rejection of, or inability to join, the natural world. She instead remains a part of her isolated, interior world.

The illustrations by Warry and Siddal emphasize the Lady's situation as an isolated, conflicted artist to a lesser extent than Hunt's and Meteyard's illustrations do. Warry's illustration, for example, does not reflect a deep interest in defining or illustrating the role of the artist. Perhaps because Warry's version did not attempt to achieve any deep artistic goal, but rather attempted to present a respectable Victorian woman, Warry gives no sign of the Lady's isolation and represents no tension between creating an inner artistic vision and experiencing life outside directly.

Siddal's illustration does depict the Lady's isolation and the conflict between the interior and exterior worlds, but Siddal does not stress these themes. Although Siddal portrays the Lady cut off from the outside world, and her stark, cramped room contrasts with the open field on the other side of her window, these details come from the poem itself.

The crucifix before the window is the only embellishment Siddal includes in her drawing. The crucifix punctuates the Lady's dilemma, for in order to see the crucifix, she must look out the window. Reinforcing the concept of shadows, Siddal places the crucifix so that the Lady may, however, glimpse the crucifix's shadow without raising her eyes to look out the window.

This conspicuous placement of the crucifix alludes to a certain inevitability of the Lady's situation, suggesting that she has no choice but to look at the world directly. Nevertheless, Siddal's drawing does not focus on the crucifix in the way that Hunt's and Meteyard's paintings assert the artist's conflict. Siddal's crucifix, at least at first glance, appears a minor detail added to her faithful, simple illustration of the poem.

Rutland makes a more blatant connection between the Lady's situation and that of an artist, wrapping the threads of the Lady's tapestry around her body. The mirror in this illustration also figures prominently, large and in the centre of the picture, framed by empty black space that highlights its significance even more. However, Rutland does not contain the Lady's reality to the space within the illustration. Instead, the Lady faces directly outward at the viewers.

In contrast to the tapestry's usual function as the shadow of a shadow, it seems as though Rutland's Lady may directly glimpse the viewer's reality, removing one layer of obstruction. This added level may be interpreted as an inventive way of handling the artistic conflict posed by the poem, or it may be that by de-emphasizing the window, de-emphasizing the Lady's removal from the natural world, Rutland de-emphasizes the Lady's position as an artist figure.

Conclusion

Tennyson's "The Lady of Shallot" inspired and intrigued many Pre-Raphaelite artists because of its tragic subject matter and treatment of the conflicted role of the artist. As a whole, however, male artists and female artists approached certain aspects of its illustration differently. Artists such as Hunt, Waterhouse, Rossetti, and Meteyard emphasized the tragic aspects of the Lady's love and her place as an object of desire, while artists such as Siddal and Warry focused more on the Lady's position in relation to her surroundings and status. Rutland's illustration overlapped these differing methods, presenting the Lady's sensuality and emotional turmoil, but to a lesser extent than did illustrations by male artists.

Rhoda L. Flaxman, defines word painting as "extended passages of visually oriented descriptions whose techniques emulate pictorial methods. Word-painters typically employ framing devices, recurrent iconographic motifs, careful compositional structures, and pay close attention to contrasts of light and dark, of colour, volume, and mass." Tennysòn was one of the most exceptional word painters of the nineteenth century and probably of all time.

In the previous passage from his "Mariana," Tennyson's use of word- painting works to create what Flaxman calls a "faithfulness to a precise and consistent perspective focused through the viewpoint of a particular spectator. This point of view often yields an effect we moderns call cinematic, implying progress from one element to the next in a 'narrative of landscape.'" The poem is marked by its static feeling - there is no climax that the poem is leading up to. Yet the use of word painting does create a "narrative of landscape."

Tennyson begins with a rather rocky first sentence, the tongue tripping over the words "blackest" and "flower-plots."

With blackest moss the flower-pots
Were thickly crusted, one and all:
The rusted nails fell from the knots
That held the pear to the garden-wall.
The broken sheds look'd sad and strange:
Unlifted was the clinking latch;
Weeded and worn the ancient thatch
Upon the lonely moated grange.
She only said, 'My life is dreary,
He cometh not,' she said;
She said, 'I am aweary, aweary,
I would that I were dead.

The imagery of "thickly crusted," with the double consonants surrounding a short vowel in both words, creates darkness and a density, setting the mood of the poem, which has already been hinted at with the word black. The use of the word "black" also serves to place the poem in an industrial setting, where the soot from the factories covered everything with a depressing, coal black. The "clinking latch" works to add sound to the image. The sound that "clinking" produces is very short and empty, just a clicking of the tongue. By the time the last line before the returning refrain is reached, the words "upon the lonely moated grange" feel hollow, especially after the "clinking" noise.

The long vowels create an expansiveness that allows one to feel the loneliness of the scene, and of the speaker. Once again, the use of pathetic fallacy allows the reader to know that the poet is trying to "dramatize grief... communicating [it] far more effectively than would the simple statement that the speaker suffers from sorrow" (George Landow, "Ruskin's Discussion of the Pathetic Fallacy," The Victorian Web).

Because the characterization in The Pickwick Papersare primarily, as Dickens says, by means of a depiction of "English scenes and people," with a large emphasis on dialogue and actions, there is not as much use of word-painting in the novel. However, at times, Dickens does use this technique. In a scene near the beginning of the novel, Pickwick stands reflecting on the Rochester Bridge. The narrator describes the scene around him: On the left of the spectator lay the ruined wall, broken in many places, and in some, overhanging the narrow beach below in rude and heavy masses. Huge knots of sea-weed hung upon the jagged and pointed stones, trembling in every breath of wind; and the green ivy clung mournfully round the dark and ruined battlements.

The word-painting in this scene is much less effective than in Tennyson, in part because Tennyson is a poet and more concerned with the individual words than a serial writer like Dickens, but also because of a difference in the function of the word-painting. Pickwick is supposedly immersed in an "agreeable reverie." Yet the placement of such a scene amidst all the hustle and bustle of the dialogue and the action creates some confusion. According to Flaxman, Victorian word painting integrates "descriptive details with thematic motifs in order to emphasize the contrast between the old and new, the past and present" (Flaxman in Smith). The man who rouses Pickwick "from the agreeable reverie" seems to be the embodiment of Romanticism.

The man is obsessed with nature and suggests to Pickwick "on a morning such as this... drowning would be peace and happiness... The calm, cool water seems to me to murmur an invitation to repose and rest". This spontaneous overflow of emotion, the commitment to passion and the utter lack of concern about how his death might affect anyone are key signs of Romanticism. Thus the word-painting here functions as a way to contrast this "old," "past" perspective with a new one that emphasizes a balance of passion with reason and a desire to connect the individual with society.

"Mariana" also addresses the issue of an individual and her lack of connection with society. Despite the loneliness and dread that Mariana feels, she still wants the connection with an other. She laments repeatedly, "My life is dreary, He cometh not... I am aweary, aweary, I would that I were dead" Her loneliness encourages her to wish her own death. The obvious bout of depression in which Mariana is immersed indicates the concern with mental health that became so important during the nineteenth-century. Having a healthy body and mind was a priority and a topic that occupied the minds of most middle class citizens. The emerging fascination with mentally unstable people, such as Mariana, indicates this growing societal obsession with mental health and sanity. This obsession stems in part from the desire to connect the individual with society.

One who is mentally unstable is largely incapable of making a connection with other members of society. They become figures like the man who interrupts Pickwick's reverie, obsessed with their own life and death in a way characteristic of Romantic thinkers. Thus word-painting in Tennyson does not work to represent a contrast between past and present, as it does in Dickens, but rather as a way to establish the depression and emptiness that come from a lack of connection with any other human being, placing Mariana firmly in the Victorian present.

Q. Give a brief introduction to Tennyson's poem " In Memoriam" ?

Or

Q. To whom does this poem is attributed. ?

Tennyson came to write In Memoriam, one of the most experimental and yet most influential poems of the century, he already had refined his characteristic basic poetic structure and needed a theme that would permit him to apply his gifts to a major-form. Arthur Henry Hallam's death in 1833 provided Tennyson with one by forcing him to question his faith in nature, God, and poetry.

In Memoriam reveals that Tennyson, who found that brief lyrics best embodied the transitory emotions that buffeted him after his loss, rejected conventional elegy and narrative because both falsify the experience of grief and recovery by mechanically driving the reader through too unified — and hence too simplified — a version of these experiences. Creating a poetry of fragments, Tennyson leads the reader of In Memoriam from grief and despair through doubt to hope and faith, but at each step stubborn, contrary emotions intrude, and one encounters doubt in the midst of faith, pain in the midst of resolution.

Instead of the elegiac plot of Lycidas, Adonais, and Thyrsis, In Memoriam offers 133 fragments interlaced by dozens of images and motifs and informed by an equal number of minor and major resolutions, the most famous of which is section 95's representation of Tennyson's climactic, if wonderfully ambiguous, mystical experience of contact with Hallam's spirit. In addition, individual sections, like 7 and 119 or 28, 78, and 104 variously resonate with one another.

One of the central resolutions of In Memoriam involves the poet's plays upon the word type, which in the poem means either "biological species" or "divinely intended prefiguration of Christ." Typology (or typological symbolism) is a Christian form of biblical interpretation that proceeds on the assumption that God placed anticipations of Christ in the laws, events, and people of the Old Testament. Typology, which had enormous influence on medieval Europe, seventeenth- century England,

and Victorian Britain, provided literature and art with an imaginatively rich iconography and particular conceptions of reality and time. According to this way of understanding the Bible, Samson, who sacrificed his life for God's people, partially anticipates Christ, who repeats the action, endowing it with a deeper, more complete, more spiritual significance. Similarly, the scapegoat and the animals sacrificed in the Temple at Jerusalem, both of which atoned for man's sins, and Aaron, God's priest, are types.

Tennyson closes his elegy with the now calm assurance that Hallam "was a noble type / Appearing ere the times were ripe." In Memoriam resolves the crisis of faith precipitated by Hallam's death by presenting him doubly as a type, because he foreshadowed both the second appearance of Christ and the coming higher race of human beings. In making this characteristically Victorian — that is, characteristically idiosyncratic — use of biblical typology, Tennyson [3]solves" the problem raised earlier in the poem where type means [3]biological species." The central sections 54 through 56, which dramatize his groping for consolation, show how the poet's doubts raised increasingly appalling specters.

He thus begins section 54 with trust that when God's plan is understood, all will see that not one life is [3]cast as rubbish to the void," but even as he tries to assert this hopeful view, his doubts wear away his confidence. Retreating, he tries in the next section to find consolation in the fact that although nature may be careless of the individual life, she is nonetheless "careful of the type." In response to this last desperate hope that nature preserves the species if not the individual, section 56 immediately replies "So careful of the type" but no. / From scarped cliff and quarried stone / She cries, "A thousand types are gone: / I care for nothing, all shall go." Thus, his friend's death, which first made the poet realise the emotional reality of loss, soon forced him to realise the possibility that not only he himself but also the entire human species could die out.

But, as the final sections of the poem make clear, Tennyson can accept the possibility man will become extinct because he has come to believe that such extinction would occur only when God was ready to replace man with a higher, more spiritual descendant. At the close of the poem, then, theological type replaces biological type, or rather encompasses it, because faith reveals that God's eternal plan includes purposeful biological development.

Tennyson, the real, once-existing man with his actual beliefs and fears, cannot be extrapolated from within the poem's individual sections, for each presents Tennyson only at a particular moment. In Memoriam thus fulfills Paul Valéry's definition of poetry as a machine that reproduces an emotion. Tennyson makes us re-experience an idealized version of his own separate experiences — and thereby become ready to accept the entirely subjective truths of religious belief.

Introduction

During the 19th century Victorians displayed an immense fondness for both ancient mythology and medieval legends. Large numbers of illustrators, painters, historians, novelists and poets enjoyed considerable success in meeting the demand for these subjects, appealing to a broad and enthusiastic public. Illustrated books, while hardly a new concept, were particularly popular during this period. This combination of visual arts and literature allowed people to gain a better understanding of their favourite characters and subject matter.

One of the most successful writers during the 19th century was Alfred Tennyson, and his poem "The Lady of Shallot" was one of the best known during this period. The subject matter, featuring the tragic fate of a young woman set against the backdrop of medieval Camelot, proved to be very popular with artists and illustrators. The popularity of his work prompted his publisher, Edward Moxon, to call for an illustrated edition of his work in 1854.

Artist William Holman Hunt had already independently worked on a drawing of The Lady of Shallot, (fig. 1) and when Tennyson requested an illustration from him for this new edition it was an opportunity that Hunt gladly embraced.

When fellow artist and friend Dante Gabriel Rossetti complained that Hunt had chosen his favourite image Hunt responded, "You know I made a drawing from this poem of the 'Breaking of the Web' at least four years ago...I have ever since been nervous lest this immature invention should be regarded as my finished ideas."

As with any illustration of a writer's work, visual artists risked not being able, or not desiring, to accurately portray a character in the context that Tennyson constructed it. Disagreements between writer and illustrator were not uncommon and these interactions are significant today for what they reveal about the period and individuals involved. The most notable conflict in conjunction with the 1857 edition of Tennyson's work involved William Holman Hunt's depiction of "The Lady of Shallot." Upon meeting Hunt after the drawing had been published, Tennyson asked, "Why did you make the Lady of Shallot, in the illustration, with her hair wildly tossed about as if by a Tornado" to Hunt replied that he was simply trying to convey the impression of her weird fate. To which Tennyson responded, " An illustrator ought never add anything to what he finds in the text."

Q. What factors were responsible for the "The Lady of Shallot"?

"The Lady of Shallot" has had and still retains an appeal that attracts writers and artists. Part of this allure started long before Tennyson began to create her mystical existence. It begins with the origins of the mysterious Camelot that served as part of the background of the Lady's drama. In the poem "The Lady of Shallot," Alfred Tennyson creates an enchanting world based on the mystery of a lonely lady and a mysterious curse that haunts her. While the specific circumstances that surround her may be the creation of Tennyson's mind, the character already existed. Where did the story come from Tennyson's source is an unusual one, but it came from an obvious origin, the legends of King Arthur.

The Arthurian legends are a mixture of mythology with a scattering of actual fact from Celtic history. The earliest appearance of the legend comes from Geoffrey of Monmouth's Historia Regum Britanniae. Written in 1185 CE., Monmouth was fulfilling the wish of Geoffrey Plantagenet to "provide the AngloNorman sovereigns with a reference point and worthy model." (Anne Berthelot, King Arthur and the Knights of the Round Table (New York: Harry N. Abrams Inc, 1997) 36.) Queen Guinevere and Sir Lancelot first appeared later in that same century when Marie de Champagne, daughter of Eleanor of Aquitaine, commissioned Le Chevalier de La Charrette, the first novel to describe the love triangle of King Arthur, Queen Guinevere, and Lancelot. (Berthelot, 36.) The connection between French and English courts allowed French literature to maintain a very close connection to the legends of Arthur.

The French romances known as the Vulgate cycle consist of the tales of Arthur, Merlin, the Holy Grail, and Lancelot. It is from these key sources that the English writer of Arthurian legends, Thomas Malory, wrote his book Le Morte d'Arthur in 1529.

While those familiar with Malory's work, especially the character Elaine of Astolat, might be convinced that his writings were the inspiration for Tennyson's "Lady of Shallot," Tennyson claimed otherwise. He did admit to their accidental similarity, stating ".

"The Lady of Shallot" is evidently the Elaine of the Morte d'Arthur, but I do not think that I had ever heard of the latter when I wrote the former." (George O. Marshall, A Tennyson Handbook (New York: Twanye Publishers, 1963) In a conversation with his friend F. J. Furnivall, Tennyson denied any intent to pattern the work of Malory. Writing to William Rossetti, Furnivall quoted an earlier conversation with Tennyson, writing "Indeed I doubt whether I should ever have put it in that shape if I had been aware of the Maid of Astolat in Morte d'Arthur." (Marshall, 59.)Tennyson's inspiration actually came from a most unlikely and obscure source, an Italian novella entitled "La Donna di Scalotta." Tennyson's son Hallam writes about this Italian source in his father's memoirs. Recounting the works contained in the 1832 volume of poems, he writes, "Among the poems in this volume were "the Lady of

Shallot" (so-called from an Italian novelette, "Donna di Scalotta")..." (Hallam Tennyson, Alfred Lord Tennyson: A Memoir vol. 1 (New York: The MacMillan Company, 1911)

The novella "La Donna di Scalotta" comes from a collection of Italian short stories commonly known as Il Novellino, Cento Novelle Antiche, or One Hundred Ancient Tales. While some of the tales are themselves much older, scholars suggest 1281 CE to 1300 CE as the date of the original compilation. Il Novellino, writes Joseph Consoli, was the "First collection of short stories to appear in Italian literature composed specifically for Italian audiences." (Joesph P. Consoli, The Novellino or One Hundred Ancient Tales (New York: Garland Publishing, Inc., 1997) While it may have been written specifically for an Italian audience, the stories did not come solely from Italian writers. Il Novellino is a collection of tales that originate from various countries. Included in this collection are stories from the Orient, French nouvelles, Provençal vidas, the crusades, the Bible, and romances of the Round Table. Because no original source remains, readers past and present must rely on the arrangement by Carlo Gualteruzzi completed in 1525.

His script and its "twin" in the Vatican are the only remaining records scholars have of the full one hundred tales.Without an original manuscript, identifying who wrote "La Donna di Scalotta" and the other tales within Il Novellino is difficult. It is likely that more then one author was involved in the process of writing the stories. It is possible that Burnetto Latini, master of Dante Alighieri, wrote the novellas that refer to Arthurian legends. Latini is thought to have owned a copy of the romances of the round table. He is also credited as being the person who brought French literature to Italy. (Paul Legasse, ed., The Columbia Encyclopedia, 6th ed. (New York: Columbia Univeristy Press, 2000) 1591.)

Depending on what edition of Il Novellino one reads, the novella of the Lady of Shallot is number eighty-one or eighty-two. The novella tells the story of the daughter of the Great Babassoro, the Lady of Shallot, who falls in love with Lancelot of the Lake. Closer in similarity to Malory's Elaine than Tennyson's Lady, Lancelot does not return her love because he already loves Queen Ginevra.

Because of her "unhealthy attachment", the Lady of Shallot at length falls victim to it and dies. Until this moment in the story, the similarities between Tennyson's work and the novella are in two characters, the Lady of Shallot and Sir Lancelot. A more conclusive connection is found in the description of the Lady after her fate is sealed. In the novella, the writer describes the lady's request upon her death:

"...her body should be transported on board a barge fitted up for the purpose, with a rich couch and adorned with velvet stuffs and precious stones and ornaments; and thus arrayed in her proudest attire, with a bright golden crown upon her brows..."

Is the poem "The Lady of Shallot" responsible for the development of the poet?

Alfred Tennyson's career as a poet "was followed closely from the start by sanguine friends who never failed to extend to him their enthusiastic admiration and encouragement..." Pleasantly encouraged by the reception of Tennyson's first solo volume, Poems Chiefly Lyrical, he was urged by his closest friend, Arthur Hallam, to produce a second volume of work.

Bolstered by their support and the confidence of his original 1832 poem, Tennyson follows the same details of the novella in lines 33 - 35, "A pearl garland winds her head/ She leaneth on a velvet bed/ Full royally appareled." (Alfred Tennyson, Poems 1833 (London: Edward Moxon, 1832). If this were not enough of a parallel the final lines of the original poem once again refer to details found within the novella. Tennyson writes in line 174 "There lay a parchment on her breast...".In the novella the author makes a similar reference, writing "...her body richly cinched with a purse attached.

And in this purse there was a letter...." In both the novella and Tennyson's poem this letter recounts to the reader and the people of Camelot the cause of the Lady's death. As similar as Tennyson's Lady may be to Malory's Elaine of Asolat, the similarities in details and wording verify that Il Novellino, not Le Morte d'Arthur, was the inspiration for Tennyson's work.

In Il Novellino the story of "La Donna di Scalotta" is a simple one. The reader knows exactly who the Lady is, where she comes from and why and how she dies. Because of the brevity and lack of background contained in "La Donna di Scarlotta," Tennyson has allowed himself and the reader more freedom in the evolution of "The Lady of Shallot." In his development of the tale, facts are few and consequently the Lady is more mysterious. The setting is the island of Shallot, which stands in the middle of a river running down to the town of Camelot.

Exactly who the Lady is and why and how she has come to be there is never revealed to the reader. The only hint of her presence to her surrounding neighbours is her singing. In line 26 the reaper in the field refers to her as a fairy. In her confinement, the Lady weaves the daily scenes that pass by her abode. Due to an unexplained curse, the only way she can proceeds in her work is by looking indirectly at the view from a mirror rather than her window. What should happen if she breaks this curse is not known to reader or heroine. One day she is drawn by the flamboyant character of Lancelot, causing her to momentarily forget the curse as she turns for a closer look.

Even though the repercussions of looking out the window have been unclear, she realises the second she looks what she has done. To remove any doubt that some fatal error has been made, the mirror cracks and her weavings unravel, reinforcing the consequences of her actions. Why she eventually breaks the curse is understandable; she is tired of watching rather then participating in the outside world. Somehow the Lady quickly grasps that the consequences of her action is death, and she quickly heads for a boat which is to be her final resting place. Knowing that no one has any knowledge of who she is, she paints her name on the prowl, floating towards Camelot and her death.

June S. Hagen, Tennyson and His Publishers new publisher, Edward Moxon, Poems 1833, which included the

"Lady of Shallot," was released in December of 1832. Another friend, Edward Fitzgerald, stated that this second publication created much more of an impression then earlier publications, as it revealed "Tennyson the person." Despite the great faith that Arthur, his friends and publisher had in his new work, critical reception was lukewarm at best. Typical was the response from an anonymous critic for Tait's Edinburgh Magazine, who stated that this new volume hardly measured up to the expectation created by the author of Poems Chiefly Lyrical. As indifferent as some critics were to Tennyson's new work, the harshest criticism of the book, including the "The Lady of Shallot," came from J.W. Crocker for the Quarterly Review. Crocker voiced numerous complaints. He went so far as to write a mocking parody of "The Lady of Shallot," referring to the Lady as a spinster with a pathetic fate.8 Distressed by criticism of his work, ten years passed before any new poems were to appear in print.

Those years were not idle, rather much time was given to polishing his writing as well as reviving his previous poems. As a result, "The Lady of Shallot" reappeared in 1842, with many altered lines and a new ending. Reception of these revised and expanded verses at least secured Tennyson's reputation, a reputation that from this point would grow with each subsequent publication. Moxon was so encouraged by Tennyson's suddenly growing fame and potential for profit that he decided to offer a deluxe edition of his work that would offer the best of Tennyson's poetry to date, handsomely bound and enriched with illustrations by the best artists of the day.

The illustrated edition that Moxon conceived of in 1854 was met with little enthusiasm on Tennyson's part. Rather, he preferred the simple, yet tasteful, arrangement of his previous publications. More to the point, he generally disliked illustrations of his work, as "they never seemed to him to illustrate his own ideas." despite these misgivings Tennyson allowed Edward Moxon to proceed with plans for this new publication, primarily because he needed the money to purchase a new home.10 As no new work was to be included in this edition, Tennyson left most of the planning to his editor. Moxon's choices for illustrators included such established artists as Edwin Landseer, Daniel Maclise, Benjamin Creswick, and William Mulready.

In addition, three young artists, John Everett Millais, William Holman Hunt, and Dante Gabriel Rossetti friends and members of the recently disbanded Pre-Raphaelite Brotherhood, were also asked to make contributions. Their work and ideals had earlier impressed Tennyson, and in turn they had long held his poetry in high regard. His new book provided them with the perfect venue to display their art.

What were the principles of the Pre-Raphaelite Brotherhood stated by William Holman Hunt?

William Holman Hunt, John Everett Millais, and Dante Gabriel Rossetti, along with four other like-minded individuals, joined in 1848 with the common goal of preserving the artistic identity of England as well as avoiding "all that was conventional in art." Their motivation lay in the belief that in the centuries following Raphael the progression of design had become stagnated by well meaning artists who continued to imitate, rather than expand upon the knowledge they had gained from previous masters. The group called themselves the Pre-Raphaelite Brotherhood or the P.R.B. in hopes of reviving the ideals, techniques and processes of artists before Raphael.

The writings and instructions of artist, critic, and writer John Ruskin, especially from his series Modern Painters, particularly influenced the philosophy of this group. In his book The Aesthetic and Critical Theories of John Ruskin, George Landow set forth three criteria that Ruskin felt poets and painters needed in order to insure that an appropriate aesthetic reaction took place. These were absolute sincerity of the artist and his work, intensity of aesthetic experience, and originality.

While the Brotherhood could not deny that there was much to be learned from the great masters of the past, it was these three criteria that they had clearly missed and that the P.R.B. aimed to attain. They were especially impressed by Ruskin's appeal to contemporary artists to "go to nature in all singleness of heart, and walk with her labouriously and trustingly, having no other thoughts but how best to penetrate her meaning, and rejoicing always in the truth." In this context nature meant much more than what is seen outdoors. Nature was also a reference to the purity of subject and colour, and foremost truth to the nature of one's self. In observing these beliefs, it was most important that the artist did not aim for the absolute actuality of detail in nature, but rather the complete faithfulness to the one received when working directly from it.

This 'Truth in Nature' became a goal that the Brotherhood aspired to in their work, in their belief emulating the goals of artists working before the time of Raphael. In addition to nature, the group almost exclusively found their inspiration for subjects in the medieval and romantic narratives of author's past and present. The brotherhood applied these beliefs to their own work in hopes of reviving "a style worthy of the wholesome English tradition."14.

Of the founding members, John Ruskin's ideas had the most profound affect on William Holman Hunt. He told fellow member John Millais: "Lately I had great delight in skimming over a certain book, Modern Painters, by a writer calling himself an Oxford graduate; it was lent to me only for a few hours, but, by Jove! passages in it made my heart thrill. He feels the power and responsibility of art more than any author I have read."

Originally begun as a defence of the work of J.M.W. Turner, Modern Painters quickly was perceived as a call for the revitalization of art, providing the criteria to do so. Great art, according to Ruskin, depended upon representation of faithful observation by the artist and the influence that its audience had upon the masses.

However, for Hunt possibly the most appealing aspect of Ruskin's ideology was the concept of the artist's responsibility in revealing evidence of God and furthering his divine plan through art. From an early age Hunt had felt the "power and responsibility" of art upon him; although discouraged by his father in his chosen profession he was never deterred from his chosen path and worked on his own to develop his talent. The declarations found in John Ruskin's Modern Painters were a confirmation and inspiration to Hunt's purpose in both art and life.

Q. What artistic lure of the Victorian age is reflected in the poem "The Lady of Shallot"?

While some of the artists were attracted to the romantic subject matter of Tennyson's "Lady of Shallot," others, including William Holman Hunt, were drawn to the underlying moral message. Many of the Pre-Raphaelites, along with other Victorian artists, created at least one version of the "Lady of Shallot" in their lifetime. Five aspects of the poem emerged as the most popular for illustration: the Lady by a window, the moment of catastrophe, the Lady leaving her island, (the Lady dying as she floats towards Camelot,) the dead Lady in her boat floating on the river."

Hunt and his colleagues particularly enjoyed the challenge of determining appropriate illustrations for this poem. Understanding the importance of who she was and what she represented was a complex issue that appealed to and challenged both contemporary illustrators and readers.

Much was and still is read into the significance of the meanings that Tennyson wished to imply in his poem. Modern theories often suggest that the Lady was a representation of society's opinion of the Victorian woman, her sexuality and her role within society. While this theory addresses valid points, Tennyson offered some clarification during his lifetime. Hallam Tennyson stated that his father said the key to understanding the poem lay in the four lines; Tennyson himself explained this pivotal text, stating that they were meant to express "The new-born love for something, for someone in the whole wide world from which she has been so long secluded, takes her out of the region of shadows into that of realities." His concern lay not in the sexuality of women but rather in the dangers of one who lives a life of isolation within a world of fantasy rather then reality.

The issue of the perils of artistic isolation was also

addressed in Tennyson's poem "The Palace of Art," which was also included in Poems 1833. In this poem a woman representing the artistic soul voluntarily isolates herself in a palace of artistic splendor. As with the Lady, solitude is enjoyed for a time until she begins to realise that the choice of total isolation is a curse rather then a blessing.

Both the Lady and the anonymous individual in the "The Palace of Art" represent the struggle an artist faces between how the artist is to retain pure ideals whilst living within the demands of society. However, the outcomes differ. In The Palace the narrator is able to escape his/her fate by learning from the lessons provided by the experience. The Lady is not so lucky for reasons not shared with the reader; her fate was determined and sealed from the beginning.

In 1850, four years before Tennyson requested that Hunt illustrate his book, the artist had already begun to explore the subject of the Lady of Shallot. His pictorial study of this time differed greatly from the final product of 1905, or even the illustration of 1857. While from start to finish Hunt's main focus was always the "moment of realization," his first attempt also included fragments of other key moments in the poem. These were represented by a series of smaller mirrors that encompassed the larger one to provide the viewer with the knowledge needed to understand how the Lady came to her realization and what transpires after.

The mirrors with their reflections of the outside world were an inspiration from Jan van Eyck's The Marriage of Giovanni Arnolfini, a Northern Renaissance artist whose work the Brotherhood long admired and whose work was readily available for study at the National Gallery in London.

At the top is a tower and wall representing Camelot, the town that plays a central role in the life and death of the Lady. Working clock-wise the next three scenes depict the Lady working at her loom, looking out the window at Lancelot, and Lancelot himself. This leads to the central mirror and its reflection of the moment of catastrophe, with Lancelot riding away unaware of what he has just set in motion. On the left side of the image the tale continues as these mirrors picture the lady preparing the boat for her death, floating towards Camelot, and Lancelot's discovery of her.

Tennyson's request gave Hunt an opportunity to once again work on "The Lady of Shallot." In the early stages of development Hunt experimented with the Lady's pose, portraying her sitting, then kneeling, all the while attempting to keep her head in proper relation to the mirror, so that the connection could be made at the appropriate moment. In the end Hunt decided to leave the Lady standing as in the previous drawing. While the Lady always remained in relation to the mirror whether sitting or kneeling, placing her fully upright added to the desired climactic outcome.

The differences in effect can be seen very clearly by comparing the image to one created by Charles Robinson. In Robinson's image the moment chosen for illustration is the same, but seated the impact is far less dramatic. Bringing the Lady directly to the foreground of the drawing ensured that while there were ensuing circumstances she is the main figure to focus upon. The viewer gets a full sense of her conflict because she is standing. Her body bends and her arms wrestle to break free of the threads that whirl up to trap her.

While her body is fighting to break free of her fate her head seems to accept it as it bows remorsefully, knowing the predicament she faces is of her own making. Her hair completes the foreground frame as it blows wildly about, framing the image reinforcing the reality that she was and still is trapped by the circumstance she has seemingly had all of her life. The large loom, where the Lady has spent all of her waking hours weaving the scenes that pass by, also encloses her. The mirror itself reveals the cause of the Lady's downfall. In its reflection you can see the ensuing catastrophe as the unaware Lancelot rides towards the distant Camelot. For the first time, this illustration includes typological symbolism to assist in explaining the scene pictured. The practice of adding elements to a painting to assist in a deeper definition of the subject was not a new one.

Heavy use of this method could be found in the work of Medieval and Renaissance artists, as well as from other periods. In reintroducing this method, Hunt hoped to "create an art that could marry realism and elabourate iconography, fact and feeling, matter and spirit." Hunt was faced with a major challenge by using this approach. Symbols that once had clear meanings to a Medieval or Renaissance audience would be little understood by his contemporaries.

In his published illustration of The Lady of Shallot, Hunt introduces the figure of Christ on the cross to the right of the mirror. Hunt fully believed in Ruskin's theory that the artist and his art must offer not only a picture, but also a deeper message, preferably one that helped to reveal God's goodness and divine plan. In this drawing Hunt has attempted to interpret the deeper moral message hidden below the surface of the image. According to Landow, "The figures of Christ and Lancelot embody the alternatives for art, defined here in a moral opposition far more absolute than in the poem."

Just as any good Christian must daily choose between good and evil in his life, the good artist must choose between accomplishing works that has no real value or art that furthered the greater good of mankind. Therefore, if an artist must separate oneself from outside influences to keep their art uncorrupted, then it is surely for the best. By making this connection, Hunt altered Tennyson's original message or intentions.

Hunt's illustration of the Lady of Shallot, along with the work of seven other artists, was released to the public in May of 1857. Unfortunately, the success of this illustrated publication was not the financial success that Edward Moxon had hoped and intended it to be. This was due in part to a delay of publication. Moxon had originally hoped the book would be available in December of 1856, just in time for Christmas, but due to the procrastination of Dante Gabriel Rossetti this was not to be.

The drawings themselves also surely played a role in the book's failure. The general feeling was that while many were fine pieces of work, they hindered rather then enhanced the work. Regarding the illustrations, a reviewer of the Art Journal declared "we are much inclined to doubt whether their aid will be generally considered to have given much additional value to the volume."

Tennyson too was not happy with the drawings included in this edition. As he had predicted, many of the drawings fell short of illustrating the text he had written. Little mention is made of specific drawings that dissatisfied him outside of those done by the Pre-Raphaelite Brotherhood. Of the works contributed by the Brotherhood Tennyson found fault with at least two of the seven illustrations William Holman Hunt had contributed to the publication, as well as work by Dante Gabriel Rossetti. Soon after the publication of the illustrated edition Hunt had an opportunity to meet with Tennyson.

It was at this time that Tennyson questioned him on the work he had contributed. During their discussion Tennyson was quick to point out that in "The Beggar Maid" he wrote simply that King Cophetua had "stepped down", rather then taken a flight of stairs as with all the work included in this volume. Artist J.C. Horsley later recalled hearing that Tennyson was greatly pleased with the works he contributed to accompany "Circumstances" and "The May Queen" While he questioned Dante Rossetti's drawing of St. Cecila for "The Palace of Art," his illustration of "Mythic Uther's Deeply-Wounded Son," for the same poem, was another that Tennyson favoured.

Hunt's illustration for the "Lady of Shallot" seems to have caused Tennyson the most annoyance. He took issue with the way in which the threads of the weaving flew about, wrapping around the Lady's body. He also questioned the way in which Hunt rendered the Lady's hair wildly flying about. Hunt replied, "I had wished to convey the idea of the threatened fatality by reversing the ordinary peace of the room and of the Lady herself; that while she recognized that the moment of the catastrophe had come, the spectator might also understand it." Hunt defended this and other modifications by arguing, "May I not urge that I had only half a page on which to convey the impression of weird fate, whereas you use about fifteen pages to give expression to the complete idea".

A fair argument, his reasoning was to no avail, as Tennyson stood strong in his belief that an illustrator should never take such liberties in adjusting an author's work. Although Tennyson was displeased with the book as a whole, understanding his acceptance of some works over others lies in the reply that Tennyson made to Hunt's above mentioned argument; "an illustrator ought never to add anything to what he finds in the text." The three drawings mentioned that found Tennyson's favour all illustrate the exact words of the poems, nothing is added or detracted from verse to image. Tennyson never asked Hunt to illustrate that particular portion of the poem. Each artist was given free reign to choose what they wished, with no specific instructions from Tennyson whatsoever. As William Rossetti later recalled, the artists were to work on their own with no comment from Tennyson.

They were to use "Their own interpretations of the poems," following their own inspiration. Why would Tennyson, who had told his editor that illustrations never seemed to satisfactorily illustrate his own ideas, neglect to offer guidance in order to insure that the outcome would meet his satisfaction without his involvement, the fact that some of the illustrations would inevitably not meet his expectations should have come as no surprise.

In the end, Tennyson's dissatisfaction could not have been entirely due to Hunt's physical renderings of The Lady of Shallot. As an artist, it was his duty to add additional information that would aid the viewer in making the transition from verse to the visual. What may well have troubled him more were the moral ideas that Hunt alluded to in his use of typological symbolism. Whether or not Hunt realised it, his additional details changed the meaning of the poem.

For Tennyson that meaning had seemed to be the idea that artists cannot allow duty to their art to entirely consume every aspect of their life, interaction is essential as it offered inspiration. Both men found something in the process of creation that had a great influence upon them. We know what Tennyson's intentions were for the message he wished to convey, but what Hunt came to comprehend was different. This alternate view led him to continue developing the subject, and while the principal figure was the same, the visual outcome would be entirely different from Tennyson's verse.

Q. Describe the "Typological Symbolism" of "The Lady of Shallot"

So what was it that Hunt saw that led him to conflict with the ideals of Tennyson's poem. In a pamphlet available at the Arthur Tooth & Sons Gallery where the finished painting hung in 1905, Hunt voiced the concern that he felt. He wrote, "The progressive stages of circumstance in the poem are reached in such enchanting fashion as to veil from the casual reader the severer philosophic purport of the symbolism throughout the verse." As one who adhered to the belief that it was the artist's duty to help the viewer be more observant and gain deeper understanding, naturally he was duty bound to lift that veil from viewer's eyes. In 1887 Hunt began to paint what would become the finished painting that now hangs at the Wadsworth Anthenum in Hartford, Connecticut.

However, taking the account of Lady of Shallot and incorporating a complex web of typological symbols based on spiritual, mythological, philosophical, and historical genres, Hunt first needed to work out his idea on a smaller canvas. This oil sketch begun a year earlier in 1886 and which now hangs at the Manchester City Art Galleries provides us with an idea of how Hunt worked out his programme so as to provoke a response that went beyond the surface of the canvas.

As with the illustration for Tennyson's 1857 book of illustrated poems, the overall composition of the painting is very similar. Yet, the addition of a complete typological program required Hunt to extend the space in the room that was once dominated by the figure of the Lady. In expanding this area the viewer not only sees the Lady's reminders of devotion but also is stuck with the notion of the nobility of the dedicating one's self to a good and worthwhile cause.

Her failure to remain true to her own beliefs is not only pictured by her present circumstances, but also by the symbols and allegories around her that reveals her fate for her failure to do so. As complex as it sounds, each attribute was chosen carefully creating an image that would leave an impact. By forcing the viewer to separate and identify each detail, in the end they were left with a message that was far more powerful than the image itself.

As in previous renderings, the Lady still stands within her loom with her body twisting and struggling with the threads that bind her. Her head is bent as her luxurious hair blown by a "stormy east wind" flies wildly about, while behind her hangs the cracked mirror an "immaculate plane of the Lady's own inspired intelligence" and the vehicle of her downfall. In this case, the mirror also provides an anchor that connects the viewer to the original tale. The additional details of the scene create a visual connection with the words written by Tennyson:

"On either side the river lie Long fields of barley and of rye That clothe the world and meet the sky, And thro' the field the road runs by To many tower'd Camelot..."

The countryside rolls gently back into the horizon and a tree lined river flows from around the island and through the fields. Reflected is Lancelot in full armor, unaware of the trouble he has just caused, riding towards Camelot sword raised in conceited exaltation, as two men walk ahead of him heralding his arrival.

Unnoticed at first glance is the Lady's own partial reflection. With just her hair and a small portion of her left arm visible, the viewer is drawn back into the room, an unobserved witness to the events unfolding.

While at the centre, a glimpse of the present is provided at either side is are commentaries on the virtues of devotion. These scenes can be seen as an admonition of the Lady's choice and a reminder of the nobility of dedication to an admirable cause. In the Manchester painting Hunt provided only biblical allegories for the images to the left and right of the mirror. At the right is Christ Enthroned a symbol of whom the Lady owes her Christian devotion.

To the left Hunt placed the scene of the Agony of Christ in the Garden. This could be seen as a reminder of Christ's struggle between his human and divine self. This scene also prompts the viewer to think of the words that Christ left with his disciples before he proceeded to the garden; "Pray God that you will not fall when you are tempted."

However, in the Wadsworth version Hunt took a curious step by combining a spiritual and mythological message. Replacing Christ Enthroned is a triumphant Hercules completing the eleventh of his twelve labours. The labours were designed to help Hercules restore his honour after killing his wife and children in a fit of insanity. Here Hercules is completing his task by picking the golden apples from the tree in the garden of Hesperides.

A feat accomplished only after the guardian serpent Ladon is slain and carried out while the daughters of Erbus sleep at the foot of the tree. By placing a halo on the head of Hercules, Hunt has turned a mythological character into a spiritual one of sorts. By defeating Ladon, Hercules becomes a mythological reference for Christ triumph over sin. Opposite Hercules and replacing Christ in Agony is the Virgin of Humility. This figure is "an early fifteenth century type of the Virgin and Child..." and it "embodies the theological concept that all virtues stem from humility..."This is a quality the Lady lacks in relinquishing her duty.

Above tying together these two orders of devotion and faithful service are the "music of the spheres." An ancient concept, the "music of the spheres" was believed to keep the universe bound together by harmony. In this theory, the "music of the spheres" "orders the heavens and music alike orders and tempers human passions and social forces." A biblical element is also mixed into this scene. One of the female figures to the right is seen stepping on the head of a snake like figure, a reference to coming of Christ and his defeat of sin. This is an allusion to the serpent that entered the Garden of Eden and first introduced sin in the world through the temptation of Eve.

By crushing the serpent's head, it becomes a symbol of hope for the Lady as well as the viewer, a promise of a return to the perfect order that once was. When asked about the similarities of his poem to the legends of King Arthur, Tennyson stated that any resemblance was a coincidence. Hunt has altered this and deliberately created a connection between Tennyson's poem and the legends of King Arthur. No longer does she weave daily scenes rather as Hunt explains; "In executing her design on the tapestry she records not the external incidents of common lives but the present condition of King Arthur's court, with it's opposing influences of good and evil." In doing this Hunt also offers some clarification of why she works in her secluded location. The Lady is unable to venture into the world, because if she does she will no longer be able to provide an unbiased record of the events of the court.

Before us is King Arthur seated on his throne in a saddened state, because he is without his Queen Guinevere, who like the Lady of Shallot, was tempted by Sir Lancelot and has failed to remain faithful to her king. However, on his right, Arthur is supported by the virtues of charity and on his left are justice and truth. Below King Arthur are his faithful knights offering their services while at the centre are the true and faithful knight, Sir offering the Holy Grail upon his shield. Lancelot too, is included in the finished portion of the Lady's tapestry, his head just visible to the far left. He is kneeling to the far left, vainly offering no gift but his lip service as he touches his fingers to his lips.

The images in the foreground are many and each provides its own message that point back to the Lady and her fate. Shall the meaning of the objects above may have been far more apparent; some images leave the viewer with questions. Exactly what the posts of the loom are meant to represent is not clear. Left unadorned in the Manchester painting, Hunt altered them for the Wadsworth piece. Opinions on this subject are few, but Samuel J. Wagstaff, curator at the Wadsworth

Anthneum, made the one that tends to make the most sense, Wagstaff suggested that the posts are meant to reference at least three of the four natural elements: earth, water, and air.

To the left is water with waves and jets of water shooting upwards and topped off by a scalloped shell. In the centre is what is to be presumed is earth, leaves at the bottom, vines spiraling upward to what appears to be a bud of some sort. On the right is air, with sunrays at the bottom and clouds billowing towards the top. The elements are meant to represent the four pillars of the universe which work together to maintain natural and harmonious order.

Just as with the "music of the spheres" above, a reference to the harmony of the earth is being made, a harmony that is obviously disrupted by the lack of the fourth element fire. It is possible that the lamp was meant to represent the element of fire. Not only would it have lit the workspace but its flame could represent the knowledge of truth and light of God. Extinguished by the dove's fearful flight, it to signify knowledge lost and the absence of divine presence.

In the Manchester painting the lamp holds candles no longer lit. In the final piece those candles are gone, and as a consequence a much stronger point is made as there is nothing left for that flame of knowledge to feed on. This unusual lamp incorporates itself into the message woven throughout the painting as well. The four owls at the top and just below the candleholders are also a symbol of intelligence and Athena the patron goddess of weaving and of divine wisdom. At the base of the lamp are four sphinxes, figures from mythology and also a symbol of wisdom. This is an odd combination; Thomas L. Jeffers points out that they along with the lamp are meant to represent "the triumph of the light of aesthetic wisdom over mystery and fear..."A triumph lost by the extinguished flame. As earlier stated it is thought that Hunt took some inspiration from Jan Van Eyck's The Marriage of Giovanni Arnolfini. In looking at the very first image he attempted in 1850, the use of the smaller mirrors reflect various aspects that have direct reference to the central one that is used.

Hunt seems to have once again returned to this piece for inspiration in composition. Just as in Van Eyck's painting, Hunt has included flooring that is incised with further allusions to the primary scene.

What some are meant to mean is to the left there are sea-like creatures ringed in a circle, each one biting onto another's tail. In the middle is a depiction of the struggle of nature as two foxes wait for a goat, a lion subdues an ox, and two men fight. Last on the right are a sword, sickle, screws, plow and a chain, but what are these in reference to, tools of war and peace or symbols of industry at the edge of each of these sections is a skull and head of Medusa, often representing death. They could tie each scene together connected with the never-ending struggle between good and evil, life and death that has been and will always be faced.

The use of the wooden patens or shoes is another reference back to Jan Van Eyck's painting. In Van Eyck's painting Arnolfini has removed his shoes as a symbol of the sacredness of the union of marriage that they have entered into. The Lady, too, removes her shoes, symbolizing the sanctity of the room and the work she has been doing. The irises are almost a contradiction to meaning of the shoes that lay beside them. They symbolize the lack of respect the Lady has come to have with her task.

In the past the iris, just as the lily, was a symbol of purity and a representation of the Virgin Mary. However,in Victorian times the language of flowers took on a whole different meaning. The iris became a reference to the messenger of the Greek gods with the same name, thus implying a warning to be heeded. They could also be associated with "lost love and silent grief, for it was Iris who led young girls into the afterlife. All meanings could be associated with the Lady's plight. There was most certainly a warning to be heeded and although she had only seen Lancelot once, there was a sense of grief and lost love about her as her actions and feelings lead her towards the curse, which appears to be death. As to the allusions to the purity of the Virgin, this is an attribute that she shared at one time; it is now lost as is represented by the flowers cast to the floor.

This excessive use of symbolism demonstrated Hunt's desire to create art that was realistic and factual yet also deeply moving to the viewer. The iconography used was not so peculiar or outdated that the audience would not be able to understand their meanings. Items such as the wooden shoes, irises, or "music of the spheres", had definitions as single objects that most educated people could understand. However, in the context of the painting Hunt's unusual combinations of these items, such as the irises thrown to the floor, combined with the fact that the methods and beliefs applied now belonged to a period now passed, caused many to question what they were seeing. Unveiled to the public in May of 1905 at the Gallery of Arthur Tooth & Sons, many were overwhelmed by the paintings typological programme.

In a review by The Times a critic wrote, "All the accessories are splendid and elabourate, and many, as Hunt explains in a note, are symbolic...but after all, the symbolism of the picture is a secondary matter. What is important is that it should illustrate the poem and that it should be in itself beautiful in composition, form and colour." This was a response that was typical of other critics who wrote on the painting, sentiments strangely echoing the very issue that Tennyson had brought before Hunt many years before.

The painting should illustrate the source from which it originated. However in 1886 when Hunt had begun to work on the final rendering of The Lady of Shallot, was it still his intent to illustrate the poem in anyway. We must also remember that in his poem Tennyson attempted to address the question of the risk of a life in seclusion in the name of art an issue, which he also explored in "The Palace of Art."

As an artist, Hunt understood these problems and perhaps this is what drew him to the subject. The difference in interpretation came from their own experiences within their chosen profession of the arts. For Tennyson the truth centreed on the ideal that the lack of life experience could prove detrimental to his work. After all it was his life experiences that made their way into the poems that he wrote. The issue was entirely different for Hunt; lack of interaction was essential to creating a pure art form as he described in his supplement to The Lady of Shallot stating"... 'sitting alone; in her isolation she is charged to see life with a mind supreme and elevated in judgment."

Conclusion

By the time that Hunt had begun work on Tennyson's illustration, his interpretations on the character of the Lady and her plight had already begun to shift. No longer was she just a figure of unrequited love or a fallen woman, she represented Hunt's own struggle for the eternal truth. The third and final painting of The Lady of Shallot had become in essence a painted illustration of the truths and beliefs he had written about in his book Pre-Raphaelitism and the Pre-Raphaelite Brotherhood.

According to Hunt it was he who played a key role in the establishment of the Pre-Raphaelite Brotherhood after encountering Ruskin's principles on the execution and function of art. Whether he alone was the one to found the P.R.B. can be challenged, but what is certain is that Hunt took Ruskin's words very seriously. He was also intrigued by Ruskin's description of Tintoretto's use of typological symbolism in San Rocco's Annunciation in Venice, Italy. From this point forward Hunt's work is a reflection of the beliefs that so inspired him in the second volume of Modern Painters.

For a time Millais and Rossetti also adhered, in various degrees, to the ideology that had brought them together as a brotherhood, but never to the degree of devotion that Hunt had for them. As Hunt's last finished work, The Lady of Shallot was a testament to the level of dedication Hunt maintained for those written doctrines of Ruskin on the function of art. The symbols of devotion that reminded the Lady of her duty also symbolize Hunt's dedication to the goals of the group. The Lady is a representation of those who failed to remain true to the calling that had been set before them, in this case Millais and Rossetti.

This painting could also be viewed as a last ditch effort to gain the recognition he lacked throughout his career. Hunt's entire oeuvre was dedicated to the illustration of religion, whether it was in Christian teachings as in The Light of the World or in Christian History as in The Finding of the Saviour in the Temple. Even in his secular works such as, The Hireling Shepherd or The Awakening of Conscious, religious references were included. Yet throughout his career, Hunt was never given notable recognition as a religious painter.

George Landow quotes Hunt's feeling on the matter from a letter written to the Reverend Robert St John Tyrwhitt quote:"why is it that I have been so persistently overlooked all my life by the very people who as Christians should have employed me I know no other artist who is so outspoken and declared as a follower of our Lord then myself. I don't boast of my excellence - only of my earnestness. I from the beginning of my career offended the great influential worldly ones by my refusal to make any compromises and I lost much fortune and much opportunity of showing my full powers to advantage".

Lack of recognition from Ruskin, the man whose work has inspired him so profoundly, was another issue that Hunt had to contend with. Despite Hunt's exhaustive dedication to Ruskin's principles, he never once acknowledged his effort, although he had spoken of those of Rossetti, Millais and even Edward Burne-Jones, a follower of the principles of the Brotherhood. In his Art of England lecture, series Ruskin eluded that it was Rossetti, not Hunt, who started the religious movement within the group and Hunt was merely his follower. Lastly and perhaps the most painful blow, Ruskin claimed that it was Edward Burne-Jones, a second generation Pre-Raphaelite, who was the greatest artist of all, realizing the goals of the Brotherhood in the work of mythology, rather than religion as Hunt had so labouriously followed.

If one is to look at The Lady of Shallot as Hunt's attempt to embody his ideals and beliefs of a life's work then his drawing of 1850 is the beginning of that realization. Hunt had not yet fully developed and attached his own principles to the piece; it was a first draft of initial ideas to come. As is stated in the introduction to this paper Hunt had not wanted this first drawing to be seen, fearing the undeveloped work would be seen as his finished idea. By the time Tennyson requested the illustrated work from him in 1854 the seeds of thought that had only begun to take hold in 1850 had begun to bloom. The Lady's disregard of the task set before her was understandable and acceptable to Tennyson, it was not to Hunt. His own struggles to carry out what he saw as his God given duty allowed him to identify and at the time condemn the Lady for her lack of faith and devotion. It is hard to say if the inclusion of details that alluded to Christian values was purposeful or not.

The illustration that was published in the 1857 book of poems is not as saturated with typological symbolism as his final work of 1905. Perhaps Hunt understood the limitations of his freedom of analysis within his commission. Although Hunt had taken artistic license on the interpretation of Tennyson's words and included religious components the original structure of the subject can still be seen.

By the time Hunt began his oil sketch for the final work finished in 1905 it was no longer his goal to merely illustrate the poem as he had in 1850. The subject is so far removed from the first rendering and poem that it is only through the central character and vague similarities that one can still tie it to Tennyson's original work. In the words, that John Ruskin offered to Tennyson on his disappointment of his book offers us an explanation of how two decidedly different views could have evolved from one subject.

"Many of the plates are noble things, though not, it seems to me, illustrations of your poems. I believe, in fact, that good pictures never can be; they are always another poem, subordinate but wholly different from the poet's conception, and serve chiefly to show the reader how variously the same verses may affect various minds..."

This is what Hunt's painting had become, another poem,

an homage to a life's work and beliefs and a lesson to us all on the value of dedicated devotion.

Q. Discuss the Ironic and Comic elements in Tennyson's poetry.

When every life becomes tragic and the element of the special case is removed, human existence itself becomes ironic. Catastrophic disillusionment and destruction are not the lot of the godlike hero, invoking by his stature the terrible laws of retribution, but of every ordinary person going about the business of common life. There are, consequently, no heroes; there are no cosmic laws to be broken; there is no possibility of fixing our pity and fear on the suffering hero. We are all victims, incapable of being "deeply moved" by what is common, uncaused, and without meaning.

The tragic emotions are not released but focused and contained, and we are forced, in ironic art, to see ourselves as victims of the trivial, both trapped and released into the "illimitable inane" ("Lucretius," l. 40). We are all caught in the same incoherence, experiencing, as Melville's Ishmael says, the contradictory ironic states, floating isolation and total bondage ("And what are you, reader, but a Loose-Fish and a Fast-Fish, too?").

Increasingly in the nineteenth and twentieth centuries, we find a myth that stresses the two images of man as caught, wriggling on the deterministic pin, or loose, accidental, with only a vague hope "that nothing walks with aimless feet."

But this is not the only myth. There was, after all, the world of Mr. Pickwick, of Jane Austen, and much of Wordsworth: the world of liberated order, settled and humane values, sanctified and full life. The comic vision stood as an alternative to the ironic, dissolving the unrelieved tension of irony by reaffirming the dignity and power of the human will, the possibility of joy, and the continuity of all life. Comedy offered a means of surpassing the insistent "facts" of irony. Against the ironic insistence on the isolation of man, comedy posed the symbol of marriage; against the contrary insistence on bondage, it posed the symbol of the dance or the party:

Christmas at Dingley Dell or Bob Cratchit's, the Mad Tea Party, cucumber sandwiches with Ernest Worthing.

The comic vision gradually becomes more difficult to sustain, perhaps, but it never dies entirely. The nineteenth century was much closer to Eden, and even its irony contains within it always the clear picture of what is lost. As Matthew Arnold says, the pain of isolation is not just increased, it is partly caused, by the memory or at least the legend of a union that once had been: "Who order'd, that their longing's fire / Should be, as soon as kindled, cool'd?" The comic thus stands against and enriches the ironic myth. Just so, irony begins to move to dominate all art, not necessarily because artists chose that myth, but because for serious writers of the last century or so. "Irony is much less often a rhetorical or dramatic strategy which they may or may not decide to employ, and much more often a mode of thought silently imposed upon them by the general tendency of the times."

But, by a striking further paradox, those artists most conscious of the advancing prevalence of the ironic view were precisely those who most aggressively resisted it. Those most sensitive to the present were also most deeply sensitive to the past: they saw that the comic life was lost but still remembered it most vividly. They continued to ask, with Hardy, "And why unblooms the best hope ever sown?" because they in part believed in — or at least remembered — the grand artistic, religious, and political hopes of the past.

The most crucial problem for these artists was contained in the perception that the present, the only thing really alive is void of meaning, while the past, which is dead, alone contains the meaning that can give life. The past is both immediate and beyond reach the comic vision refused to yield completely to the ironic, and we find, in artist after artist, these forms existing side by side. One could argue, in relation to the past, from full and resonant comic grounds:

The Present is the vassal of the Past:
So that, in that I have lived, do I live,
And cannot die, and am, in having been —

Here our bondage to the past is made cause for an extension of personality throughout time, so that our being "a portion of the pleasant yesterday" helps define us in relation to time and insures that we "cannot die,". Implying not only that we have life in the past but also that we will, by irrational but very compelling analogy, continue to live in the time that has defined us.

But "portion of the pleasant yesterday" recalls nothing so firmly as the grim lines from "The Lotos-Eaters": "All things are taken from us, and become / Portions and parcels of the dreadful past" (ll. 91-92). It is not just that this "pleasant" past has become "dreadful"; time the protector has become time the ravager. This transformation locates for us the centre of Tennyson's major poetry: the interplay and conflict of the comic and ironic modes. No other nineteenth-century writer is more responsive to the intense presence and distance of comic life, the memory that seems to make life possible in its promise of continuity and yet turns it into a mockery of genuine life, a literal death-in-life.

Tennyson's career can be seen as a and courageous resistance to the demands of ironic art, an art he had, moreover, mastered very early. If one sets aside his minor poems - the political and public verse, his English and domestic idylls, and his dialect and humourous poems — something like a semicircular pattern may be traced. The *Poems by Two Brothers* and the volumes of 1830, 1832, and 1842 all contain a few comic poems but show, in the main, a steady development toward more compact and rich ironic statement. Beginning with *The Princess* however, and continuing through *In Memoriam* and Maud, Tennyson tries various and often unique comic strategies, only to return to irony in the late poems, and particularly in *Idylls of the King*, surely the major ironic work of art of the century. This development is neither simple nor pure - comic and ironic forms are used throughout his career – but the main outlines seem reasonably clear.

This suggested pattern differs markedly from that implied by what was once critical orthodoxy: the view that Tennyson and his poetry could best be apprehended by a series of contraries. Harold Nicolson made an admirably strategic division of the lyric, morbid, and mystic Tennyson from the public bard, and we have had, since, a good many developments and refinements of this view[4]. At present, critics frequently deny the dualism and assert one or another unity in its place. It is, however, surely just as dangerous to ignore the tension in Tennyson's poetry as to go on inventing new labels for it.

One can, of course, see how apt and expressive descriptions such as "life-weariness," "despair," "frustration," or "melancholia" are in explaining the basis of Tennyson's art. Even more basic, it seems to me, is a larger formal battle carried out in his poetry between two alternate myths. One of these, irony, does express itself in the form of balanced, but unreconciled, opposites; the other, comedy, takes a firm, single direction. The first myth has often been approached indirectly by means of the dualistic view mentioned before; the second has largely been ignored.

The narrative pattern of irony, what Northrop Frye calls "the mythos of winter," frequently been characterized in discussions of "open" or "general" irony and distinguished there from the "specific" or "closed" irony that is more properly thought of as a technique. This general irony is non-corrective, presenting, like all irony, some conflict but insisting always that the conflict cannot be resolved. This is the irony of the impossible situation, an irony that includes us all as victims — characters, readers, even the ironist.

Art rooted in "unidealized existence" is likely, then, to formulate its structural principles and its narrative patterns in reference to general irony. There are no heroes and no heroic action; worse, there is no coherence to support any purposeful action whatever. Such heroism and such coherence are, however, often recalled in this irony in order that they may be parodied. In fact, parody seems to be the basic principle of this narrative irony.

It feeds on the affirmations contained in the other traditional patterns: romance's idealizations, tragedy's cathartic sacrifice, comedy's liberation. Practicing always rhetoric of deception, this pattern forces us to anticipate resolutions that never come. Such rhetoric is deliberately unstable, seeking to disarm us, to include its audience with its victims. The characteristic themes are of disillusionment and meaningless defeat, the fall from freedom into bondage.

While there is some specific irony in Tennyson — one thinks of "The Last Tournament" or the verse epistles — he is, clearly, not Donne. But he does utilize extensively the more general narrative pattern, especially in the depiction of dominant opposites which cannot be coordinated or made to cancel, but which demand equal and contradictory responses. The tension between the religious, hopeful symbol on the one hand, and the tragic or melancholic symbol on the other, marks the centre of Tennyson's poetry, the point being that his irony is not merely gloomy, almost never simply macabre. The contraries exist together, as brothers, an early poem says, stealing "symbols of each other".

The result is that no emotion can flow outward from us. The comfort of comedy and the perverse comfort of decisive negativism are alike denied, and the reader is suspended between alternate emotional and intellectual responses to alternate, unreconciled themes. Whatever Tennyson may have meant by his cryptic remark that "what the public do not understand is that the great tragedy is all balance throughout." The "balance" he achieves and transmits is the ironic one presented in *Moby-Dick,* where the *Pequod,* tilting dangerously to one side under the weight of a whale's head lashed to it, hoists another on the opposite side, thus regaining her "even keel; though sorely strained, you may well believe."

Ishmael goes on to point out the usefulness of this image as a symbol for the human mind, poised, paralyzed, and unable to "float light and right." Irony, it may be said, causes so much horizontal strain that it makes any free forward movement impossible.

At its most obvious, Tennyson's ironic vision did insist directly and openly on the alternate truths: death is all, life is all — "All Things Will Die..... Nothing Will Die," as the poems from 1830 put it. But we find the unresolved oppositions in much less dramatic and ostentatious form throughout his career. In the beautiful poem, "To the Marquis of Dufferin and Ava" (1889), for example, he deals with both the greatness of the Indian Empire (Lord Dufferin had been governor-general of India) and the sense that India was the treacherous fate that drew his son Lionel to his death. Toward the end of the poem, these views coalesce as Tennyson dwells on the terrible fact that his son died so far from him, with strange rites and in a strange sea:

Not there to bid my boy farewell,
When That within the coffin fell,
Fell-and flashed into the Red Sea,
Beneath a hard Arabian moon
And alien stars.

The strong romantic associations packed into "Arabian moon" and "stars" are juxtaposed against the brutality of "hard" and "alien." But the romantic associations are not canceled by the adjectives, just as the speaker's belief in the Indian enterprise or in the continuation of life through death is not shattered. The lines describing the death are, after all, contained in a tactful public utterance, which celebrates first the virtues of a good colonial ruler and ends in a vision of love in this life and the next. The poet-and the reader-perceives both visions with equal force: the private, despairing clarity of the image of a remote death, suggesting the alien universe and the absurd, causeless nature of life, along with the public, hopeful vision of reasonable and kindly political activity and a religion of love. Neither wins. It is the great virtue of Tennyson's art that, as he matures, the diffuse and obtrusive "All Things Will Die" – "Nothing Will Die" dichotomies become compacted into phrases as suggestive and haunting as "hard Arabian moon."

Irony does not dominate all of Tennyson's poetry, but it does control the early poems (up to 1842) and many of the late ones, most prominently *Idylls of the King*. In the great middle period, the period of *The Princess, In Memoriam,* and *Maud,* Tennyson searched for means to transcend the ironic tension of vividly presented but unreconciled opposites. Transcendentalism helped, of course, and we find lively statements of it attributed to him: "Nothing worthy proving can be proven" or "Poetry is truer than fact," for instance. But transcendentalism is likely only a small part of the major cause of Tennyson's liberation, which is the discovery of the possibilities of comedy.

In fact, it could be argued that transcendentalism was convenient not primarily for its doctrine but for its ability to provide a happy surprise behind every false appearance, exactly paralleling the ending of comedy, where the disguises come off and reveal familiarity and promise. In any case, Tennyson spent the central part of his career writing comedy; imaging the very form he could also parody so completely. The movement from liberty to bondage was for a time reversed, as Tennyson sought to forge a unique and lasting comic vision.

Q. Describe the comic element in Tennyson's work. ?

Comedy" here is taken to mean the mythic pattern, not that which is funny. In this sense it duplicates in quality our sense of the term "irony"; that is, it is a narrative pattern, supported by an appropriate formal but unstated convention (or conventions). It clearly emphasizes liberation, freeing the ego from traps which are external and, especially, internal so that it may find, in its rejuvenation, a more or less exuberant social and personal life.

Comedy finds its source at the close of the basic myth, in the resurrection of the dead god and his restoration of fertility happiness to the community. It transforms an inhibiting condition, usually a social condition — symbolized by an unjust king, law, parent, personal vice or illusion — to a clarified and liberated one: from "law to liberty," as Frye says. Comedy is especially satisfying because of its sense of completeness, its location at the very end of the myth, but also because of its magical way of solving problems that hinge on the contrary demands of the private self and of society.

It takes as its hero a figure who confronts an unjust law boldly, and endures a period of neglect or even hostility in order finally to overcome injustice and gain recognition and reward from his society. By means of a focus on the liberation and rewarding of the hero, comedy feeds the isolated egos of us all. At the same time, by attacking relentlessly all misanthropic and overtly egoistic tendencies and by regarding all extroverted and social traits as laudable, comedy supports community."

This union of the personal and the communal is effected partly because we can easily identify both with the egoistic hero and with the society he redeems, but it is also true that comedy works very carefully to keep that heroic ego within certain bounds. One must, it suggests, be expansive in one's joy and, above all, charitable. Charity and forgiveness take the place of tragedy's iron justice and retribution and often stand in conflict with them. Comedy emphasizes the miraculous and improbable; tragedy the necessary and inviolable.

Thus, the hero is rewarded with gifts that will tend to social expression: marriage, which supports and prolongs the social order, and money, which is seen almost entirely in terms of its allowing the hero to give gifts, hold parties, and the like. In other words, if we are willing to define ourselves socially and accept [8/9] certain minor restrictions on our pride and our tendencies toward tyrannical or blind behaviour, we can be rewarded with gifts that are both social and personal. After all, in comedy marriage implies a beautiful lady.

Comedy thus works against social definition seen broadly and impersonally (i.e. in terms of modern social science or the nineteenth century's political economy) and supports social definition seen narrowly and personally. Finally, comedy's position at the end of the myth means that, with the shadow of death and sacrifice behind it, it retains a very strong feeling about the preciousness of life itself and is always dedicated to it.

It is not often recognized that Tennyson's poetry contains a large element of this zest for experience, usually expressed indirectly but often coming to the surface in lines like, "One only joy I know, the joy of life". As Georg Roppen very perceptively argues, "Tennyson's obsessive preoccupation with death is the negative aspect of an insatiable life-zest which informs a considerable part of his poetry and seeks expression in various directions.

His craving for immortality... is not an aspiration to beatitude, but to continued, happy life." But the comic sense that controls the major poems of the middle period is often realised in ways both puzzling and unique. The comedy is maintained only in the midst of difficulties so large that the form and even the values must be continually won and re-won. The conventional certainties of comedy are very difficult for Tennyson to accept, despite the fact that he had a strong artistic — and certainly personal — instinct to do so.

As a result, we have comedies which are not only highly specialized but which are haunted by their inverse: very sophisticated parodies of that comedy. The comic vision is never as purely expressed as is the ironic, and its tentative quality checks the resounding confidence that is usually necessary to bring off comedy's miraculous, nonlogical leaps. I am not suggesting that ordinary comedy can work only by establishing a mindless euphoria, but it seems clear that very little comedy is as dubious of its own affirmations as is Tennyson's. This very distrust, however, can make the affirmations all the more striking. Easy as it is to make jokes about Queen Victoria's comparison of *In Memoriam's* comfort to that [9/10] of the Bible, no one can doubt that the queen spoke sincerely and out of the depths of real need. It is no small thing to offer hope in the face of death; comedy has always tried to do just that.

But the tentativeness of Tennyson's great comedies helps to explain why he was never fully comfortable in that form. Despite the fact that *In Memoriam,* for instance, is a finer poem than "Rizpah," the latter is more unified and generically resonant. Tennyson could growl on with "grim affection" about "Bones" it is a fully finished and formed utterance — but he apparently disliked talking of *In Memoriam.* Partly, I suppose, because he was so close to it, but also because it is highly complex, almost generically mystifying, offering various directions for our emotions. *In Memoriam* is Tennyson's version of *The Divine Comedy*, but it lacks entirely the total confidence and the resultant easy coherence of Dante's poem. Tennyson, one feels, could have written ironic poems like "Rizpah" forever. It is a wonder and perhaps a clue to his greatness that he tried with such skill and against such odds to write a poem about a world that could be rescued for sense, loyalty, and love.

It is a great wonder principally because Tennyson seemed unable to delude himself, except in minor poems. Even Dickens could bluff-witness John Harmon and Bella Wilfer in *Our Mutual Friend* — if the genre so demanded. But Tennyson, in his major poems, is always turning over the comic coin, seeing if the affirmation can stand its own negation. This ironic tendency in his comedy is both remarkable and unsettling. Every comic generalization stands, but not on very steady legs.

First of all, while Tennyson could accept completely the necessity and even the beauty of a social or domestic life – "Come down, O maid,". For instance, is one of the most complete lyric expressions of domestic comedy in our literature — he perceived at the same time that this vision could operate as a trap, killing the spirit of man and encasing him in deadly trivia. There is a strong sense of this opposition in *The Princess*, "Ulysses" is a full statement of the problem, and *Idylls of the King* explores the pressures of the social life as subtly as *Middlemarch* and with very much the same view.

Second, Tennyson felt most uneasy about the principle on which comedy reverses tragedy: time's renewal. Time triumphs not only in *The Winter's Tale* but in every comedy, by having its linear march expose the false, restricting society, by its realization of a transcendent joy that lies outside time, or by its denial of time's dominion: they lived happily *ever after*. Tennyson's ambiguous attitude toward the past has already been mentioned; it seems, however, that there was a larger ambiguity, involving change, which he could see both comically and ironically.

For instance, the comic expression asserts that change is comfortable, that it is for the better, and, most important, that it does not alter our real being: "We are all changed by still degrees, / All but the basis of the soul". The comic view of stasis and change takes as its symbols, respectively, eternity and regeneration. Turned about, however, these assurances become the two ironies that dominate much of Tennyson's poetry: comfortable change is transformed into meaningless flux; solid and unchanging being becomes an image of man trapped and unable to help himself.

Further, though comedy always has managed its defeat of time by a projection into future it has generally done so successfully only by convincing us of the powerful happiness realised in the present, "They lived happily ever after" has meaning only if they are happy now. Tennyson seemed constitutionally unable, however, to imagine genuine and full comic happiness materializing for a long, long time; sometimes, one gathers, not until a few eons have passed.

It is a peculiar comic satisfaction that one can obtain from waiting for evolution to solve problems. Evolution is not nearly as rhetorically persuasive as, say, sex. Still, this is to oversimplify a more complex issue that involves what Spedding called Tennyson's "almost personal dislike of the present, whatever it may be." Existentialism is a modern term, but all effective comedy has contained more of it than Tennyson could muster.

Tennyson's tendency to complicate the comic mode is apparent even in minor issues. His use of repetition, for instance, is, on the surface, highly appropriate to comedy, where the recurrence of events gives us a sense of the deep continuity of life and growth. In Tennyson, however, the lulling reassurances contained in the repetitions of "Come down, O maid" can just as easily become the compulsive, desperately negative "Let us alone" of "The Lotos-Eaters" or "Tithonus," where the suggestions of life, ever awakening in similar patterns, are made hideous by burlesque.

Similarly, there is in Tennyson a distrust of the comic

principle of prodigious abundance, of wild, almost uncontrolled generosity. He spoke of being appalled by "the lavish profusion... in the natural world... from the growths of the tropical forest to the capacity of man to multiply, the torrent of babies." Still, though it is complicated and even tortured, comedy is central to Tennyson's vision, so remarkably strong that it could be maintained and finds long and continued expression despite ironic pressures from without and within. It is the interplay of these two forms that I wish to examine.

Tennyson mediates between the two great myths that have become the dominant modes of modern artistic expression. The development of the ironic situation is even more elabourately indirect in "The Lady of Shallot." It is possible to discuss the poem in terms of rhetorical irony, emphasizing the problem of whether or not we are made to approve of the Lady's isolation or of her leaving. But this is a problem externally imposed by critics, probably by analogy with most of the other poems in this volume, where the means and terms of judgment are indeed key issues. Here, however, the ironic situation is balanced in such a way as to suspend judgment absolutely. Unlike, say, the Soul in "The Palace of Art" or the mariners in "The Lotos-Eaters," the Lady presents no arguments and has no real choices. She is in isolation; she is lured away; she invokes the curse. Artistic withdrawal is neither condemned nor approved. The necessity for judgment is just what marks the difference between rhetorical irony and the complex but basically contained thematic irony in this poem.

One might, interestingly enough, have made a good case for rhetorical irony in the 1832 version of the poem. At least it would have been a better case, since the revisions for the 1842 volume almost all act to broaden the focus of the poem by removing our attention from the Lady herself and directing it to her environment. The changes emphasize the sense of a determined situation and deemphasize the image of a personality making a decision. To take one of many instances, lines 24-26 are changed from

A pearl garland winds her head:
She leaneth on a velvet bed,
Full royally appareled to 1842's
But who hath seen her wave her hand?
Or at the casement seen her stand?
Or is she known in all the land?

It is this "land," the external world of Camelot, that emerges in the 1842 version as a major force and symbol in the poem, suggesting the principal lure and promise that draw the Lady out of her isolation. But active terms like "draw" are misleading; for the movement is only apparent, not real. The broadest, most general irony of the poem is that the Lady simply exchanges one kind of imprisonment for another; her presumed freedom is her death.

The Lady is most commonly seen as a form of the artist, and doubtless her absorption in weaving the beautiful web suggests that. But her story also, as in "The Book of Thel," symbolizes the birth of the soul, the movement out of childhood protection into adulthood, the development from innocence to experience, the promise of social and unified being to the isolated ego; Hellstrom,, sees the Lady as choosing mortality, but he does argue that the poem is quite un-ironic.

All these possibilities coalesce around the central ironic pattern: the carefree but incomplete self, imprisoned in that self and cut off entirely from any direct experience, is drawn by the lure of sexuality, beauty, growth, and change — life itself — not into freedom and expression but into obliteration. The real dilemma is one that can be neither judged nor solved. The Lady must obey and must defy the curse.

The opening of the poem quickly establishes the ironic contrast, setting up a picture of the world that is both true and false, true in objective fact but with terribly misleading implications:

On either side the river lie
Long fields of barley and of rye,
That clothe the wold and meet the sky;
And through the field the road runs by

To many-towered Camelot;
And up and down the people go

"On either side" of the Lady is the promise of fruitfulness and warmth, gentleness and motion. The abundance of nature is connected to heaven and to man, the grain *clothes* the field, joining the earth both to man and to heaven, and the field contains the road on which all human activity takes place. The centre of this microcosm is Camelot, many-towered as a temple, the source of the apparently benign and unified activity. In contrast, the Lady lives on a "silent isle, imprisoned within "four gray walls, and four gray towers".

It is true that within this tomblike home there is a "space of flowers" and that her song "echoes cheerly" from it, but the force of this contrast between her island and the outside world is so strong that such contradictory details are nearly swept aside. Even the suggestive revelation that the curse is connected not to isolation but to life, that she is not cursed now but will be if she chooses to live, is submerged in the continuous development of the basic ironic contrast.

Part 2 creates an image of life at Camelot, the irresistible world of "realities," as Tennyson so enigmatically puts it, that "takes her out of the region of shadows." (*Memoir*). The main reality presented here is motion itself. In contrast to her stasis, the pictures of the world she sees are "moving," "winding," "whirling," "ambling," "riding." This static-dynamic dualism is crucial: she believes the lying promise of the mirror, progressing from her death-*like* isolation into the whirl of movement that is literal death. The most important of these perceived images of dynamic eternal life makes her "half sick of shadows" and prepares her for the final destructive lure:

For often through the silent nights
A funeral, with plumes and lights
And music, went to Camelot:
Or when the moon was overhead,
Came two young lovers lately wed;
"I am half sick of shadows," said
The Lady of Shallot.

Notice the indiscriminate *or* that connects the funeral and the lovers. Life offers funerals or marriages; both are equal: love is equivalent to death.

The next section is dominated by the image of Lancelot. For the Lady, he is the symbol of personality and fulfillment in the vast scene of the world's growth and beauty. He seems to her to provide an even more specific promise: the achievement of individual identity. He is the first person to be named in the poem, and he seems to guarantee the validity of names and their ability to give permanence and meaning to the self. He comes, riding "between the barley-sheaves" with all the abundance of nature.

Lancelot carries with him a shield, in which "A red-cross knight for ever kneeled / To a lady", an image of perpetual promise, invoked in terms of courtly love. The emphasis in Tennyson's lines on "for ever kneeled," however, also implies that it is only the promise, not the fulfillment, that is perpetual. The "blue unclouded weather" in which Lancelot appears conspires to make this image as beautiful and blinding as possible: like a "meteor, trailing light" he "flashed into the crystal mirror". The first "reality" the Lady actually meets after invoking the curse is the truth of this mocking nature, which is no longer blue and unclouded but dark, with a "stormy east-wind" and a heavy low sky over the "pale yellow woods").

Images of oppression and waste surround her. Pathetically, she still tries, by writing her name on the prow of a boat to claim the promise of personality Lancelot had held out to her. But her personality is not confirmed, even by her death, and the tragic assertion of being is burlesqued. As she floats by Camelot, the knights "read her name" but respond only with misunderstanding:

Who is this? and what is here? And in the lighted palace near Died the sound of royal cheer; And they crossed themselves for fear, All the knights at Camelot. She manages to create only a flurry of superstition. Lancelot, however, is presumably differentiated from this confusion and muses quietly a moment — only to exhibit how undifferentiated he actually is;

He said, 'She has a lovely face;
God in his mercy lend her grace,
The Lady of Shallot'

"She has a lovely face is absurdly inadequate to the mystery and potential tragedy of the Lady's story. We move only from one level of incomprehension to another. Lancelot is a structurally heightened parody of those figures at the end of a tragedy — Horatio is an example — whose duty it is to interpret, clarify, and keep alive the story of the tragic action, thus ensuring the institution of a new order.

Here the death is uninterpreted because there is no context to give it meaning an no interpreter. Lancelot turns from the Lady after a perfunctory benediction, dismissing her and thus permanently fixing the absurdity of her death. This, then, is what the parable of growth and development amounts to: not criticism of the Lady, or Lancelot, or "isolation," or the world; only an ironic equation of development with decay. The Lady is born into death.

Perhaps "The Lady of Shallot" marks the limit of this form of Tennyson's indirect, thematic irony; not that he was to abandon it, but it was to be subsumed in the search, for more inclusive ironies, ones that would contain even the reader. Surprisingly, he found the means for this subtle rhetorical irony not in the further dissolution of his readers' judgment but in an insistence on judgments. The secret of this extension was not in the abolition of old certainties but in the reinforcement of them.

Still, and it is a large qualification, these certainties are never unopposed, they are never adequately supported, and they never provide solutions. They are certainly present and we are asked to make judgments based on them, but these judgments are either contradictory or, more commonly, trivial. They go nowhere. They never answer the questions that were raised in the poem, though they do create others. Most of all, these judgments do not provide comfort or release; they construct the ironic prison.

This rhetoric clearly involves a refinement of irony's traditional control of perspective and distance. It is nothing new for irony to vary our perspective abruptly, asking us to see as immediate and painful what we had supposed was comfortably distant and secure. Still, though the reader is often moved against his will, he always knows where he is. In the 1842 volume, however, Tennyson is striving to project the state which irony embodies, to create the suspension and discomfort the poems discuss. Previous poems had been made ambiguous by structural or thematic means; here the ambiguity is achieved rhetorically, by making our perspective on the poem uncertain. He removes the solid position from which we can make judgments and then urges on us both the necessity for judgments and their futility.

The most radical form of this uncertain perspective is found in the dramatic monologue, where the removal of context makes it extremely difficult not only to know how to judge but to be sure if one should judge at all. Certainly, the creation of a solid position from which one can observe how the speaker "contradicts himself" or is subject to the poet's satire is a critical fiction, a convenience that distorts the effects of the poem.

Robert Langbaum's *The Poetry of Experience,* a brilliant discussion of the problem of perspective in the dramatic monologue, uses a very open appeal to our *experience* in the poem to demonstrate that an overtly satiric reading of a dramatic monologue is a possible, but rather crude and uninteresting response.

To see that Ulysses's comments on Telemachus are contemptuous is one thing; to argue that this contempt acts to condemn Ulysses is something else. 'there is no way we can find within the poem a morality that allows for such certain judgments. By removing rhetorical securities, the dramatic monologue does, as Langbaum insists, force us to experience the speaker himself, not a meaning which is external to him.

Still, the tendency of this form to find the extreme case, in fact to be generally effective in direct proportion to the outrageousness of its argument and the distance of the speaker and action from conventional moral and social norms, means that our instinct to make judgments is very strongly activated.

Langbaum argues that the tendency to the extreme case and the bizarre subject reduces judgment to absurdity and further indicates the widely accepted need of the poet to resuscitate, to drive through customary associations and revivify life.

One can grant these arguments but see them as subservient to another principle he mentions but then seems, in particular analyses, to ignore: the tension between sympathy and judgment. It seems to me that, contrary to what I take to be the implications of Langbaum's argument, judgment is not an attendant or superficial response but an immediate and powerful one.

But it is also given no place to rest, no terms with which to deal, and this very fact accounts for the ironic rhetoric. We are asked to respond simultaneously on two contradictory levels: that of distant critical judgment and that of absorbed, direct experience. We must and we cannot do both; and we realise, therefore, the tension between the now disjoined meaning and experience.

The dramatic monologue manifests a special form of the ironic rhetoric, which works to to suspend the case of judgment by making perspective unstable. Though many of the poems that follow in my discussion here are not pure. dramatic monologues but uncertain mixtures of monologue and soliloquy, they contain the essential features of the rhetoric of the dramatic monologue: the uncertainty of context, the demand for judgments, and the absence of support which makes judgments significant.

But cease to move so near the Heavens, and cease
To glide a sunbeam by the blasted Pine,
To sit a star upon the sparkling spite;
And wine, for Love is of the valley, come,
For Love is of the valley, come thou down
And find him; by the happy threshold,

"Ask me no more: thy fate and mine are scaled: / I strove against the stream and all in vain: / Let the great river take me to the main." These lines occur in the last of those intercalary songs which Tennyson called "the best interpreters" (*Memoir*, of *The Princess*.

I am not, by the way, speaking of the blank verse lyrics, like "Tears, Idle Tears," which are part of the main body or the poem, but of the six intecalary songs added in 1850.One would expect these climactic lines, then, to interpret the solution that is about to come. Insofar as they do, however, they expose how the comedy, *The Princess*, nearly turns into an irony, *The Defeat of Ida*. Overcome by the powerful forces against her, the heroic Ida sadly accepts her fate and abandons all resistance.

The obvious plan of the poem seems to make such a response perverse. Ida is not defeated but finds her way into a triumphant union. Such a union will allow her both to fulfill her distinctive femininity and to fight more effectively for her ideals. She is not sacrificing her heroic identity, it is supposed, but making it communal and thereby strengthening and guaranteeing her selfhood.

Read in this way, the poem steers a course between the futuristic and abstract goals of the female university and the conservative, brutally concrete and instinctive views of the men. Lady Blanche and the prince's father represent extremes of these alternatives.

On one side is the primitive male conception that sees human [58/59] relations in terms of hunting, mastering, killing:

Man is the hunter; woman is his game:
The sleek and shining creatures of the chase,
We hunt them for the beauty of their skins;
They love Its for it, and we ride them down/;

These lines expose, with remarkable bluntness and precision, the secrets of the male position. The argument is not unique to the stupid old king, however; we can see it reflected in Cyril's aggressively obscene song, and especially in such unconsciously patronizing actions as Walter's patting Lilia's head. "We ride them down" is not a peculiar but a universal masculine attitude, one that the poem vigourously rejects.

On the other side, so the plan implies, is the equally dangerous counter-reaction: Lilia's primitive anger and its projected symbol, the university. This university represents a response on the same impossible grounds of battle and conquest; the women isolate themselves in protective hatred and strike out in wild, impotent fury. Thus, each party is, in the old sense, "humour-ridden," dominated by basic male or female humours. The action, as in all humour comedies, breaks the rigidity of these humours by ridiculing them and proposing a new being that is flexible arid humane.

But this balancing action is not unopposed, and the poem is not so simple. Princess Ida is much closer to genuine heroism than to humourous Amazonism; her position demands a respect never given to the male argument. As her world begins to crumble from within and the external pressures mount against her, she begins to appear more a symbol of defiant and heroic will than a mere spoiled, petulant girl.

Beneath the overt pattern, then, runs a counter-theme which embodies, in the battle between Ida and the world, a profound conflict between two forms of comedy, *The Princess* represents an attempt to forge a new genre by putting in opposition heroic and domestic comedy, the aloof princess and the voice of "Come down, 0 maid," the visions of "Ulysses" and "The Miller's Daughter."

Gerhard Joseph's chapter on *The Princess*,, also provides a reading in terms of "a contest of genres, exploring the range of comedy in two directions". Joseph's two types of comedy, however, are quite different from the ones discussed here. He describes Tennyson's exploration of "the spirit" of two poles of Shakespearean comedy, "the late dark comedies and the earlier romantic ones". *The Princess*, he maintains, does "begin in a festive spirit of *Love's Labour's Lost*... and gradually darkens toward the mood of near tragedy, as in *The Winter's Tale*".The chapter is a suggestive one and forms a good alternative in the argument presented here.

Tennyson is again dealing with the dilemma that dominated the 1842 poems: the inability to merge the fully matured and complete human ego with the communal values demanded by comedy. Like "The Two Voices," "A Vision of Sin," and "The Palace of Art" before it, *The Princess* attempts to bridge this gap. It is no longer enough, however, just to dissolve this irony. Here Tennyson attempts to solve the problem by re-forming and redefining the central comic symbol: marriage.

The poem tries to make the heroic vision yield to the domestic without sacrificing the heroic emphasis on personality. Marriage becomes a literal growth toward a oneness which does not obliterate difference. But it is very difficult, for us and for the poem, to grasp this unique argument very firmly or for very long. *The Princess* fails to sustain the purity of comedy and finally becomes another mixture of comedy and irony.

The domestic vision is as fully embodied here as in any poem in the language, but by being directly juxtaposed to the heroic, its defects are strangely highlighted. The poem insists on being true to both sets of values and thus cannot escape giving a curious sense that its solution is both a victory and a defeat. Ida gains a great deal, but the poem is unwilling to ignore what she must leave behind: the lofty, appallingly cold but magnificent height of the undefeated personality.

Criticism of the poem has certainly not ignored evidence of basic conflict or disunity, but it has generally located that conflict only in the poem's tonal diversity and has almost without exception seen that diversity as a weakness. In many ways the definitive criticism on this point is given within the poem, when the narrator comments in the Conclusion that he had, in order to please both "the mockers and the realists", arranged the narrative "as in a strange diagonal, / And maybe neither pleased myself nor them".

Though the poet later argues that excesses in action and, by implication, in tone, point toward eventual harmony, this positive verdict has had little support, either outside the poem or within. Most critics agree, instead, with the "Tory member's eldest son," who, though a fool whose general views are specifically repudiated, provides a most influential comment on the poem's tone: "Too comic for the solemn things they are, / Too solemn for the comic touches in them".

The point is worth belabouring simply because the tone

is so intimately related to theme. *The Princess's* attempt to reconcile warring social, psychological, and generic elements is symbolized by the effort to bring together alternate demands as to the poem's tone. The "maiden aunt" first pompously asks for a tale which is "Heroic... / Gravе, solemn!", a notion that invokes the instant ridicule of the young. Later, the contest becomes one between the mocking men and the serious women, whose silent influence "had ever seemed to wrestle with burlesque". The traditional war between old and young and between men and women becomes, thus, a challenge to poetic tact. Insofar as the tone can harmonize such contraries, the extremes of youth and age, the future and the past can blend into a mature present; more radically, the differences between men and women can be resolved into "the single pure and perfect animal".

By suggesting that the resulting poetry "maybe" pleased neither faction, then, the poet is suspending the entire movement of the poem and confirming the tentative quality of its solution. The problem of tone is here a problem of total vision; it is, in this sense, the only problem of the poem, and it can be solved only by examining the thematic and generic issues it is made to include.

But one preliminary point needs to be made: the usual argument that the poem begins as "mock-heroic" and then changes abruptly to the serious distorts both the nature of the burlesque and the nature of the tonal change. In the first place, the mockery is not of the heroic. Only the excesses of false heroism are mocked, and that is done only to ensure the protection of the legitimate form of heroism. The banter protects and moves us closer to Ida, the figure of genuine heroism, by reducing her detractors.

The two old kings, for instance, attack her so bluntly and stupidly that potential criticisms are invalidated. The prince's father puts the antifeminist position in the crudest possible terms, arguing that women are inferior but useful animals to be hunted and tamed, subdued, if all else fails, by the misery of child-bearing and child-rearing:

A lusty brace
Of twins may weed her of her folly. Boy,
The bearing arid the training of a child
Is woman's wisdom.

His obscene diction threatens to give the game away; he puts the common male position so bluntly it cannot be accepted, instinctive objections to Ida are thus dismissed.

Similarly, the sting is removed from her own father's criticism. It is cast in the form of anti-intellectualism that is so feeble it is simply silly: her "awful odes," he says, are called "masterpieces: / They mastered me" Any force the parody of Ida's odes might carry and any objections based on a more pervasive anti-intellectualism are blunted by repudiating their source. Finally, even her brother's mild criticism of her, "She flies too high", is balanced against his admission that he may be too crude to understand her and also against his rough but fine sense both of her stature and of the basic justice of her cause:

"She asked but space and fairplay for her scheme". Throughout, then, Tennyson exercises various rhetorical means to promote our regard for heroism and for its advocate, Princess Ida. Even such direct burlesques of the school as those connected with the "daughters of the plough" are deliberately separated and kept distant from Ida, and thus they suggest only aberrations, not basic faults, in the heroic scheme.

The usual interpretation of tone denies even the linear development implied in "diagonal" and argues for an abrupt change from one mood to another. While the threats to comic fulfillment, which demand a solemn tone, are somewhat more strongly emphasized and also more protracted in this comedy than in most, the tone in all romantic comedies develops away from the banter that is necessary for the preliminary attack on the humourous, blocking characters toward the calm acceptance that comes with the victory of resilience.

The movement from attack to acceptance is most marked in those. comedies we are likely to think of as warm and optimistic, *A Midsummer Night's Dream*, for instance. "Jest and earnest working side by side" is the traditional slogan of integration, not dislocation.

The attempt to find the point of this presumed alteration in the poem, then, seems to be self-defeating. Edgar F. Shannon, Jr., for instance, points to the interlude between sections 4 and 5 as a "transparent" means by which Tennyson "sharply marked the shift from levity to sobriety." But section 5, far from being sobre, seems easily the most humourous of all, opening in "unmeasured mirth" at the sight of the men disguised as women, and moving to the must extensive funny attack on the two old fathers and such slapstick episodes as that between the unfortunate male herald and the eight daughters of the plow.

The tone moderates, but it does not change abruptly; neither does it become "dark." It moves toward serenity, the mood that combines joy and earnestness. Whether it quite achieves this union is questionable, but that is a matter which must be settled by considering more than just tone.

The major problem remains: the conflict of the two impulses of comedy and the effort to harmonize them. Though the poem finally attempts to solve the dilemma by leaning heavily on the concept of the natural, it also maintains the image of the heroic princess, whose heroism is defined largely as her ability to resist for so long the lure of the natural. It is a comedy of normality, but in its secret heart it seems to lament the failure of the grandly abnormal. As a result of this disjunction, almost everything in *The Princess* carries with it contrary signals: positive acts are negative; victories are also defeats. This complex dualism is apparent throughout the poem in its images and themes, perhaps most obviously in its action. Even the most ludicrous action of all, Ida's plunge into the river, cuts in two directions. On one hand, it functions as well-deserved ridicule of her pretensions, her slightly absurd readiness for tragic death:

> We were as prompt to spring against the pikes,
> Or down the fiery gulf as talk of it,
> To compass our dear sisters' liberties.

The stage is set for the comic catastrophe, the comeuppance. She is brought low, significantly, by a trivial event, Cyril's ribald song; she does not spring against the pikes but clumsily misses the plank and rolls into the river. Instead of finding glorious martyrdom, she must suffer an inglorious rescue by a man she hates.

On the other hand, the ridicule is so extreme that it suggests not so much corrective action as a brutal assault. Why, for instance, does Cyril do such a gross and stupid thing? It is one of the issues the poem ponders — and ponders very awkwardly but cannot resolve. The obscene song seems merely a meaningless assertion of male supremacy, a primitive attack on femininity itself.

From this point of view, Ida is not only ridiculed but trapped, not for any particular purpose, but simply by some basic malignity. Heroism is completely denied by the episode but to no real educational purpose, and the result can as easily be to increase our sympathy for Ida as to ridicule her. The action is as absurdly meaningless as it is comically justifiable.

This same mixture also attends the central symbol: the pursuit of knowledge. Ida's university is legitimate, as is her dedication to learning; but tier scheme invokes not only the support of heroic comedy but the ridicule of domestic comedy and its insistence on the physical and intuitive as opposed to the cerebral and rational.

The university, then, is its most fundamental enemy; the union of learning and implied asexuality in the female college is simply a variation of the usual anti-intellectual equation of pedantry and sterility. Turning the pedant into a woman simply reinforces the primitive appeal by invoking the atmosphere of locker-room masculinity. It makes our own response all the more tense and ambiguous.

Further, Ida's search for knowledge involves the creation of a new society, a world that is specifically utopian, bringing with it a divided response to utopias. She is, however, made specifically heroic by her loneliness and by the suggestion that she is bringing order where there was chaos, taming the beast.

The parallels between Ida and the quite unambiguous King Arthur of the *Idylls* are clear, But Ida's new society, heroic as it is, liberates only in order to impose new restrictions. We hear a great deal about discipline and duty, virtues that are perhaps necessary but that are invoked almost always in comedies as enemies of the free and flexible human spirit.

The prince begins the action of the poem by disobeying his father and following the "voice" of nature, thus outlining the whole course of the action of domestic comedy, the rejection of the artificial, the planned, and the rigid for the values of nature and spontaneity. It is the wily and dishonest Lady Blanche who is constantly mouthing the principles of obedience.

"And she replied, her duty was to speak, / And duty duty, clear of consequences" but it is the undutiful and disobedient Lady Psyche whom we are asked to approve of Rules must always be broken in the spirit of anarchic comedy, and duty wan with love. The prince accuses Ida of barring "Your heart with system out from mine". It is Ida's devotion to system that creates the heroic world and also the enemy of that world.

At the centre of this difficult mixture of irony and comedy is Ida herself, the most fully developed and yet the most problematic character in the poem. For, despite the apparent ridiculousness of her plan, she is not portrayed as ridiculous. Even her plan, in the end, is seen as absurd only in the sense that irony renders all the best hopes pointless. The princess is conceived of as remarkably calm and rational, considering how deeply she perceives injustice and how firmly she believes in her cause.

She almost never rants, and her speeches exactly invert the rhetorical pattern common to fervent crusaders. Instead of building to more and more excited flourishes, even Ida's official speeches of indoctrination begin with rhetorical excess and move to greater simplicity, clarity, and moderation. Since her lieutenants, Lady Blanche and Lady Psyche, both employ the more traditional strategy of gradually increasing the voltage, Ida's comparative calm is made even more noticeable. The rhetorical pattern of her speeches suggests the development beyond the mere excrescences of format radicalism to a genuine heroic simplicity. She always ends with a position that is so moderate it is made to appear emphatically sensible.

Even the purpose of the university is not what we would surely expect in a burlesque, that is, the reversal of tyrannies and the creation of a new race of Amazons; rather, Ida wants to do away with tyranny, or at least to minimize it. Her university does not seek to combat marriage but to make it just a little less like slavery. She is not preparing celibates or man-haters but those who "may with those self-styled our lords ally / Their fortunes, just balanced, scale with scale". This goal seems almost pathetically limited, but it brings down on her in full force the. world of men.

Whatever she herself may be, her institution is hardly antisocial; she seeks only a readjustment in society, a movement toward balance. Ida herself never speaks of dominance. She offers merely a chance to "lose / Convention", that is, to revive and free society. But it is precisely the moribund convention that men live by, and her very reasonableness thus incurs their most instinctual wrath. If she were more radical, she would be less of a threat; *The Princess* would be a more straightforward comedy but a much less interesting poem.

Ida's refusal to be satisfied with ranting marks her deep seriousness. It guarantees the. validity of the promise she holds out: "O lift your natures up:/ Embrace our aims: work out your freedom". The "freedom" here is very much like the inner freedom Ulysses finds in the face of the external inhibitions of old age and death. She really means to make a new world, not by re-creating society but by providing to others the secret of rebirth she herself has found:

We touch on our dead self, nor shun to do it,
Being other — since we learnt our meaning here,
To lift the woman's fallen divinity.

She hopes to give back to women the individual Edens they have lost.

Tennyson is very careful to give Ida no motive other than

simple heroism. The other possibilities, her being spoiled by her weak father or perverted by the teachings of the sexually frustrated Lady Blanche, are entertained only to be dismissed as trivial. Her offer to her students is precisely that of Ulysses to his mariners, and she has Ulysses's insight into the necessity for absolute devotion to the unfettered, noble self. "Better not be at all / Than not be noble". The human will is made triumphant by assertion, and women, Ida promises, who are now "laughing stocks of Time", may be conquerors of time and death. Heroic comedy allows a destruction of the ultimate trap.

The question is, then, why the plan is so easily upset. Ida resists courageously, but the rest of the university topples with absurd readiness. One answer, given before, is that the university is too rigid, too schematically conceived, a sure sign in ail comedy of vulnerability to the forces of nature. Ida holds things together, as Lady Psyche says, with her "iron will" it is clear that her system gains coherence only from laws and rules. And comedy hates all rules.

Still, there is more to this "iron will" than simply a violation of comic precepts. We sense that Ida's will is hardened because there is little genuine response to her heroism. Her enemies are not only the men without but all that is selfish, cowardly, and indolent within. In one revealing scene, the narrator discusses the flow of students after lectures and very quietly provides the proper diagnosis of the university's illness.

The picture begins with "One walking reciting by herself', then one who "In this hand held a volume as to read, / And smoothed a petted peacock down with that". Then, however, the view shifts from the single figures to large groups of students, who are clearly not interested even in faking seriousness: some run to row on the water or merely to sit in the shade under the bridge, or in the thickets, or on the lawns. The more energetic toss a ball back and forth. The climactic picture in this gallery of presumed spiritual revolutionaries shows how ridiculously impossible the task is: the

Older sort" "murmured that their May

Was passing; what was learning unto them?
They wished to marry; they could rule a house;
Men hated learned women.

The new world is ruined not by Ida's excesses, clearly, but by a sad mistake she has made in trying to share and make communal her own heroism. She has never had a chance, and all the flurry of the wars is the result of a ludicrous hysteria on the part of men who really have no cause for fear. Nothing can throw off the dead hand of convention.

The chief enemy, therefore, is time, most specifically the past. Ida wants to pull free from this bondage, but she is defeated by its attractions. She cannot combat the psychic force of time., the power and passion engendered by the most important of the lyric songs in the poem, "Tears, Idle Tears," The poem, as Ida recognizes, offers, a kind of melancholy luxuriance that is regressive and imprisoning. The past sings with "so sweet a voice and vague, fatal to men". In her view, the poem has power, but of an inferior and dangerous kind. It is a sentimental poem, masking as ironic honesty an appeal to self-indulgent introspection and maudlin self-pity. It is, she says, "a death's-head at the wine", a trembling poetry that is contemptible. "Let the past be past; let be / Their cancelled Babels", she proclaims, but no one hears her, Even the prince, who might have understood a little, carries with him in his invasion certificates of the imprisoning past, the absurd contract made long ago by the two fathers.

The past controls in the most outrageous forms, and eventually the prince-or his father-or time-wins. There is, from this point of view, no possibility of change. Ida fails not because she has been rigid, but because she strove to free us from the days that are no more. Her insistence that women are "Not vassals to be beat, nor Pretty babes / To be dandled, no, but living wills, and sphered / Whole in ourselves and owed to none" is both self-evident and ridiculous. By asserting so clearly the importance of the human will, she has demonstrated its impotence against tyranny, convention, instinct, and, most generally, the past. Since she cannot shut out the forces of the past, then, all she can do in her desire to liberate is to build a new prison.

This invasion of the past that turns her comic world into an ironic one conics, in its most insidious form, as a "voice"- not only the passionate voice of "Tears, Idle Tears" but the tired one of all conventional language. One of her most perceptive and most impossible wars is a linguistic one. When the disguised men are first presented to her, Cyril takes the opportunity to remind her of the old kings' contract, saying that the prince is "The climax of his age! as though there were / One rose in all the world, your Highness that, / He worships your ideal"). Ida is indignant, not about the prince but about the language, the frozen clichés that come from equally frozen attitudes:

We scarcely thought in our own hall to hear
This barren verbiage, current among men,
Light coin, the tinsel clink of compliment.
Your flight from out your bookless wilds would seem
As arguing love of knowledge and of power;
Your language proves you still the child. Ida sees that the language of men is just like, indeed is, the imprisoning voice of the past. Love songs, she says, "mind us of the time/ When we made bricks in Egypt"), The platitudes of love have within them the deceptive lures of slavery. The lute and flute fantastic tenderness, And dress the victim to the offering up,

And paint the gates of Hell with Paradise,

And play the slave to gain the tyranny. She tries to counter this conventional language with a new one, forging Valkyrean hymns or songs of prophecy, urging that song

Is duer unto freedom, force and growth of spirit. The academy is primarily a school of new poetry, hoping above all to remold the language: "And everywhere the broad and bounteous Earth / Should bear a double growth of those rare souls, / Poets, whose thoughts enrich the blood of the world"). But it is the old unpoetic language that tears apart the university. Ida is defeated by voices, by words.

So that we do not miss the force of this theme of

imprisonment in language, Ida's own downfall is foreshadowed by an exactly parallel defeat of Lady Psyche. When she discovers the identity of the three men and resolves to tell the princess, the men turn on her with their world of words. They deliberately combat her new self with stereotyped images of a generalized female. The prince begins the assault with, "Are you that Lady Psyche?" and proceeds to cite a fixed image, a portrait that hangs in his father's hall, an idealized version of womanhood).

This tactic is so obviously the right one for their purposes that each speaker uses it in turn, picking up with a repeated "Are you that Lady Psyche?" when his predecessor has run out of breath. She is thus recalled to an imaginary, womanized, selfhood, quite at odds with the independent woman she has, with Ida's help, presumably become. She is pushed toward an unreal past, toward sentimental images of marriage, nurturing care, and passivity. The men finally entrap her so firmly in tire assumptions contained in this world of conventional language that she paces about "like some wild creature newly caged" and at last yields to their absurd conception of what she is, thus betraying Ida. She had broken away with her princess into a new freedom and a new tongue, but here she is "newly-caged" in the old clichés of sentimental tyranny.

In a similar fashion, then, Ida herself is beaten down by words, by the relentless assault of the most instinctive of men: her brother and the two kings. She is threatened, flattered, denounced, but the one image before her always is that of "woman": tender and submissive.

"O if, I say, you keep / One pulse that beats true woman, if you loved /The breast that fed or arm that dandled you"), Cyril begins, and the others chime in with similar appeals, climaxed by Gama's sentimental evocation of Ida's mother on her deathbed gasping out, with her last breath, "Our Ida has a heart". She is simply dragged down:

But Ida stood nor spoke, drained of her force
By many a varying influence and so long.
Down through her limbs a drooping languor wept:

Her head a little bent. Having forgiven Lady Blanche, the princess is then vulnerable to the same tactics, a point the prince is not slow to grasp. He realises the efficacy of repetition and pressure:

Nor did her father cease to press my claim,
Nor did mine own, now reconciled; nor yet
Did those twin-brothers, risen again and whole;
Nor Arac, satiate with victoryNowhere is the ironic image of the lonely hero ingloriously assaulted more firmly set than in this theme of language and its culmination in Ida's fall.

But the ironic defeat is also a comic victory, depending on our angle of vision and whether we respond more fully to the collapse of the heroic or to the fulfillment of the domestic comedy. This ambiguity is apparent even in the figure of the child, a symbol Tennyson used quite deliberately, strengthening it through the various revisions, presumably to clarify the meaning of the poem.

"The child is the link thro' the parts," he said (*Memoir*) and indeed that is true. It is the most important and complex symbol in the poem and thus the most important key to interpretation. From the point of view of domestic comedy, the child is an essential and nearly perfect symbol. It can be used both statically, as a symbol of innocence, or dynamically, as a symbol of growth and development. The actual child, Aglaïa, is a static image used to evoke responses of tenderness and maternal warmth in Ida, but the symbol has much broader applications in the poem that suggest process and an acceptance of change.

Disturbances, then, can be almost automatically set aside as youthful excesses, not only excusable but valuable as educational preludes to growth. This is the exact argument used by the narrator at the very end to explain the poem's relevance:

This fine old world of ours is but a child
Yet in the go-cart. Patience! Give it time
To learn its limbs: there is a band that guides. Ida's utopian radicalism is thus reduced from a threat to a mistake,

and not a serious mistake at that. All of comedy's charity and generosity (even if, as here, it is an evasive, patronizing generosity) are thus implied by the child symbol, which clearly gives very useful support to one side in the comic battle. The support to domestic comedy is not only useful; it is continuous. The child is central to most of the songs that link the sections and anticipate so sharply some of the issues about to be raised.

Tennyson's comment that the importance of the child was "shown in the songs which are the best interpreters of the poem" (*Memoir*) may, however, be misleading; for while the appropriateness of the songs is usually clear enough, they often seem far more simple than the action they are presumably interpreting so well. They distort things a great deal, though they are still noteworthy for the half-light they throw.

The first, "As through the land at eve we went," presents the major and reiterated use of the child symbol in the songs. Here the couple who have fallen out "kiss again with tears" when they see the grave of their child. The child acts as a force for unification and reconciliation. It is also, here. and in the main action of the poem, a natural and physical symbol, inciting the kisses in this song and Ida's reawakened sexuality. Apart from this, the child also suggests that unity is even stronger after the experience of disunity: "And blessings on the falling out /That all the more endears".

This notion supports the argument of domestic comedy to the effect that Ida's experiment is valuable when abandoned because, though abnormal and therefore to be rejected, it acts to expand the boundaries of life, to extend what we think of as normal- Ida, of course, might very well call this song sentimental and evasive; and she would, no doubt, be right.

But she is allowed no direct comment, and the next linking song, "Sweet and low," is much more subtle in its evocation of the child as a binding force between man and wife. The father is drawn back from the "dying moon" to home and new life, apparently not by the wife in the first stanza, but by the child in the second. "Father will come to his babe in the nest", even if he resists the call of his mate. There is the mildly subversive suggestion that the only genuine male response is to a child, since men themselves are children; but the principal linking is of the child with love and unity.

The third song, "The splendor falls on castle walls," does not specifically mention a child, but it does deal directly with the associations developed around that symbol. The song expressly denies the power of fame to combat time (that is, it denies Princess Ida's argument), as well as the sustaining power of heroism. The terms associated with the heroic vision here-splendor, castle, wild cataract, cliff, sea -evoke echoes that diminish as time passes.

Against this decay is the personal, introverted domestic love whose power grows as time goes on and thus is served by time, not defeated; "Our echoes roll from soul to soul, / And grow for ever and for ever" In the next two songs, which belong among the least effective lyrics Tennyson ever wrote, the child symbol is reinforced without much development. In "Thy voice is heard through rolling drums," the warrior gathers courage and strength from imagining "his brood" and then goes out and hacks his enemy to pieces.

There is in this song, as in the narrative itself, a curious connection between children, men, and barbarism, but it is not developed. The last song to deal with a child, "Home they brought her warrior dead," simply reaffirms the child's ability to minister to life, love, and personality. Rather than committing suicide, the newly widowed woman looks at her child an her knees and weeps sustaining, life-saving tears. It is easy, as I said, to see that poems like this have some bearing on the problems Princess Ida faces, but it is not easy to see bow they are the "best interpreters" of these problems. They seem, rather, to give support, less and less effectively as the poem goes on, to those aspects of the child symbol that serve the argument for domestic comedy.

But there is another side and another argument. From the standpoint of heroic comedy, the child is associated with regression, defeat, and deadly traps. Against the arguments of domestic comedy for the natural and ordinary in marital affairs, heroic comedy insists that the present relation between men and women is grotesquely perverted and unnatural:they had but been, she thought,

As children; they must lose the child, assume

The womanTime and again the child image is brought up not in reference to sweetness and tenderness but in reference to ugly containment. Ida's chief aim, one might say, is to invert the values that collect around this symbol and to rob it of its enormous sentimental force.

In order to mature, to "lose the child," women must abandon, not children of course, but the tradition of falsifying sentimentality associated with that image. And that tradition is located exactly with domestic comedy. Again like Ulysses, Ida's stern realism refuses to ignore the fact that heroic life is a life of exclusions; the comforts and values of domesticity are among those things excluded. The child, as the emotional centre of domestic life, is the central trap, and Ida uses the symbol in reference to all her enemies. Even in attacking the barren language of love she refers to this symbol: "Your language proves you still the child".

The child which can, in one way or another, promise eternal life for domestic comedy is seen by Ida as the very prototype of the time-bound. In her most impassioned speech she admits the force of the symbol, arguing that it is because the suggestions that surround children are so powerful that their appeal must be resisted: "Yet will we say for children, would they grew / Like field-flowers everywhere! we like them well: / But children die; and let me tell you, girl, / Howe'er you babble, great deeds cannot die".

"But children die" is the difficult admission at the heart of her heroism. She rejects the sentimental illusion of permanency which, to her, is all normality can offer, and she sets out really to destroy time, not evade it. When men use. children as weapons — "Children -that men may pluck them from our hearts, / Kill us with pity, break us with ourselves" sthey are instinctively denying not only heroism but genuine life to women.

They are pulling them back into the shadowy world of

ignorant childhood, where there are. only hints and counters of basic being. The famous advice of the prince's father — "Man for the field and woman for the hearth: / Man for the sword and for the needle she: / Man with the head and woman with the heart" explains just why Ida must pursue life away from men. They are out to kill her.

Finally she collapses: "Her iron will was broken in her mind; / Her noble heart was molten in her breast". But this climactic fall, strangely enough, bears no overt relation to the child. The removal of Aglaïa softens her up, but her will cracks only when she sees the prince and imagines him to be dead. The capitulation of Ida and her followers is symbolized by their all becoming nurses, not directly of children but of men. The princess, it seems, has lost one child, Aglaïa, only to have her replaced by another, the prince, her future husband.

The basic relationship imaged here is clearly not that between man and woman but between mother and child. Men expose their childlike natures to trap women and form them into children too. Ida is defeated not by the bloody war, the image of man's might, but by his prostration and weakness.

Wanting so much to lose the child, Ida is attacked by one, and she loses her heroism: "azure pillars of the hearth / Arise to thee; the children call" At the end, when the prince argues for the wonderful new state they can achieve together, one cannot help wondering how exactly to take his many references to children.

It is one thing to urge women not to lose their "distinctive womanhood", but he defines that distinguishing quality as the ability not to fail "in child ward care, / Nor to lose the childlike in the larger mind". Beneath all the fine words is a deeply regressive tendency. Perhaps we are traveling right back to where we began.

We cannot really know, I think, since the form of the poem is finally as ambiguous as its central symbol; but there are some possible answers given in the crucial seventh section. At the beginning of this last section, Ida's new Eden is shown transformed into a wasteland: "So blackened all her world in secret, blank / And waste it seemed and vain". Her isolation now is arid and she succumbs to the lure of the valley. The conclusion presents a brilliant case for domestic comedy, but it does not allow the arguments to remain unopposed even there.

The most effective arguments for domestic comedy are not really "arguments" at all but the two seduction songs in this seventh section, "Now sleeps the crimson petal" and "Come down, O maid." These mark both the occasion and the cause of the princess's final yielding.

The first song is, most obviously, a celebration of sexual release and fulfillment, appropriate since, as the force of domestic comedy becomes more and more dominant toward the end, Ida is seen less as an idealist and more as a virgin. But the song also operates to urge. an openness to all experience, not just sexual experience. Ida's isolation now appears to be fearful withdrawal.

As a counter to this assumed fear, the poem offers very elementary reassurance, soothing her and promising that comic existence is both beautiful and, more important, secure: "So fold thyself, my dearest, thou, and slip / Into my bosom and be lost in me" It offers both excitement and protection.

The poem's emphasis on now, the word that begins each of the four stanzas, creates a tone of sweet urgency to the reassurances and defines the movement of the new comedy away from the bondage of the past and futuristic abstractions alike.

The present, both in its intensity and comfort, its combined images of waking and sleeping, and its unification of the remote and the transient with the immediate and permanent, is the basis of the new solution.

This solution is reemphasized and completed in "Come down, O maid," which directly follows "Now sleeps the crimson petal." The poem presents most clearly the opposition between the two kinds of comedy: the heroic world of the cold and splendid mountain, and the domestic, pastoral world of the valley. It is also a fine and subtle rhetorical work, of course, which seeks to demolish the world of heroic comedy; its "splendour") is granted, but it is a splendor that is alien to man and to nature-finally to life. Heroic comedy, it suggests, may move "near the Heavens" and elevate man to the company of the stars, but it is not pleasant: "What pleasure lives in height (the shepherd sang) / In height and cold". 'the simplicity of the appeal is deliberate. Against the grandeur of isolation is placed mere comfortable joy.

Death, ice, and blasted pines, wild eagles, and especially the image of great waterfalls that break up a mighty stream into diffusive foam "that like a broken purpose waste[s] in air" make up the pointless, lonely world of irony. Domestic comedy offers fulfillment, sexuality, and, most of all, an integral place in teeming life. All nature awaits the maid's coming and participates in her welcome. The final promise is contained in the merging of the sweetness of her own voice with the sweetness and abundance about her. The poem embodies the unified harmonies it discusses and thus revivifies pastoral clichés. The new comedy, in fact, works by asking that clichés be deliberately accepted as such, just as Ida accepts the cliché of feminine tenderness, the child, and the prince accepts the cliché of masculinity, "the blind wildbeast of force"). The clichés are not confirmed but made over, so that childhood and age merge into maturity, the past and future into the eternal present.

The best part of the new solution, certainly, is that Ida does not completely abandon her dream:

She still were loth to yield herself to one
That wholly scorned to help their equal rights
Against the sons of men, and barbarous laws. Tennyson wants still to keep alive the hope of heroic comedy. Both the Poem's greatness and its major difficulties are due to this insistence. The fullest argument for the reconciliation of the two comic principles is found in the prince's long closing speech, but even that does not make such an impeccable case as one could hope for.

He maintains, as one would suppose, that they should forget the past and all wasteful opposition between the sexes. "The woman's cause is man's," he says; "they rise or sink /

Together, dwarfed or god-like, bond or free". But the prince goes further: this unification is to be accomplished by a preservation of important differences.

Man and woman should each protect his "distinctive" uniqueness (thus the child and the war) in order to form a more perfect bond: "Not like to like, but like in difference. By doing so, they will quite undeliberately become more like each other, rising toward the ultimate goal:

The single pure arid perfect animal, The two-celled heart beating, with one full stroke, Life. Opposites are reconciled not by superficial, overt compromise but by a crystallizing act of the creative imagination. Their universality is ensured by their being most fully realised in their finite particularity; the poet attains to full creative participation in the universe not by denying but by fulfilling his personality. The prince's paradoxical solution may baffle us, but it would have made good sense to Shelley and Keats.

The prince ends this climactic argument with a benedictory "May these things be!". One would suppose that all that remained would be an "Amen" and a wedding. But there is neither. The harmony is disrupted by the most startling and important lines in the poem: the princess responds to the prince's hope that all these things will be accomplished with a sighing "I fear / They will not". The prince argues some more, but the princess again sighs and calls it "a dream". He then becomes less abstract, citing his mother as the type of perfection that can be realised in Ida and completed in marriage. Still, she resists: "It seems you love to cheat yourself with words: /This mother is your model".

The old theme of language reappears at the end to reassert the ambiguity of the situation and to hint at the final irreconcilability of the two comic modes. Ida suggests that the rhetoric is wearing a little thin, that the deceptive language can create a trap for them both. Ida cannot easily be mother or child to this child-man, She does not deny him, of course, and the fact that all her objections are put "tremulously" at the end does suggest that she is about to yield.

But her questions are never answered, and her doubts

remain unresolved. The prince simply reasserts the vision of glorious comic existentialism- "all the past / Melts mist-like into this bright hour" and stops arguing. The final line of the narrative proper reinforces only the ambiguity: "Lay thy sweet hands in mine and trust to me".

This is not what we would expect as the inauguration of "the single pure and perfect animal." We never hear Ida's answer. The poem thus ends on a question mark, with this image of the prince's condescension taking us back to the very source of all the trouble, indeed of the poem itself. 'Where,'

Asked Walter, patting Lilia's head (she laid Beside him) 'lives there such a woman [as the feudal warrior] now?' [The poem that arises from an act of condescension may, then, close with one, hinting at an ironic circularity that mocks the ostensible educational progress of the poem's narrative. Perhaps no one learns anything.

These questions concerning the poem's efficacy, as well as its cause and relevance, are, surprisingly, points dealt with by the poem itself. *The Princess's* frame, the elabourate modern idyll, not only surrounds the story of Ida but also explains it; The importance of the frame is also kept before us by Lilia's interruptions midway through the poem, between sections 4 and 5. By maintaining an extensive series of parallels to characters and themes in the narrative, the frame acts as a commentary on that narrative and as a confirmation of its final ambiguity.

The prologue, the first hall of the frame, provides a strong impetus to the argument for domestic comedy. It presents an image of discontinuity contained within and yielding to a larger continuity, the union of diverse elements in a single unit. The poem opens on a scene of harmony: the broad, sunny lawns of Sir Walter Vivian are given over to his tenants. The house itself is a unified medley of styles, of places and times. It provides, a sense of continuity and control, of complete mastery: fossils become ornaments; lava is made into "toys".

The images of nature's awesome destructive power are thus made safe and manageable in the domestic atmosphere.

Though the tenants are there partly to learn, the comic pedantry later to be associated with Ida's scheme is carefully removed from these lessons. There are references to teachers and "facts," but the real purpose is enjoyment.

The "patient leaders of their Institute" collect all manner of scientific equipment, but it is used for quite unscientific purposes. The telescopes show beautiful views, the electrical demonstration unites a group of girls in a dancelike ring, and so forth. Sport and science are joined, with sport, clearly, out in front. There is thus a good deal of light cast forward, anticipating the power of the domestic comedy later to be fulfilled. But against this background of harmony is the disharmony among the young people, who forecast the tension and disunity of the tale of Princess Ida. The argument among them is caused by their response to a legend of female heroism, a story of a lady fighting to preserve her will: "O noble heart who, being strait-besieged / By this wild king to force her to his wish, / Nor bent, nor broke".

Objectified by history, such a person becomes a pleasant joke to the men, but she is a serious figure indeed to the women. The resistance of the historical lady to the wild king's desire to "force her to his wish" is subtly echoed in Lilia's contempt for Walter's pat on her head. As in the main body of the poem, women struggle against the smothering assumptions of male dominance. Male courtesy is equated with brutal power, war with love songs. The central conflict between heroism and gentle submission is thus begun. The group becomes an image of ironic tension yearning for resolution, divided against each other and against themselves

The plan for the medley is a brilliant idea, for it promises to provide an end to the quarrel and a new unity of time: "Why not a summer's as a winter's tale?" The seven men are to speak as one, with the women's voices separate and distinct but harmonious, foreshadowing the unity of the prince's final argument. There is also, in the very spontaneity of the poem's composition, a strong echo of domestic comedy's insistence on natural development, natural values. Finally, the lighthearted sense of game or interlocking dance is also suggested, providing a context that is implicitly critical of solemnity, isolation, and rebellion.

But the ancient tale itself does not so single-mindedly support the values of domestic comedy. The historical lady, forced against her will, is the type both for the lonely figure of the princess, hammered at by men and held to a contract she considers "invalid, since my will / Sealed not the bond", and also for little Lilia, who alone resists the aggression of the seven men.

The ambiguity of the young people's position is made apparent immediately on the ending of the narrative in the Conclusion, where, after a moment of quiet, Walter, the male supremacist who had begun the conflict, is stirred to a deep and startlingly compassionate insight: "I wish she had not yielded!" All the prince's rhetoric has not been enough to erase from his mind the image of heroism dragged down. That Walter, of all people, should be the one to represent this response shows how deep the generic split has become and how impossible has been the task of merging heroic and domestic comedy.

The Conclusion proceeds, then, to the feud over tone and the decision to remold the work so as to find a unifying attitude toward its subject. Interestingly, Lilia, the frame's parallel to Ida, takes no part in the dispute but sits musing, plucking the grass, and wondering. Her sudden question to the aunt, "You - tell us what we are", is left unanswered, both because the workmen are now noisily taking their leave and because no answer would help. The lovely vision of harmony and satisfaction, then — "The happy valleys, half in light, and half/ Far-shadowing from the west, a land of peace" is mocked by the unsettled dispute, the inadequate solutions, and the unresolved questions.

The poem focuses on Lilia for its close: "Last little Lilia, rising quietly, / Disrobed the glimmering statue of Sir Ralph / From those rich silks, and home well-pleased we went". The feminine silks are removed from the noble Sir Ralph. The heroic and the domestic, male and female, thus safely disjoined, we could perhaps be "well-pleased," were it not for the fact that the poem has illustrated the price we pay for the easy pleasure of domestic comfort. Like Walter, we are haunted by Ida's fall and by the poem's refusal to evade the consequences of that fall: the sacrifice of the heroic will.

Of all Tennyson's early poems, "Ulysses" seems to come closest to breaking this ironic tension, Though there is more to the poem than the "need of going forward" *(Memoir)* Tennyson offered as his motive in writing it, the central power to which we respond is that of romantic heroism. There are complex modulations in tone, certainly, but for most readers the poem moves toward an expression of serene confidence:

Though much is taken, much abides; and though. We are not now that strength which in old days Moved earth and heaven; that which we are, we are But Ulysses is much more than another indomitable superman, beyond the reach of time and death.

He, in fact, grants the power of circumstance, even of age and physical weakness. He does not stand above these forces but is caught by them, and he knows it. Yet he refuses to see himself as a victim and thus provides an answer to irony: the undefeated will; see Charles Mitchell, for a reading that emphasizes this point. The will accepts its own condition unflinchingly — "that which we are, we are" — but does not allow the force of external terror to negate it. In the face of death, the comic will asserts an irreducible ego; the acceptance of reality amounts to a triumph over it.

The great modern hero is this old man, who has already had his heroic adventures and who now achieves his personality and defines the hope of ours simply by refusing not to be. The comic and heroic will is the poem's subject; its primary motive is the relaxation of ironic tension.

But the tension is relaxed only within, not outside, the poem; for Ulysses, but not for us. The view of heroism is made comprehensive as well as intense, and it is this completeness that causes the escape to be closed to us. The force of the will projected here is enormous, but it is also, we sense, highly specialized. The poem lacks entirely comedy's usual sense of inclusiveness. "Ulysses" deals just as powerfully and rigorously with what the hero cannot accept as with what he can; nearly half the poem is devoted to sloughing off the encumbrances that stand in the way of this narrow solution. Because the poem is so explicit about this pruning, we can see the magnitude and variety of the human spirit being sacrificed for its heroic but naked endurance.

The result is the only heroism and the only solution to irony now possible, both compelling and impossibly restrictive. Despite the resounding, positive conclusion, the poem has worked to deny us the ability to participate in it uncritically. Though apparently an alternative to "The Lotos-Eaters," then, "Ulysses" operates in much the same way; it presents an answer that dissolves tension for the speaker and increases it for the reader.

The two poems also seem to have similar strategies for attacking the ironic dualism by heightening one-half of it: they both magnify the isolated, individual ego. Though the means of satisfying the ego are very different, perhaps even opposite, in the two poems, both solutions are equally exclusive and equally extreme. Some commentators, in fact, argue that these extremes meet, that Ulysses's desire for life is rooted in a desire for death," This reading, perhaps, sacrifices too many important distinctions for this striking similarity, but it is true that both poems are very uneasy with social demands, especially the sense of social acceptance that is central to comedy. In place of this society they are forced to offer substitutes: the extraordinary fellowship of death in "The Lotos-Eaters" or, in "Ulysses," what appears to be some highly dexterous faking.

For "Ulysses" seems to insist absolutely on the final separation of the individual from communal values: the only hope for the existence of the self is in isolation. The rejection of community begins at once:

It little profits that an idle king,
By this still hearth, among these barren crags,

Matched with an aged wife, I mete and dole
Unequal laws unto a savage race,
That hoard, and sleep, and feed, and know not me. The values associated with unity, order, and harmony, with love, family, and nation, are treated with lofty and imposing contempt. "Little profits" catches exactly the sneer of aristocratic understatement that is so disarming and so insusceptible of argument or reproof. What strikes us here is the control and the breathtaking rapidity with which all these civilized values are swept aside by the rush of the demands of the primitive self. The correctives we might apply are based on moral and social values that have been made irrelevant.

Ulysess proceeds in the next lines with an expansive, positive tone that provides us with a kind of rhetorical breather. His affirmations of a life-hunger act as a form of flattery, emphasizing the indiscriminate richness and value of simple experience. But the real work of this second section is to reinforce the independent power and value of the ego: "I have enjoyed / Greatly, have suffered greatly, both with those / That loved me, and alone" Love and all other mere externals are flattened and reduced to insignificance. The affirmations are all on the surface; underneath, the paring away continues as we approach nearer to the pure, undisguised self.

When he turns to Telemachus, there is little disguise left. The naked scorn of the opening lines has simply changed to a more confident, if bored, patronizing. Ulysses "accepts" Telemachus and his duties, certainly, but he accepts them as inferior, hardly deserving of his attention. This sense of casual superiority is carried largely by his diction, which is weary, cliché-filled, "official" language.

The tinge of parody is most apparent in his compliments: Telemachus is "most blameless" that is, most mediocre. Ulysses's evident relief at having dismissed this tiresome subject — "He works his work, I mine" emphasizes the enormous elevation he has attained. The key is "I mine." Ulysses has by now accomplished his own goal: the rigorous and careful definition of the heroic self.

The final section completes the pattern, presumably, by incorporating the triumphant ego of Ulysses into the fellowship of his mariners. From another point of view, he must now turn to the reader and include him in his plans. It is all rhetoric, both in the best and worst senses: it is eloquent persuasion and also mere cajolery. In these lines we hear must clearly the echo of Dante's sinner, who, after a stirring call to his comrades — "Ye were not form'd to live the life of brutes,/ But virtue to pursue and knowledge high" — turns and with a different voice entirely proudly announces the issue of his persuasive powers:

With these few words I sharpen'd for the voyage
The mind of my associates, that I then
Could scarcely have withheld them

There is more than a touch of this self-assured rhetorician in Tennyson's figure. Master of all experience and, by this point in the poem, master of his own situation, Ulysses proceeds to overpower his men — and he nearly overpowers us. But we sense the great control and assurance in his language, the uniform public rhythms so very different from the jagged, varied movement earlier. Lines like, "It may be we shall touch the Happy Isles, / And see the great Achilles, whom we knew", are striking partly for their quality of heroic understatement, but also for the self-consciousness of this understatement.

We apprehend the exhilaration of the lonely and triumphant ego behind all this, and the very magnificence of the language alerts, our critical sense and heightens the tension between sympathy and judgment.

Ulysses finally offers not comic union but absorption into his own ego. Everything in the poem has demonstrated how resistant he is to being reduced to "one equal temper of heroic hearts". The heroic will can triumph only by cutting itself off from the very values it now seeks to affirm. He has defined himself by casting away all communal, ego-reducing ties, and he thus leaves us with no real solution.

The final lines sadly reinforce both the greatness and the inaccessibility of the hero. With a finer irony even than the

Lotos-eaters' appeal to their "brother mariners" to join them in oblivion and death, Tennyson shows the existential hero able to create by his supreme will a unity he cannot join simply because his will is supreme. Ulysses leaves irony behind, but he pays a great price for his escape. And he makes it impossible for us to go with him.

Maud pushes comedy to its ironic limit; it marks the end of Tennyson's attempt to work seriously with that form. After *Maud*, nearly all of his major poems are ironic. This is not to say that the comic vision failed Tennyson or vice versa; there was simply little more for him to do in that genre.

Tennyson's moods or emotional states may or may not supplement his poetic instincts; they hardly exist on the same level. Most major nineteenth-century art was becoming ironic in form, a fact that seems far more important than anything that may have happened to Tennyson personally.

Still, there does seem to be in Tennyson a remarkable desire to resist the generic dominance of irony. His major poems after *Maud* are ironic, but there are not many of them that can be called major. *Idylls of the King* and a few dramatic monologues stand against a barrage of domestic idylls, political poems, occasional verse, and miscellaneous minor poems. "Lucretius" is counterbalanced by many poems like "De Profundis," poems which are nominally comic but which restrict the range of their appeals very narrowly, to those who can, for instance, be moved by lists of paradoxes:

Of this divisible-indivisible world
Among the numerable-innumerable
Sun, sun, and sun, through finite-infinite space
In finite-infinite Time. "De Profundis" is a poem that might be called technically happy:

Hallowed be Thy name - Halleluiah!-
Infinite Ideality!
Immeasurable Reality!
Infinite Personality!
Hallowed be Thy name-Halleluiah! One can recognize a kind of dusty exuberance here, the sort of pedantic flight one

associates with amateur nineteenth-century metaphysics, which, of course, is exactly what this poem and others like it consist ofThe remarkable quantity of the late comic poems is as important as their uneven quality. Tennyson did keep trying in comedy, but if not quite all the late poems that matter are ironic, the qualification is so trifling it can be ignored for now. Irony dominates the later major poems, so much so that it invades even poems which are clearly intended as positive statements.

For instance, Tennyson obviously admired Sir Richard Grenville's lone fight against fifty-three Spanish ships. The poet's imagination was deeply stirred by the Hemingwayceque image of valor in defeat. But, while perceiving fully the heroic aspects of Grenville's endurance, Tennyson cannot entirely exclude from "The Revenge" [1]a glimpse of the ironic extension of that heroism. He catches, therefore, both great determination and also mania, the sense that heroism itself is fascinating but unnatural. Grenville's full-toned speeches about not giving in are played off against flat details like: "But in perilous plight were we, / Seeing forty of our poor hundred were slain, / And half of the rest of us maimed for life".

The poem even hints at a suicidal quality in the hero, a perverse delight in self-destruction, presented in such a way as sometimes to seem slightly callous, even absurd: "Sink me the ship, Master Gunner — sink her, split her in twain! / Fall into the hands of God, not into the hands of Spain!" (ll. 89-90). The heroism contains a touch of vulgarity, a crude and narrow irrationality at odds with the expansive serenity common to the heroic tone. Sir Richard Grenville's sacrifice, further, spares no one and therefore comes to seem a trifle wild:

And a day less or more
At sea or ashore,
We die-does it matter when? To any human being in his senses it matters a great deal. It matters very much, surely, to Grenville's men; they say so:

We have children, we have wives,
And the Lord hath spared our lives.

We will make the Spaniard promise, if we yield, to let us go. Not so anxious to fall into the hands of God as their leader, the brave men leave Grenville to die if he likes - and of course he does. This odd disagreement and separation of Grenville from his men at the end of the poem upsets the directness of its predominant motive: the celebration of devoted and single-minded patriotism.

But irony is the enemy of the single-minded, and here mixes into the heroic celebration the token images of domestic comedy - children and wives. And the two cannot easily be mixed. The poem takes as its centre the celebration of what we think of as modern qualities: the acceptance of defeat and isolation. Even so, the image of defeated nobility is too complacent for irony. Sir Richard Grenville is not satirized, of course; but very strategically, just at the end of the poem, we are made to question the real desirability of his virtues.

Irony is nearly omnipresent in these late poems. The deliberately or overtly ironic poems are not really improvements over those in the 1842 volume; in many ways they are not even fundamentally different from them. What is apparent in the later poems is a more intricate and also less dramatic irony. The same themes and situations are there and the same rhetoric, but they are developed with more complexity and quietness.

Such changes are, in a general way, to be expected; what is surprising is the extent of this development. Tennyson's assurance in the form is such that he is able to extend it and establish its essential parodies less obviously. In the case of some early poems that were revised and published later, we have a good basis for examining this change. Poems like "The Captain," "The Voyage," and even "Tiresias," originally written in the mid-1830s though not published until much later, are interesting ironic poems, but they are, I think, quite simple in comparison with the other late poems.

"The Captain" is not an unsubtle poem, but the source of its power is blatantly clear. A certain beleaguered crew conspires to turn the tables on a brave but stern and generally unlikeable captain. When a roaring fight comes, they fold their arms and refuse to take part, grinning at the captain and gleefully dying: "over mast and deck were scattered / Blood and brains of men".

The poem pretends to supply a moral to the effect that severity is an ineffective tactic for leaders to adopt but such cautions are absurdly inadequate, failing entirely to explain the central action. The grotesque juxtaposition of such gory results with motives that are in every way childish defies any explanation. The poem emphasizes this pointlessness by picturing at its close both the ironic fellowship of the crew and captain "side by side beneath the water" and their final triviality:

There the sunlit ocean tosses
O'er them mouldering,
And the lonely seabird crosses
With one waft of the wing. The poem has a dark power, but its strategies are fairly simple.

Just as direct is the ironic structure of another of these early-late poems, "The Voyage." Eleven of the poem's twelve sections present a virtually untroubled vision of the pursuit of the "Ideal," a vision and a goal that are as soft and mellow as they are vague. These sections avoid giving any concrete picture at all but simply exude an atmosphere of warm acceptance. The final section none too subtly disrupts all this with some grim actuality: "Now mate is blind and captain lame, / And half the crew are sick or dead".

The conclusion picks up lines from the first section and echoes them with a loud, sardonic jeer: "We know the merry world is round, / And we may sail for evermore" "The Voyage of the Maeldune," published in 1880 and written in the same year, provides a good contrast to these two earlier poems. Though quite similar in its subject, the late poem demonstrates Tennyson's development toward compression and certainty of tone, largely by means of the technique of ambiguity he had mastered in the *Poems* of 1842.

On one level, "The Voyage of the Maeldune" presents a very clear picture: a progress through various temptations to a highly appropriate moralistic conclusion, the holy saint's rebuke of vengeance. The men of the Maeldune presumably learn, after passing through the symbolic ordeals of the Isle of Fire, the Isle of the Double Towers, and the rest, the virtue of forgiveness.

It is characteristic of Tennyson's later ironic poems that the obvious and non-ironic statement of the poem, like the one just outlined, should be given greater and greater strength: the ironic counterstatement is put with much more reserve than in the earlier poems. Here, the vengeance-forgiveness motif is not subverted at all; rather, it is rendered inadequate to explain the poem's details. It is not, finally, vengeance that causes the men to kill one another but simply life's experience. The islands themselves have no connection to the purpose of vengeance (except for the first isle, and the wind blows them away from that one). These strange lands suggest, in their diversity, the complex of sensations and acts that make up all of life, particularly a good life. But all impulses act the same on these men, as they do on all men.

Silence makes them yearn to kill each other; noise makes them actually do so. They are frustrated by the Isle of Flowers, but the fulfillment they find in the Isle of Fruits leads to something worse than frustration: "And we stayed three days, and we gorged and we maddened, till every one drew / His sword on his fellow to slay him, and ever they struck and they slew".

The Isle of Fire and the Paradise tinder the sea cause more deaths; even the Bounteous Isle, which encourages them to play, leads to war games and the inevitable result: "we slew and we sailed away" This grim absurdity is climaxed in the episode of the Isle of the Double Towers, where, because there is some division, no matter how arbitrary, the men choose sides, naturally in order to kill one another; "and all took sides with the Towers, There were some for the clean-cut stone, there were more for the carven flowers".

The saint's verdict about forgiveness at the end, then, touches only a part of the problem. The final lines are brilliantly ambiguous, supporting the moralistic warning of the saint but also

Suggesting that vengeance for these men is not so much wrong as superfluous after so much murder, that it is not morality but simple weariness that renders the whole quest pointless:

And we came to the Isle we were blown from, arid there on the shore was he, The man that had slain my father. I saw him and let him be. O weary was I of the travel, the trouble, the strife and the sin, When I landed again, with a tithe of my men, on the Isle of Finn. The indirectness of this late irony is highlighted by comparison with one more of these early-late poems, "Tiresias." This poem is a good deal more complex than poems like "The Captain" or "The Voyage," perhaps because it was later revised more extensively; still, it does have a somewhat greater directness than is usual in poems composed later. The poem is partly about sacrifice; but the form, structure, and context all call into doubt the nobility, even the purposefulness, of such a sacrifice. Presumably, Menoeceus will, by killing himself, appease Ares, end the slaughter, and create for himself an enduring fame.

None of this is exactly denied, but the loud voice of heroism is accompanied by ironic whispers that tell us that Menoeceus's death merely supports a senseless and bloody order and ensures the extinction of his own name at the hands of a fickle populace.

Further, Menoeceus and his free sacrifice are clearly displaced from the centre of the dramatic monologue, which is occupied by Tiresias and his bondage. Tiresias has been cursed, in Tennyson's version, for presuming to search for beauty and knowledge. He wanted to see "that more than man / Which rolls the heavens, and lifts, and lays the deep". This aesthetic and religious longing takes him to the heart of life and to the centre of all wisdom, where he finds the Goddess Pallas Athene. She reveals to him the principles on which the universe operates: malignity and pettiness. Because he dared to worship, Tiresias is made the subject of a vicious joke. His religious desires are cruelly completed: his inner sight is made perfect, while his outer sight is destroyed.

What more could a transcendentalist want? Because he now has 'the secrets of truth, Tiresias is effectively isolated from all men;

there is no need for any further curse than the ability to see what is and will be. He call "only speak the truth that no man may believe". The phrase is significantly ambiguous. Tiresias speaks the sort of truth men will not believe; or he speaks the truth, and therefore [so that] men will not believe him. Tiresias is given the answer to all human prayers, but what a bitter and cynical answer it is. He sees all essential truth — that is, all "famine, plague, / Shrine-shattering earthquake, fire, flood, thunderbolt, And angers of the Gods" and therefore no one hears him.

Tiresias himself only partly understands that he has been cruelly tricked. He has slipped farther into the hands of the mocking gods than he realises. He can still recall with pleasure the vision of Pallas Athene, that alien deity who denied all mankind by denying him. There is, in other words, a dramatic irony working here that asks us to perceive Tiresias's position as even more terrible than he himself acknowledges. He fails to see, for instance, that Menoeceus's sacrifice really only allows Ares to win and thereby confirms what Ares, "whose one bliss/ Is war and human sacrifice", represents. Ares can be satisfied with Menoeceus's sacrifice only because it is, in itself, an emblem of the senseless slaughter that delights him.

Ares and Pallas Athene, the two deities mentioned in the poem, form a grim unity, supporting the principles of trickery and absurdity. Yet the climax of the poem is a paean to these gods, a hopeful vision, in fact, of an eternity spent in praising these agents who have made him such a pitiable victim.

On the other hand, Tiresias does see, though he can do very little about, the ineffectiveness of truth itself. But he blames this not so much on the gods, on the very nature of things, as on the people. Cosmic injustice becomes, in his blindness, a matter of political ranting against the stupidity of the populace. The poem is framed by these very important complaints. He early laments that casting "wise words among the multitude / Was flinging fruit to lions"), and argues bitterly near the end of the poem that "the wise man's word Here trampled by the populace underfoot". Yet in the centre of these attacks are his pious exhortations to

Menoeceus to slaughter himself for the good of these very people.

It is interesting that he rests his appeal to Menoeceus so very little on altruistic or ethical grounds; almost his entire argument is based on Menoeceus's achieving fame with the people, and thereby a kind of immortality. These people, so unable to hear truth and so feeble, are suddenly, in this argument, endowed with wisdom, courage, and stability. Tiresias is forcing Menoeceus into art even more horrible version of the fate he himself has experienced: a useless public life. The heart of truth is deception, whether it lies in Tiresias or in the gods. Tiresias's greatest curse was not to be disbelieved but, in this one instance, to be believed. He has unwittingly but surely become Pallas Athene herself

The full achievement of the late ironic work, other than *Idylls of the King,* is represented very well by two poems, "Lucretius" and "Rizpah." Both are essentially dramatic monologues; both demonstrate Tennyson's growing ability to manipulate the two rhetorical poles of the dramatic monologue, sympathy and judgment, so as to include us more surely in the final irony.

The first thing to notice about "Lucretius" is Lucretius's wife, or more exactly, the frame of the poem in which she appears. Such frames almost always function in a dramatic monologue to add a necessary context and thus to strengthen the reader's judgmental response. These tactics are necessary in order to maintain the conflict between sympathy and judgment, to keep the poem from being rhetorically direct. When the central figure or the argument is implicitly outrageous, judgment is automatically brought into play; but when, as here, the speaker is given great intellectual power and dignity, it is necessary to do something more to call forth our judgment and ensure the proper tension.

That something more, in this case, is the story of Lucilia and her passion, which surrounds, although it does not explain, Lucretius's tortured soliloquy. The incongruously flat, domestic opening of the poem "Lucilia, wedded to Lucretius, found / Her master cold" acts to focus our attention on the human passions and needs Lucretius is denying. Tennyson boldly uses the stock comic figure of the sterile pedant for very serious purposes. Lucretius's denial of the passions is seen, right from the start, as a denial of all that is human. We see, too, that his unnatural excision of passion, his rage for intellectual placidity, must inevitably evoke the retribution of nature and humanity, symbolized here by Lucilia's potion. The potion acts directly to check "his power to shape". The ordered, rational world of this heroic and potentially tragic philosopher is destroyed by the simple jealousy of his wife. As in *In Memoriam*, then, instinctual feeling overcomes controlled, rational system, the difference being, of course, that "Lucretius" completely burlesques *In Memoriam's* solution.

The force of this burlesque is maintained in Lucretius's soliloquy as well, though we do very much need the clearer ironies of the opening twenty-five lines of domestic actuality to alert us to the sad contradictions that control his life.[4] He is caught in the indifferent universe he has created-or rather perceived; for there is no indication that he is wrong about the universe or about the remoteness of the power that control it. What mocks him, at least in this central section, is the chaos that underlies all human life and makes ridiculous the ideal of calm indifference after which he has sought.

"I thought I lived securely as yourselves"), he cries to the gods, but such glorious serenity is denied to man. It is not that Lucretius errs in imagining the world as cold and atomistic; he miscalculates only in supposing that man has an integral part in that world. He prays to "The all-generating powers and genial heat / Of Nature", but it is just this force which creates a mixed and unsettled life. In his dream he is haunted by visions of a universe whose genial heat has become a raging fire.

The most remarkable of these visions is that of the naked breasts of Helen overpowering and turning to the ground a threatening sword.[5] Masculinity, particularly masculine control, is powerless in the face of utter sexuality, perhaps, but it is also "all that beauty" (l. 64), as he sees, which masters control and force. This is a completely ambiguous symbol. Furthermore, the power over out sort of violence — the sword-issues riot in peace but in another form of violence:

and as I stared, a fire, The fire that left a roofless Ilion, Shot out of them, and scorched me that I woke. [ll. 64-66]

For man, all beauty, desire, power, destruction, nurture, and murder are intermingled, not in real unity but in a wild, unmanageable chaos.

Lucretius is not satirized, then, nor is the heroism of his attempt to save a coherent universe denied. In trying to save humanity, however, he has abandoned it. His dying response to his anguished wife is the terrible issuance of the desire to make men gods: "Clasped, kissed him, wailed: he answered, 'Care not thou! / Thy duty? What is duty? Fare thee well!'. This black denial of care, duty, and need is what comes of a philosophy that attempts to make sense of the universe and man's place in it. Lucretius is mistaken not because he adopted the wrong explanation of coherence but because he tried to find coherence at all.

He betrays human nature, to be sure, but the human nature we see in Lucilia is that of a murderess. Sympathy and judgment work together to keep before us with equal force the grandeur of Lueretius's attempt and the trivial but disastrous nature of his failure. His betrayal is our own, and he is, in another sense, betrayed by us, All our dreams of hope and meaning, the poem finally asserts, are canceled out by our glaring insignificance.

"Rizpah" works for a similar inclusiveness in its irony, though its rhetoric operates very differently. Despite a certain false staginess, the poem achieves an effect that is very rare in Tennyson's dramatic monologues. It is absolutely direct in its appeals, rejecting almost entirely the intricate imagistic and structural movement of the early dramatic monologues in order to force us into full identification with the speaker.

There is no ironic structural order, no reversals, and no tricks in this poem, simply a linear movement of intensification, The images become more and more concrete, but all to the same purpose. In one sense, "Rizpah" supports Langbaum's arguments on the dramatic monologue: it makes us into the speaker. Most kinds of judgments are rendered trivial by the sheer emotional power of the mother's language and by the carefully arranged dramatic context.

By presenting her case to a Protestant do-gooder, Rizpah shows how desperately inadequate mere benevolence is. The general level of concern and understanding, she suggests, cannot touch flit primitive feelings that control human life. The charitable lady parodies genuine charity; she can only prattle on about sin, retribution, and election, abstract and meaningless catchwords when weighed against the concrete source of Rizpah's knowledge: feeling her son's bones move in her side).The dramatic situation seems fashioned to disallow conventional responses.

The visitor represents not so much the failure. of Christianity (the poem goes on to demonstrate that she understands Christianity as little as she understands maternal love), as the failure of social being, our conventional selves, The charitable lady constantly makes judgments, invoking the grand symbols of religious justice. But these have no meaning to Rizpah and do not touch her experience; like her, we are forced to leave them behind. Conventional judgment is made to appear callous and, most of all, blatantly superficial.

The poem carefully connects this conventional religious and moral judgment to the legal judgment that has sentenced Rizpah's son. just as the Christian lady is removed from Rizpah's elemental reality, so is social and ethical justice remote from true justice. The law is invoked as an instrument of decision so cruel and indifferent to humanity that we must reject that judgment and the whole complex of social institutions it represents — for instance, the asylum where they beat the mother in order to cure her. This last, hideous nonsequitur is emblematic of all our customary responses and kindnesses. We must cast aside our social judgments and our social beings, it appears, in order to live with the elemental love and devotion of Rizpah.

But the rhetoric of the poem is not, I think, quite this simple. Though we do reject a whole range of judgments, we retain others. The tension in the dramatic monologue between sympathy and judgment is preserved, but the judgment evoked is of a very special kind.

Unlike almost all of Tennyson's other dramatic monologues, "Rizpah" does not evoke a judgment from outside the speaker; there is no appeal to any of the normal responses that create the pole of judgment in "The Lotos-Eaters" or "Ulysses." Here the speaker herself generates both the sympathy and the judgment. Though the poem appears to be stripping away our superficial, social facades, it is actually just selecting a possible social framework for us.

Rizpah counters the charitable lady's Calvinism not only with the terrible, chaotic image of a grim contest for her son's bones, which would in itself seem to repudiate all religions, but with a different religious interpretation. Rizpah has not turned her back on God; she has "been with God in the dark" She has found the more basic arid real Christianity:

Sin? O yes — we are sinners, I know - let all that be, And read me a Bible verse of the Lord's good will toward men — Full of compassion and mercy, the Lord' — let me hear it again; Full of compassion and mercy — long-suffering.' Yes, O yes!.

For the lawyer is born but to murder — the Saviour lives but to bless. We reject lawyers and Calvinism and asylum-keepers - that is, one *form* of existing social being but in its place we are given a different social plan: one of mercy, forgiveness, rewards, and happiness. The strict world of law is replaced by what, in its implications, is a comic world with comic order. Rizpah provides us with a new standard for judgment, a new context which, though given only in outline, can easily be created in full by the reader.

The ironic tension, then, is provided by the split between the actuality of experience presented and the joyous vision of the Christian frame of values that is evoked. Only one kind of judgment, the comic kind, is appropriate to human life; but, then, what does comedy have to do with such things as scratching for bones? We are forced to see the absolute validity of two quite different worlds: the world of nightmare and the world of forgiveness and mercy.

Instead of raising a critical judgment, this poem disallows criticism altogether. But it does preserve a more profound conflict between the judgment, or the image, of a comic world of desire, and the sympathetic identification with the terror of the world of experience.

There are, as I have said, many late poems that are probably comic, though one would not want to so classify such works as "The Ancient Sage" with much conviction. Virtually all these poems are generically incomplete, lacking the confident vision of harmony and the ability to project solutions that are both concrete and evocative. They tend to rely instead on sonorous abstractions: again and again we are asked to accept as a climax lines like

A deep below the deep,
And a height beyond the height!
Our hearing is not hearing,
And our seeing is not sight. ["The Voice and the PeàkSuch generalized assertions may be presumed to have a cheering effect; they are a kind of transcendental "Good morning." When Tennyson's late comedy does move toward specifics, it either degenerates into Polonius-like aphorisms — "Nor roll thy viands on a luscious tongue, / Nor drown thyself with flies in honied wine" ("The Ancient Sage,") - or else dissolves into the anomalous "sunnier side of doubt" ("The Ancient Sage,") he often recommends. Cleaving to doubt, sunny or not, suggests a tentativeness which properly belongs to irony, not comedy. Tennyson developed the habit of adding question marks to nearly every affirmation he could bring himself to make in the late poems, for example,

A whisper from his dawn of life? a breath. From some fair dawn beyond the doors of death. Far—far—away? ["Far—Far—Away,"

The best he can do now is to offer the hope that all is not quite lost—yet. The facts of existence seem to him so overwhelmingly uncomic that he can support comedy only by an act of faith, and a weak act at that. The happiest expression he can honestly find is a wary hope against hope:

Chaos, Cosmos! Cosmos, Chaos! who can tell how all will end? Read the wide world's annals, you, and take their wisdom for your friend. Hope the best, but hold the Present fatal daughter of the Past, Shape your heart to front the hour, but dream not that the hour will last. ["Locksley Hall Sixty Years After,"]

This particular poem is a vivid illustration of the general inability of these late poems to find peace. Though Hallam reports that the poet had "endeavoured to give the moods of despondency which are caused by the decreased energy of life," Tennyson himself said that "the old man in the second 'Locksley Hall' had a stronger faith in God and in human goodness than he had had in his youth." (*Memoir,*)

These explanations seem to me slippery at best. The old man who speaks in the second "Locksley Hall" tries very hard to put things in a positive light - at least some of the time — but he keeps falling back into the negations that dominate the poem. The uniquely personal comedy of the first "Locksley Hall," where progress and the dynamic movement of the age were used to call the speaker out of himself, is now repudiated:

Good, this forward, you that preach it, is it well to wish you joy? Is it well that while we range with Science, glorying in the Time, City children soak and blacken soul and sense in city slime? The general solutions have failed, interestingly, not so much because of city slums and city slime, but simply because such solutions have not helped him:

Poor old voice of eighty crying after voices that have fled! All I loved are vanished voices, all my steps are on the dead. All the world is ghost to me, and as the phantom disappears, Forward far and far from hence is all the hope of eighty years. As in the first poem, the focus is intensely personal; the speaker is not asking for a social utopia (or really even for social improvement) but for some happiness. The pleasantest things he can find to say-"Follow Light, and do the Right — for man call half-control his doom" - hardly indicate the strong "faith" Tennyson ascribed to him, nor do they provide sufficient assurance to support a comic poem.

There are a few poems which, whether or not they are major, do manage much more certain comedy. "Vastness," for instance, is an interesting late attempt to repeat the comic formula of In Memoriam. it puts irony on trial, allowing it to display its own climactic insufficiency. The ironic platitudes are given more than free play; they are presented in the harshest and most stinging way: "What is it all but a trouble of ants in the gleam of a million million of suns?".

The compressed bitterness and, at the same time, the range of allusion represent ironic technique at its most effective. Still, the long line and the fast meter, made generally more regular and thus quicker as the poem proceeds, suggest a mounting frenzy; as does the increasingly frequent use of inclusive words like all and every:

"Spring and Summer and Autumn and Winter, and all those old revolutions of earth; / All new-old revolutions of Empire — change of the tide — what is all of it worth?". Such lines give a subtle hint of a loss of control that is less and less well hidden. Instead of the expected cool detachment, the tone becomes more heated, and after thirty-five lines of this the ironic momentum peters out.

In one line, then, only one-half of a stanza, the calm assurance of love is stated: "Peace, let it be! for I loved him, and love him for ever: the dead are not dead but alive. Exactly as in *In Memoriam's* section 57, the fury is silenced by the word *peace,* which allows a new tone and a new attitude to take over. In *In Memoriam,* of course, more than seventy lyrics go on to support and define this new tone; here, there is only this one line.

The power of that line and the force of the comic solution depend, in a negative sense, on our perception of the mounting fury and weakness of the irony and, in a positive sense, entirely on the word love and its ability to evoke a whole range of experience and values contrary to those of irony. The assertion here is necessarily bald because it cannot be supported by logic or the emotional turmoil that accompanies irony.

Love gives "peace," as the poem says; therefore further words are superfluous, really impossible. Tennyson is, one could argue, more tactful here than in *In Memoriam,* allowing the cumulative force of irony to backlash and to provide by inversion a borrowed energy to the comic term "love."

This poem is, at any rate, a unique and, I think, successful comic experiment. What needs to be emphasized, however, is not the success of this sort of poem but its rarity in Tennyson's late work, Even here Tennyson had enormous difficulty persuading himself to put the last line in a positive form. Earlier versions arc strongly qualified or are stated negatively. We can see, in fact, each of the four versions (the last is the published one) growing gradually but surely stronger and slightly more affirmative, as if the poet were expending a great deal of effort to work himself up to write a single comic line:

Save for a hope that we shall not be lost in the Vastness, a dream that the dead are alive? *MS 1st reading.*

Peace, for I hold that I shall not be lost in the darkness, the dead are not dead but alive. *MS 2nd reading.*

Nay, for I knew thee, O brother, and loved thee, and I hold thee as one not dead but alive. *MS 3rd reading.*

Peace, let it be! for I loved him, and love him for ever: the dead are not dead but alive. Perhaps the almost pathetic hesitancy recorded here gives some indication of why there is so little comedy in Tennyson's late poems. "Demeter and Persephone," in fact, seems to me the only fully realised comic poem written in conventional terms (unlike the very special form of "Vastness"). It is a mellow and, surprisingly, quite simple and undisturbed comedy.

There are complex implications in the myth, of course, which is not simple at all, but Tennyson's presentation of that myth, even with his much discussed frame, follows a direct comic form. The poem may, as James Kissane points out, have some connections with an essay by Walter Pater,

"The Myth of Demeter and Persephone." Tennyson had a copy of this essay, which he marked rather carefully, noting, among other things, Pater's suggestion that the image of Persephone "is meant to make us in love, or at least at peace, with death."

Such an attitude, we know, is not foreign to Tennyson; it is one major effect of "The Lotos-Eaters." "Demeter and Persephone," however, does a good deal more, celebrating not death but full and harmonious life. Even in her painful search for her daughter, Demeter finds that death and life, good and evil, are interrelated, not in conflict:

"The Bright one in the highest / Is brother of the Dark one in the lowest". Out of this basic unity the myth resolves itself by making Persephone queen of both life and death. This classic belief does not, however, fully satisfy Tennyson, who augments it with a vision of the future, where "kindlier Gods" will bring these related opposites of death and life into an even fuller and more complete unity:

Till thy dark lord accept and love the Sun,
And all the Shadow die into the Light,
When thou shalt dwell the whole bright year with me.

The comic wholeness of the present is not denied, but it is made prefatory to the richer comedy to come.

All that remains are those short and highly evocative religious poems which are among the very last poems Tennyson wrote. The series of brief lyrics written at the end of his life are very different from anything else in the corpus. They have about them a quietness and peace totally absent from the earlier poetry.

Poems like "Faith," "The Dreamer," and "The Making of Man" present solutions which are still general but have a solidity that is missing from the vague abstractions he had depended on in other late poems. Especially in "God and the Universe" he achieves a suggestiveness and confidence that recall the religious comedy of George Herbert and Milton:

Spirit, nearing yon dark portal at the limit of thy

human state, Fear not thou the hidden purpose of that Power which alone is great, Nor the myriad world, His shadow, nor the silent Opener of the Gate. Tennyson thus continues, right up to the time of his death, to strive for comedy. But on the whole his late poetry after *Maud* really belongs to irony.

Chapter 9

Critical Essays

"Mariana" likewise portrays and engenders a suspended position. The poem is, in the first place, remarkably adrift from its presumed Shakespearean source. As John Stuart Mill said, "There is no mere amplification; it is all production, and production from that single germ" ("Review"). It is certainly "all production," developing from an intense and single-minded imaginative speculation on the short and evocative phrase, "Mariana in the moated grange."

By separating Shakespeare's character so completely from the play, Tennyson achieves the intense focus that also makes the desolation seem uncaused. There is no point in looking to *Measure for Measure* in order to find out why "he will not come," much less to determine that he will, as he does in the play, come after all, Here there is no narrative movement at all, the whole point being that Mariana's love is senselessly denied, that her fruition is cut off without reason.

At least, by restricting the poem to her baffled ignorance, Tennyson makes it clear that any reasons are radically disproportionate to the implications of pointless imprisonment. "He cometh not" is all that matters, and the poem thus develops die purity of a cosmic statement of irony.

For though the poem is often treated as a picture of sheer desolation, a "giving in" to melancholy, our response is surely not so simple and very definitely not so easy and relaxed as the word melancholy would suggest. The poem seems to move to a climax, but it actually mocks climactic structures. The picture of a bondage that cannot be broken is created and reinforced by all the details of the poem. The thick, clogged opening lines, for instance, or the metrics of the refrain, where the quick, regular movement of "She only said, 'My life is dreary,/ He cometh not,' she said" is interrupted by the unexpected sluggishness of the next line-"She said, 'I am aweary, aweary' — a line which not only suggests the very hopelessness and weariness it is talking about but also retards and thus emphasizes the decisive last line of the refrain—"I would that I were dead!"

One should also note the brilliant way in which Mariana's heightened sensitivity is suggested: she both sharpens small details and obliterates the distinction between large ones. She knows all about the patterns on the bark of the single poplar tree but confuses waking and sleeping states. The distortion here resembles that of nightmare, with its horrifying clarity of detail and its absolute lack of boundaries, its absence of familiar context.

Similarly, her stasis is supported even by the slight ambiguity of "she only said," repeated in every refrain and suggesting either that this was all she said, or that all she did was to say this. It is an arresting ambiguity that goes nowhere. There are no choices to be made; either meaning is equally appropriate, or equally inappropriate. The notion of her doing nothing all day except saying this, or the notion that the terror of her situation evoked only this minimal response, strike us as uncoordinated but equally applicable meanings.

But in the image of desolation and weariness finally is balanced by the poem's remarkably strong support of Mariana's associations with youth, growth, and hope. The poem's irony is defined by the pressure of the undeniably just claims of love and comic promise against the equally undeniable fact of denial. The positive side is, of course, implied very strongly by the enveloping situation: Mariana's youth and hope are supported by the fact that she is waiting for a lover, as they are also by her connection with a pastoral landscape and with romantic terms like "casement."

Primarily, though, the positive level is presented by inverting the usual images of comedy and the pastoral. The poem is filled with references to beauty, order, and hope-all, of course, bitterly distorted but nonetheless there. The opening lines give a parody of a beauty that is ordered and controlled. Man's capacity for both enjoying and arranging nature is mocked in the image of sluggish decay overcoming the flower-plots, rust and disorder invading the carefully controlled growth of the ornamental pear tree. The image of man as master of nature's beauty is thrown against that of man as victim of nature's anarchy.

Mariana, it must again be insisted, is not caught by this last image only; she is caught between the two. On one hand there is the "blackest moss" but on the other is the poplar tree, one of the poem's most important symbols. In the midst of the dark and stagnant waters of the marsh grows a single poplar tree, "all silver-green", the only relief in "the level waste, the rounding gray". One entire stariza is devoted to the shadow of this tree and the implications of this teasing symbol of the growth and promises that are denied her but are *ever* present to her, falling "Upon her bed, across her brow", and making itself a part of her mind.

It is a symbol of genuine hope that can be neither claimed nor forgotten; it stands for all that makes release impossible for Mariana. Also supporting this mocking, positive side of the poem is the recurrence of the day's cycle, with each morning bringing a renewal of the bitter knowledge of what is not there and, more important, the taunting reference to "the sweet heaven", a heaven of which she is constantly aware, even though it is closed to her.

This same conjunction of illusory hope and a knowledge of hopelessness is mirrored in the intricate structure of the poem. The only motion is the merely apparent one within actual stasis. Though the refrain does suggest a genuine development in its change from "He cometh not" to "He will not come," we recognize that these are not really separate perceptions, that they simply state the tension that defines her entire existence, the waiting with the certain knowledge that there is no point in waiting. And we see, too, that is poem is narrated from such a distant perspective as to describe not a climactic movement but a slice of life, a typical day with its recurrent hopelessness, rising to a finality that will be dissolved by the renewed hopeless hope of a new day. The action, then, is ironically recurrent, not tragically complete. The tragic simplicity of a climax is distorted to a conclusion only of a mouse squeaking and a fly buzzing. The tragic sensibility has now only these materials; only trivia surround her.

This poem is a prototype of Tennysonian irony, formulating many of the techniques and attitudes that appear later, but it is also a highly instinctive form of a vision which, even in later poems, is often put more obtrusively. When the ironic dilemma is stated more overtly, the poetry appears more obviously thematic, sometimes even thematically "divided." Because of this, it is easy, but I think wrong, to approach it as merely dualistic. Such an approach ignores the potential unity provided by ironic tension. Tennyson is not on one side of the argument or the other; like all ironists, he is on neither side-and both.

A good example of a poem that appears to be but is not a "thesis poem" is "A Dream of Fair Women," which establishes its irony partly in reference to its apparent source, Chaucer's The Legend of Good Women. Tennyson's poem resembles Chaucer's only superficially; the earlier poet's comforting, stable framework is removed, and the cosmic resonance of the tales, comforting or not, is implicitly denied. Taking the place of Chaucer's coherent series of portraits of faithfulness, love, and tragedy, Tennyson's group emphasizes the discontinuity of history and the pointlessness of presumed grandeur. The catastrophes here are either paltry or uncaused. The ironic conjunction is put immediately in the deceptively limpid introductory lines:

In every land
I saw, wherever light illumineth,
Beauty and anguish walking hand in hand.

The downward slope to death. What ties the portraits together is the "hand in hand" union of beauty and anguish. There is no further thematic point.

The dream itself takes place in the mocking familiarity of the narrator's memory, a continual symbol in Tennyson for comedy, here used to create a distorting framework: "The smell of violets, hidden in the green,/ Poured back into my empty soul and frame / The times when I remember to have been /joyful and free from blame". And all this happy nostalgia prefaces a nightmare. The first figure, Helen, begins by putting in clipped, disconnected, and very dramatic phrases the essence of her ironic function. Because she was beautiful, carnage resulted: "Where'er I came / I brought calamity".

Though the narrator naïvely tries to twist this into a romantic framework, claiming that he too would have died for such a face, such escapes are disallowed. He is soon overwhelmed by the march of hideous and meaningless deaths: Iphigenia relates the grim, realistic details of the knife moving "through my tender throat" in a sacrifice which led only to further desolation. Cleopatra reduces her potentially tragic position to ludicrous capriciousness, saying that death really is not so bad except that "I have no men to govern in this wood: / That makes my only woe She turns her grand suicide into an act of petty revenge: "Of the other [Caesar]: with a worm I balked his fame. /What else was left?" Jephtha's daughter, who follows, is the most complex case of all.

Her sacrifice had depended on a grisly kind of gambling, her father having promised God that for victory over the children of Ammon he would kill the first person he saw leaving his house to meet him. Though she continues after death to defend her father and to proclaim the rightness of God's law, the narrator ignores all this and responds only to the monstrousness of the situation:

My words leapt forth: 'Heaven heads the count of crimes With that wild oath.'The absurdity of Jephtha's sacrifice is that perceived by Browning's Caliban, for whom divine justice is represented by the decision to murder every twenty-first crab: "Let twenty pass, and stone the twenty-first, / Loving not, hating not, just choosing so." The girl's pathetic defence of her murderer is further undercut by a long simile comparing her voice to the sound of a "holy organ" in a cathedral.

The Christian context mocks the Old Testament ruthlessness without offering any further hope, for the last sad portrait is of the Christian Rosamond, "whom men call fair" The poem ends with a typical ironic capping: the naive narrator adds that he unfortunately woke before the good part of the dream, before he was able to see Margaret Roper, Joan of Arc, or Edward I's wife, Eleanor, "who knew that Love can vanquish Death".

The ingenuous persona blandly makes the point that all heroic and comic aspects of death are denied. The last gruesome twist is his complaint that poetic language is insufficient to describe his dream. Such language is too pure; it fails to provide adequate tension, particularly "to give the bitter of the sweet" as if the terrible vision we have just seen has been "sweet."

Accompanying this irony is a persistent strain of comedy, which is found here in many poems, most of which are deliberately understated, self-conscious, and very light in touch. The self-parodying "O Darling Room" seems simply an extreme of this, not, as Croker assumed, too ridiculously self-indulgent and self-centreed, but rather too detached, self-aware, and apologetically trivial. just as specialized and partial is the comic impulse behind a poem like "Lilian," which plays off against the slavish adoration implied in most of the poems in this extended female gallery — "Isabel," "Adeline," "Madeline," and so forth-by treating the tinkling laughter of the cruel "Airy, fairy Lilian" as a cause for irritation rather than romantic languor.

Instead of being mastered by her gay coquetry, the lover adopts a masterful tone himself, warning her that lie is becoming so borcd with her laughing that if praying won't stop her he will stomp on her, "crush" her. There is a limited but genuine comic satisfaction provided here, not only in the burlesque of the essentially ironic lover-slave tradition, but in the bolstering of the human (especially the male) ego by suggesting that the will can control any emotion.

There are instances of much fuller and genuinely liberating comedy in these volumes, most notably in the lovely paired poems, "The Mermaid" and "The Merman." These poems confront explicitly the image of the isolated self and move to the celebration of joy and union. Both poems open with a brief stanza that is part invitation, part pure song, emphasizing both the beauty (thrones, golden crowns or curls) and the loneliness ("Sitting alone, / Singing alone") of the magical state enjoyed by, the mer-creatures.

The second stanza not only admits the isolation but emphasizes it, carefully restricting it, however, to the daytime, to the rational, dutiful part of the merman's life, and the self-absorbed alienation of the mermaid. This admission out of the way, the full force of the poem can fall on the nighttime life, the life of the complete imaginative self, of irrational fulfillment:

Oh! what a happy life were mine
Under the hollow-hung ocean green!
Soft are the moss-beds under the sea;
We would live merrily, merrily. It is true that the merman and mermaid envision somewhat different nighttime paradises: his is free, open, promiscuous — "I would kiss them often under the sea, / And kiss them again till they kissed me" while hers is quieter and more controlled" But the king of them all would carry me, / Woo me, and win me, and marry me".

But there is no real conflict here; the discrepancy is part of the gentle joke, bringing up the extra force of the comedy-of-manners sexual battle to support the principal Edenic comedy. More important, this compartmentalization of the solitary from the communal self is an important strategy and an important part of comedy's answer to irony.

The poems here admit the argument that all men are isolated, but they see that isolation simply as a past of a multiplicity of conditions, a multiplicity, furthermore, which contains not only isolation but happiness and freedom. The ironic strategy is to focus and solidify; comedy's is to expand and free, to reject entirely the absolutism of irony.

But, comedy is just as susceptible to attack from irony, and it is certainly more usual in Tennyson to find the comic solution subverted. The ironic poems are often generically pure; the comic poems very seldom are. One may offer plausible biographical or sociological reasons for this fact, but simpler reasons are implicit within the forms. Irony is based on parody and thus is, in a way, parasitic. It is, further, defensive and hides its premises; comedy, at its best, is expansive and exposes all its secrets. When the two modes are competing, as in Tennyson, it is difficult for comedy to survive. Irony with a comic twist results in the sheer peculiarity of "Mariana in the South"; comedy transformed to irony results in the uniform power of "Mariana."

This ability of irony to attack comedy is more clearly illustrated in the contrasting poems, "The Poet" and "The Poet's Mind." "The Poet" is certainly a comic poem, though exclusively public and social in its emphasis. Still, it provides a strong and effective image of the force of poetry, expressed in the specifically comic terms, "hope," "youth," "spring." The grand object is to recapture. Eden, not just for the poet but for the entire world: "Thus truth was multiplied on truth, the world / Like one great garden showed".

It would be an Eden ruled by the expansive goddess of comedy, "Freedom". But "The Poet's Mind" shows a garden that is shrunken and delicate, threatened by a very dangerous enemy the rational mind, the dry and shallow wit of the "dark-browed sophist", The flowers "would faint", the plants would be blighted, the "merry bird" would be killed if the sophist were to enter. Most important, the source of all this life and joy, the large fountain in the centre, fed "from the brain of the purple mountain") and recalling the great symbol for poetic energy in "Kubla Khan," would itself "shrink to the earth if you came in". Great images of power, lightning and thunder, are associated with this fragile and threatened fountain.

In the middle leaps a fountain
Like sheet lightning,
Ever brightening
With a low melodious thunder. But there seems to be only an illusory union of power and beauty, only a faint echo of the confident and not endangered voice of Wisdom set loose

by the garden in "The Poet": "Her Wisdom's words did gather thunder as they ran, / And as the lightning to the thunder So was their meaning to her words".

"The Poet's Mind" is thus an inversion of "The Poet"; it suggests the ironic trap that may await the too-certain vision of comedy.Though comedy never entirely disappears and though it later reaches full expression in Tennyson's poetry, it is irony which came to dominate his writing of this period. It controls *Poems by Two Brothers,* the volumes of 1830 and 1832, and, to an even greater extent, *Poems* of 1842.

Bibliography

Ormond, Leonee. Alfred Tennyson: A Literary Life. New York: St. Martin's Press, 1993.

Thorn, Michael. Tennyson. New York: St. Martin's Press, 1993.

Brantley, Richard E. Anglo-American Antiphony: the Late Romanticism of Tennyson and Emerson. Gainesville: University of Florida, 1994.

Philip Collins. ed. Tennyson: Seven Essays. New York: St. Martin's Press, 1992.

Joseph, Gerhard. Tennyson and the Text: The Weaver's Shuttle. Cambridge: Cambridge University Press, 1992.

Tucker, Herbert. Critical Essays on Alfred Lord Tennyson. New York: G.K. Hall, 1993.

Andrew, Aletha. An Annotated Bibliography and Study of the Contemporary Criticism or Tennyson's Idylls of the King. New York: P. Lang, 1993.

Buckler, William Earl. Man and His Myths: Tennyson's Idylls of the King in Critical Context. New York: New York University Press, 1984.

Simpson, Roger. Camelot Regained: the Arthurian Revival and Tennyson. Wolfeboro: D.S. Brewer, 1990.